# Not Quite Like Home

# Not Quite Like Home
## Small Hostels for Alcoholics and Others

**Shirley Otto**
*Research Director,*
*Detoxification Evaluation Project,*
*The Maudsley Hospital,*
*London.*

**Jim Orford**
*Senior Lecturer in Clinical Psychology,*
*University of Exeter and*
*Principal Psychologist, Exe Vale Hospital,*
*Exeter.*

JOHN WILEY AND SONS
*Chichester · New York · Brisbane · Toronto*

41620

*Library of Congress Cataloging in Publication Data*

Otto, Shirley.
    Not quite like home.
    Includes indexes.
    1. Alcoholism—Treatment—England—London.
    2. Halfway houses—England—London. 3. Halfway houses.
    I. Orford, Jim, joint author. II. Title.
HV5283.G7L656      362.2′92′09421      77—12664

ISBN 0 471 99589 4

Printed in Great Britain

# Contents

# Preface

This book is divided into two parts. To us the second part came first, and indeed readers with a special interest in research may care to look at it first. It gives an account of a fairly intensive piece of research carried out simultaneously at two small hostels which specialized in the care of men who had had recognized problems in controlling their drinking of alcohol.

The present authors were specialists in alcoholism research and undertook this project in comparative ignorance of parallel developments in other fields. During the course of the work, however, and particularly when analyzing and attempting to interpret data, it became abundantly clear that whilst some of the issues arising were peculiar to alcoholism, most were not. We began to read about hostels for people who had been psychiatrically ill and about hostels for young offenders, for example, and realized that many of the matters which concerned us about alcoholism hostels were of concern in those fields also. Hence, when it was suggested to us that the detailed research report should be preceded by a more general discussion about small hostels and some of their problems, we were easily persuaded of the sense of so doing. It is such a discussion that forms Part I of the present book.

Origins of the Research

The early decisions to do the research on a particular topic and with a particular sample or in a particular location are the most irrevocable and crucial in the process of doing research. They are always only partly made on scientific grounds; they are influenced by the personal predilections of the research workers and factors such as research funding and administration. In any event the origins of research often remain obscure, and for this reason it may be useful to outline the origins of this research, if only briefly.

The present research was based at the Institute of Psychiatry (part of London University and attached to the Maudsley Hospital) situated in the Camberwell area of South London. The Institute and Hospital complex has a wide reputation for teaching, research and innovative applications in psychiatry and clinical psychology. Camberwell Green lies a few hundred yards to the North, and the Elephant and Castle a mile or so further on in the same direction. Both are notorious congregating points for vagrant men and women. Little more than a mile to the East is situated the largest Government reception centre for destitute men in England. The centre can accommodate 900 men nightly, many of whom have drinking problems (Tidmarsh et al, 1972).

The origins of the present research lie in developments taking place on both the research and practical fronts in the mid-1960s. A small hospital grant, and later a more substantial grant from the Nuffield Foundation, were obtained to start a small research unit on alcoholism at the Institute (the Alcohol Impact Project). This later expanded into the Addiction Research Unit funded by the Department of Health and Social Security and by the Medical Research Council. At about the same time was founded the local Camberwell Council on Alcoholism which was a major influence behind the setting up of the two alcoholism hostels that were to become the main objects of the present research.

One of us (J.O.) joined the Alcohol Impact Project as a recently trained clinical psychologist at the end of 1966. It was not long before he had what was for him the quite novel experience of meeting hostel residents, and not long before he was encouraged to take a research interest. An early intention was to 'research' 3 hostels simultaneously. However the manpower resources did not permit that and the first exercise was an investigation of a single 30 to 35-bedded residential project which had already been operating in the South London area for 8 years (it appears later on as House C). The data gathering part of this initial exercise ran for 9 months, between July 1968 and March 1969. The results have been published in the form of six articles (Orford, 1974; Orford and Hawker, 1974a, b; Orford et al, 1974, 1975 a, b).

The investigation at House C represented an exploratory, rather uncertain approach to the job of trying to marry research and alcoholism hostels. The intention was to 'research' the hostel. With hindsight, such a broad brief was stimulating and yet ludicrous. One might as well try and 'research' a hospital or a factory. The notion of research which was adopted was informed, and in many ways limited, by the research worker's training in clinical psychology, with the latter's emphasis (no longer so exclusive now as it was then) upon separate individuals and their problems. Several of the articles which emerged, whilst interesting, had more to say about the individuals staying in the hostel (their symptomatology, their motivation, and characteristics making it more or less easy for them to mix with others, for example) than about the hostel itself. Others began to describe relatively superficial features of the hostel, such as the lengths of stay and ways of departing of residents (Orford, 1974), and the features of hostel life which residents found most and least important (Orford et al, 1975b). One article began to approach a more social psychological issue, namely the framework within which hostel staff evaluated and described their residents (Orford et al, 1975a).

Nevertheless it was this investigation at House C, which we later started to refer to as a 'pilot study', which provided the background for the studies to be reported in Part II of this book. A number of workers in the Addiction Research Unit contributed to the study at House C, but in each instance their involvement was part-time, and accordingly a successful application was made to the Medical Research Council for a grant to employ a full-time worker. The small team of present authors was completed in late 1969 with the appointment of a recent psychology graduate (S.O.).

Since then the research perspective has changed markedly. A full-time research worker was able to become much more closely acquainted with the reality of small hostels, and the interests and perspectives of the researchers have become more 'social' and less 'clinical'. We were forced to become aware of, and started to take a greater interest in, such matters as the dynamics of selection processes, the informal social structure of residents, the differing ideologies of staff and residents, and even such 'extraneous' factors as committee and overall project organization. This, rather personal, developmental process and some of the inconsistencies which inevitably resulted may be apparent throughout the research report. The research techniques employed were necessarily decided upon at a relatively early stage and would probably not be those that we would choose now. Furthermore, the perspective on hostels with which we ended up was not at all the type of viewpoint with which we started at the outset.

There was even uncertainty over what to call the research project. In the grant application to the Medical Research Council in 1969 the term Hostels Project was used. However, the use of the word 'hostel' opens up the possibility of confusion between the small, informal, houses with which this research is principally concerned, and large lodging houses and other institutional settings. In North America the term 'halfway house' has been used widely, and indeed this was the term preferred when the report of the 'pilot' study at House C was written. But the term halfway house seems to imply a particular model of how these facilities should work; it contains assumptions that many would wish to avoid. Later we tried calling the study the 'alcoholism communities project' but the term 'alcoholism community' is not one that is used at all widely, and the word 'community' has more than one meaning. In general we shall avoid the issue by referring throughout to 'the present research'. The places themselves we prefer to call simply 'houses' although this word has been used interchangeably with the word 'hostels' often qualified by the adjective 'small' (even this is misleading as some are much larger than others). The difficulty of finding a suitable word is indicative of the in-between nature of these facilities; they do not easily fit into any of our preconceived notions about organizations for care. The British Home Office Working Party report which recommended hostels for persistent drunkenness offenders (Home Office, 1971) refers awkwardly to 'relatively small therapeutically-oriented hostels' and a recently inaugurated Federation (FARE) is open to those who work, in Britain, in 'Alcoholic Residential Establishments'.

The Study of Houses A and B

The main component of the research to be reported was an intensive study of two small alcoholism hostels, which will be referred to as Houses A and B. Both were set up in the mid 1960s, were situated in South London not far from the Institute, and through the voluntary Camberwell Council on Alcoholism had a special link with the research unit where the present authors were employed.

A major problem at the planning stage was the dearth of literature devoted specifically to non-institutional residential facilities for alcoholism. Other than published accounts of Houses A and B (Cook et al, 1968; Edwards et al, 1966) to which lengthier reference will be made later, published work appeared limited to a single long-term follow-up study which had very little to say about hostels themselves (Myerson and Mayer, 1966), and the occasional report of research examining a very limited issue such as the relationship between past treatment contacts and lengths of stay in a halfway house (Rubington, 1970).

It is probably fair to say, therefore, that the research team felt forced to operate as if they were breaking new ground, without any

previous research work to guide them. The general approach was therefore somewhat atheoretical. We can now see, with hindsight, that this
approach may have been misguided, and that a more explicit theoretical
framework to the study, derived from a related theoretical or applied
field of study, would have been beneficial.

This is not to say that the research was totally uninfluenced by
other work. Thinking was particularly influenced by a number of unpublished accounts of alcoholism hostels, noteably one from Canada
recounting in great detail early experiences at Bon Accord (Collier
et al, 1970). Possibly the most important influences were accounts of
research into related forms of residential care or treatment. Rapoport's work on the therapeutic community at the Henderson Hospital
(Rapoport, 1960) was counted a key work, but particularly stimulating
was Apte's report of research into English halfway houses for the
rehabilitation of ex-mental hospital patients (Apte, 1968). Sinclair's
(1971) work on juvenile probation hostels was not available whilst the
present research was being planned but was made much use of later, when
the results were being interpreted. Certain issues in theoretical and
experimental social psychology were instructive: for example, relationships between group cohesiveness, conformity and attitude change
(Kiesler, 1969). We were also influenced by a number of developments
in the measurement of relevant parameters in the area of social treatments generally. For example, work by Moos on measuring ward 'atmospheres' (Moos and Houts, 1968), Ellworth's work on the measurement of
staff attitudes and reputations (1965), as well as various developments
in the measurement of individual contributions to group discussions or
therapy sessions (e.g. Bales, 1950).

The various research techniques which were finally employed will not
be described in detail here. They are each introduced at appropriate
points in the chapters in Part II and are described in greater detail
in the Appendices at the end of the book.

A Rapid Survey of Alcoholism Hostels in London

The choice of Houses A and B as the objects of research was dictated by historical associations with the research unit rather than by
any more logical consideration. By the time the study at Houses A and
B was being planned in detail the research team were aware of the existence of a number of other small alcoholism hostels in the London
area and were anxious to know something about the range and diversity
of these facilities, and particularly to know how typical or atypical
Houses A and B were. To this end a rapid survey was mounted during the
Summer of the same year in which the study proper at Houses A and B
commenced. The survey was carried out by a psychology undergraduate
on placement at the Addiction Research Unit, the aim being to survey
all small hostels then existing in the London area which made special,
but not necessarily exclusive, provision for 'alcoholics'. The hostels
included numbered 9 (making 11 with Houses A and B).

The interview schedule (see Appendix E) used was divided into 2
parts. The first was administered to the staff member in charge only
and concerned itself with such matters as the origin of the house, the
categories of people it was intended for, staff numbers and qualifications, selection criteria, the nature of the program, and aims and
goals.

The second part was administered to one or more members of staff
and to a small sample of residents at most of the houses and was con-

cerned with perceived patterns of decision-making within the hostel.

The findings of this survey will be presented at appropriate points in the discussion chapters in Part I. Each of these chapters (Chapters 1-4) will be in two halves; the first devoted to a general discussion of hostels, the second to a specific discussion of alcoholism hostels.

We are indebted to more people than we can name for encouragement and support during the course of the research and the writing of this book. In particular we would like to mention members of the Alcoholics Recovery Project and the Helping Hand Organization who went out of their way to collaborate with us - Philip Lemon, David Whitehead, Danny Levine, Chris Conway and David Kitchen. Tim Cook's continuous support over the years is particularly warmly remembered, not least because of the detailed and highly valuable comments which he made on the first draft of this book. A number of former colleagues at the Addiction Research Unit contributed in various ways. We thank them all but can only mention 4 by name. Griffith Edwards, as head of the unit, supported us throughout. Indeed the idea of research in this area was initially his and he was responsible for the initiative necessary to get it going, as he has been for so many innovative developments in the field of alcohol problems in Britain. David Robinson has been a most stimulating colleague and we are particularly grateful for his comments on the draft. Lynda Gaines was a vital and creative member of the team at the stage of collating and analyzing data. Joyce Oliphant deserves our warmest thanks for her patience and skill in acting as project secretary, in typing drafts, and finally in providing the publishers with camera-ready copy of the whole book - a more than usually exacting task. We would also like to thank the Medical Research Council and the Department of Health and Social Security for their financial support, and also the Institute of Psychiatry, London University, for accomodating and supporting the work of the Addiction Research Unit.

Our most important acknowledgement we have left till last. We wish the hostel residents who patiently endured our presence and answered our questions, as well as all present and future residents of alcoholism hostels, the sobriety they wish for themselves. We are doubtful that their condition is best described by the words 'illness' or 'disease', but of their sufferings we have no doubt.

Shirley Otto
Detoxification Evaluation Project,
Maudsley Hospital.

Jim Orford
University of Exeter and
Exe Vale Hospital, Exeter.

June, 1977.

# Acknowledgements

Permission to reproduce extracts from the following works is
gratefully acknowledged:

Vagrant Alcoholics by T. Cook, 1975, Published by Routledge
and Kegan Paul Ltd., London.

Halfway Houses: A New Dilemma in Institutional Care by R.Z. Apte,
1968.  Occasional Papers on Social Administration, No. 27.
Published by George Bell and Sons, London for the Social
Administration Research Trust.

Setting up a Therapeutic Community by G. Edwards, A. Hawker
and C. Hensman, 1966.  The Lancet.

Varieties of Residential Experience by J. Tizard, I. Sinclair
and R.V.G. Clarke, 1975, Published by Routledge and Kegan Paul
Ltd., London.

The Halfway House Movement: A Search for Sanity by H.L. and
C.L. Raush, 1968, Published by Irvington Publishers, Inc., New
York.

# Part I

# A Critical Appreciation of Small Hostels

# Chapter 1

# Foundations of the Recent Hostel Movement

The ethos of the halfway houses, while differing from one
another, have a peculiarly indefinable quality; they are
neither like a traditional...institution nor a 'home'
(Apte, 1968; p.58).

## THE REACTION AGAINST LARGE INSTITUTIONS

This book is about small residential communities, or hostels,
which have a caring or rehabilitative purpose. Yet it is important
to start elsewhere, with a discussion of institutions, because it
is only by appreciating the reaction that has taken place against
the large institution that the hostel or halfway house movement
can be understood. Sooner or later the enthusiasm which is now
associated with small hostels may change into a critical awareness
of their inadequacies, and a movement for further reform. But for
the moment they are popular, and it is in the direction of the
increasingly unpopular large institution that we must look to understand why.

Most people's homes are small and informal, and there is no
hierarchy, at least amongst the adult members. There is much contact
with the world outside and the expectation is that members will
interact much, will show a great deal of friendly and supportive
behaviour towards one another, and will feel that others care about
them and that they can rely upon them. How true this image is does
not matter. What is important is that it is the image that most
people hold about what constitutes the right set of circumstances
under which to live an active and responsible, free and dignified,
life.

However, this book is about living arrangements for people who
are considered, if only for the moment, in need of non-family care:
principally the orphaned, the physically and mentally handicapped,
the elderly infirm, the mentally ill, the delinquent or criminal,
the addicted, and our special subjects of study - those who suffer
from alcoholism.

### The Nature of Large Institutions

The following description draws mainly upon accounts which
have been given of large institutions for the adult mentally ill.
Such institutions have been particularly fully described by a num-

ber of different writers, and they provide one of the most relevant contrasts with that special category of small residential community with which this book is particularly concerned - namely the alcoholism hostel or halfway house. However, what we intend to describe is the stereotype of a traditional, 'bad', institution, whether it be a mental hospital, a mental subnormality hospital, a prison, an orphanage or a large old people's home. The description that follows represents an amalgam of observations made by different people, but draws particularly upon accounts given in the following books: Institutional Neurosis (Barton, 1959), Asylums (Goffman, 1961), Institutionalism and Schizophrenia (Wing and Brown, 1970), and Social Therapy in Psychiatry (Clark, 1974).

Size and Structure

The sheer size and structure of .the institution are perhaps its most impressive, and least home-like characteristics. Large institutions can be very large indeed, catering for hundreds or even thousands of inmates at a time. Inevitably there is a large staff who specialize in different tasks. Various hierarchies of superordinate and subordinate staff are in evidence, and there is a special class of administrative staff. Even though the institution may be broken down into relatively small units, such as the wards of a mental hospital, the effect of these staffing arrangements is to rob staff who are in closest contact with inmates of the autonomy necessary to react in a flexible and personal way.

There are other features built into the institution which emphasize the distinction between staff and residents or inmates. Staff may be required to wear a uniform style of clothing, and residents may be required to adopt a different, but still uniform, style if only for reasons of convenience or finance. There may be an enforced non-reciprocal manner of addressing other people, with inmates addressing staff by a title, and staff addressing inmates simply by name or even number. Spacial arrangements within the institution often reinforce the staff-inmate distinction. There is usually strict segregation of eating and toilet facilities for example, and inmates are denied access to special staff areas, such as offices and lounges.

There is likely to be a multitude of formal rules and regulations about all manner of matters. But of particular significance are regulations restricting the freedom of movement of inmates both within the institution itself and to and from the world outside. Greater freedom of movement may be given to a restricted number of residents as a special privilege. The 'closed' nature of the large institution is a key feature distinguishing it from other types of living arrangement, and hence movement towards 'open doors' in mental hospitals, and towards 'open prisons', is particularly crucial in its reform.

Perhaps even more important in understanding the reaction that has taken place against it are the types of social organization and forms of social behaviour which have been described as taking place within the institution. Barton (1959) summed it up by referring to the poor 'atmosphere' to be found in the typical ward of a large mental institution. The following are some of the main ingredients of such an atmosphere.

## Authoritarian Position of Staff

First and foremost is the fact that staff make all decisions about institution or unit policy, and most decisions about individuals. Decisions affecting inmates, about which the individuals concerned have little or no say, range from the large, such as matters of admission and discharge, to the small, such as when to take a bath or change clothes. Much of the behaviour which staff display towards inmates is disciplinary, punitive and 'bossy'. There is no fair and equitable discussion with individual inmates about their behaviour, and certainly no open discussion with groups of inmates.

## Staff-Resident Social Distance

A related, second, element of the poor atmosphere is the great social distance between staff and residents. As Goffman (1961) has vividly described for a large mental hospital, staff and inmates live in two separate worlds with rather little friendly contact between them. They have different points of view about all manner of things, including what the institution itself is for and how people in it should conduct themselves. They are likely to acquire narrow, hostile, stereotyped views of each other. Residents may develop a code of conduct which is directly contrary to the values and wishes of staff; the 'inmate code' of large prisons is a well-known example. Inmates mostly inter-react with those specialist staff whose role is principally that of custodian and disciplinarian, and have relatively little contact with other specialist staff or people from the outside world whose roles have more of a treatment or befriending element

## Depersonalizing Routine

A third ingredient is the uniformity and regimentation of inmates' lives, and the strictly planned schedule which governs life in the institution. Life is controlled by routine, and a routine which is uniform and inflexible from day to day. It follows from the lack of freedom of inmates to move outside the institution, that all activities of day and night - working, eating, recreation and sleeping - are carried out in the one institutional setting. This is a feature of institutional life that particularly sets it apart from the type of lives that people lead in the outside world, where different functions are usually carried on in different places and with different people, and is the feature that gives the 'total institution' much of its special character (Goffman, 1961). What is particularly important is that all activities are carried on under one authority, and in accordance with one master plan. In addition to wearing uniform dull clothing, inmates may be stripped of, or at least discouraged from having, many personal possessions of their own, and in general have little or no opportunity to stamp their own individuality on self-appearance or on the arrangement or decor of their living space. The effects of this uniformity, coupled with lack of opportunity for making decisions about matters which affect their own lives, has been aptly described as 'depersonalizing'.

## Inactivity

Particularly damaging is thought to be a fourth element of life in the large institution, namely the inactivity of inmates and their lack of practice of normal community roles. Inmates may spend much of their time in idleness, or else occupied with irrelevant, useless activity. Hence they are not compensated for their loss of contact with the outside world by being given extra practice in the roles they might be expected to play if and when they leave the institution. The inmate is just an inmate, and no longer a father or mother or an employee, or even a customer with real money to spend, or a traveller who has to negotiate the public transport system. Even ordinary quite everyday skills are not practised, and habits not maintained. Loss of contact with the outside world, combined with loss of the skills required there, lead to a loss of confidence in the ability to get by outside the institution, and a decided reduction in prospects of doing well in a competitive world.

This rapid portrait of the archetypal large institution gives a picture of an arrangement for living which is not only inhumane by most people's standards, but is in addition now recognized to be harmful in a clinical sense, in the long run. In the large mental hospital, for example, it is thought to contribute to a state of being, almost amounting to a clinical syndrome, that has been variously termed 'institutionalization', 'institutionalism' and 'institutional neurosis'. Much of the characteristic behaviour of those long-stay mental hospital patients labelled schizophrenic - the apathy, the withdrawal, and the apparent disinclination to leave the institution - is now thought to be the result of long periods living in the typical environment of the large institution.

## Custodial Ideology and Staff Attitudes

It is probably most important to realize that the nature of the typical institution, as of all institutions, is under-pinned by a corresponding set of ideas about the purpose of the institution, and change is unlikely to take place or alternatives arise unless those ideas are challenged or an alternative ideology takes their place. The custodial structure and social organization of the typical old-fashioned mental hospital, or typical closed penal institution, derived from an emphasis on the custodial function of the institution. Security and custody have probably always headed the list of priorities in the design and management of prisons, and the same was probably true of mental hospitals during a long 'custodial era' which followed the (now seen as enlightened) era of Moral Treatment in the early 19th century, and which has only relatively recently been seriously challenged (Raush and Raush, 1968, p.11; Wing and Brown, 1970, Chapter 1). It is the ideological position of those who plan and manage the institution that principally affects the institution's organization and, most importantly, its staffing (Tizard et al, 1975, pp.6-8).

Crucial variables connected with staffing include numbers of staff, the training and status of staff, and staff attitudes towards their job and their charges. A custodial ideology probably leads to the appointment of a relatively small number of staff , but particularly to a preponderance of relatively poorly paid staff who are untrained, or at least not trained in one of the healing, helping or educating professions, and who are unable to compete for jobs of higher status and greater satisfaction. In mental hospitals many such staff are likely to hold custodial or traditional attit-udes (Gilbert and Levinson, 1956; Pearlin and Rosenberg, 1962; Ellsworth, 1965). As with all organizations, the ideological con-formity of the majority of staff may be maintained by selective recruitment and selective discharge or leaving of staff members whose personalities are more or less receptive to the institutional ideology, and to an unknown degree of attitude change during the time that staff work in the institutional environment (Gilbert and Levinson, 1956, p.271; Etzioni, 1964).

The foregoing description of the large custodial institution is of course a stereotype, and is no more true of all large instit-utions at all times than is the image of the happy family, with its warm, caring atmosphere, true of all family groups at all times. Institutions have always varied (variation is the main theme of Chapter 3 of this book) and no doubt even at the height of the custodial era of the mental hospital, some institutions were better than others. Yet, there can be no doubt that the ideology, struc-ture and organization of many larger institutions encouraged the sort of social atmosphere that has been described, and made it difficult to achieve the kind of informal, democratic, atmosphere for which the planners of many small residential hostels aim, and which from time to time they achieve. Even institutions which are not 'total' and which are highly regarded by many, such as schools and general hospitals, as well as large total institutions which have been thoroughly reformed, such as modern mental hospitals and open prisons, undoubtedly share some of the features of the bad traditional institution, on account of such characteristics as their largeness, their bureaucratic administration, and the division and distance between staff and consumers.

## Non-Traditionalism in the Mental Hospital

One of the main factors behind a change in thinking about how the mentally ill should be treated has been the application of the social, as opposed to the clinical, sciences (Raush and Raush, 1968, p.29). Anthropologists, sociologists and social psychologists are trained in traditions, and study phenomena, which impress them with the importance of the social environment in modifying behaviour. The notion that behaviour constitutes a personal condition which is appropriately labelled and which can be treated without much regard for the rest of a person's social environment, is not one that they find it easy to accept. By way of contrast, medical doctors and many clinical psychologists and social workers are trained in such a way, and have experience of such phenomena, that they are more comfortable thinking in terms of individual diagnoses and individual treatment. There are perhaps areas of human behaviour where one or other approach is more obviously applicable than the other. In the case of mental illness, however, lively debate is possible. Hence the increasing application of the social sciences has made a diff-erence, particularly in their emphasis upon the environmental determinants of behaviour.

There have of course been many progressive developments in

recent years in fields connected with education, treatment and corrections. There can, however, be no doubt that one of the single, most significant, influences in the mental health field has been the development of the Therapeutic Community model of treatment at a unit (later known as The Henderson) at Belmont Hospital in England. The method was pioneered by Jones (1952, 1968) and studied by Rapoport (1960). The very term 'therapeutic community' has become a key one in the developing movement towards alternative ways of caring for people who might formerly have been placed in large custodial institutions. The term has been much used and misused, but for many has become synonymous with a form of social organization which is open and democratic and provides a contrast with the large institution.

Rapoport developed a questionnaire to test the commitment of both staff and patients at Belmont to the ideology of the therapeutic community. Amongst statements indicating agreement with this ideology were the following:

> Patients should help to decide how their fellow patients should be treated.
> If a patient is very abusive or destructive in hospital, it is better to discuss it with him than to discipline him.
> If it were possible, staff and patients should share all facilities and activities in common - cafeterias, workshops, socials, meetings etc.
> Everything the patients say and do while in hospital should be used for treatment.

Two of the major ingredients of the therapeutic community, which served to mark it off from the typical institution, were the high value placed upon free emotional expression, and an emphasis upon a democratic organization of the community. Patients were not to be held down by a controlling, disciplinary staff, but rather were to be encouraged to express themselves even if this involved out-bursts of anger and destructiveness. Such behaviour would then constitute the substance of group discussion with the focus sometimes upon the individual and sometimes upon the social organization of the community. Patients were to be fully involved in decision-making about day-to-day community policy, and even about the admission and discharge of fellow patients. Hence staff were relieved of much of the authoritarian position which they would have had in a more typical institution. Patients were also involved in a great deal of activity in the therapeutic community, and had plenty of opportunity to practise social, work and other skills.

Yet in many ways the therapeutic community at Henderson retained certain institutional features, even some elements of the 'total institution'. It was on hospital premises, its senior staff person was a medical doctor, and its users were called patients. Although much time would be spent by patients in small groups, the total residential group (between 40 and 50) was too large to be home-like. Freedom of movement between the hospital and the outside world was by no means unrestricted, although it was less restricted than many people considered desirable for the type of person it was caring for (mainly young adults, many of whose problems took an anti-social form). Whilst being informal in some senses, in other senses it was rather formal with many expectations about the detailed program of the therapeutic and administrative groups, work assignments, and other activities which patients would follow for much of their waking life in the community. As in the total institution described by Goffman, all activities followed a plan and were conducted under one authority - in this case the authority of the all-seeing community for whom all behaviour was grist for the therapeutic mill. The therapeutic community is a very specific model which can indeed be criticized for being over-rigid (Whiteley, 1972, p.40). There have been few attempts to copy this model of the 'therapeutic community proper' (Clark, 1965), but there have been numerous instances of the partial liberalization of institutions or parts of institutions involving the introduction of some elements similar to those used at Belmont. This Clark (1965) refers to as the 'therapeutic community approach'.

Of the many more-or-less radical innovations that have taken place in the mental hospital in the last 20 to 30 years, the one reported by Fairweather (1964) in his book, Social Psychology in Treating Mental Illness, is worth more than a passing mention for two reasons: firstly, this innovative program was extremely well described and the immediate effects upon patient behaviour observed and measured in great detail; and secondly, the program was designed for a fairly typical mental hospital population - patients were of mixed diagnoses, but a large proportion had been diagnozed 'schizophrenic' and many had been in mental hospitals for some years. The experiment involved the comparison of a 'traditional' and a 'small group' ward in the same hospital, to one of which patients were assigned on a purely random basis. On the traditional ward patient problems were discussed individually with staff members who made final decisions about all important matters. A psychologist was responsible for scheduling daily activities and for leading meetings, and other members of staff (nurses, psychiatrists, social workers) occupied their traditional roles. On the small group ward, on the other hand, a new patient was immediately on admission introduced to a task group of fellow patients who were made responsible for orienting him or her to the ward. Task groups were responsible for certain work assignments on the ward and the group was responsible for the completion of tasks as well as for the individual progress of its members through a number of graded steps. Privileges were assigned in accordance with this stepwise progress and recommendations about promotion, and even about ultimate discharge, were made by the group. On the traditional ward staff assigned jobs to individual patients, and staff were responsible for disciplining and progress of patients. The total experiment lasted for 6 months and staff switched wards half way through.

Although the traditional ward was probably quite unlike the worst of the large institutions, there were dramatic differences in patient behaviour on the two wards. Social activity was at a much higher level on the small group ward with much more talking and joint activity amongst patients, and much less inactivity or sleeping. Both wards held a daily large ward meeting of all patients and staff, but the atmosphere in the meetings on the two wards was quite different. On the traditional ward there was much silence, more talking by staff, and when patients spoke they were more likely to direct their comments towards a staff member. In the meetings on the small group ward there was scarcely any silence, much lively discussion with two or more patients often speaking at once, less staff talk, and many more patient comments directed toward fellow patients. There were effects also on staff satisfaction, particularly for nursing staff who evaluated their experience on the small group ward more highly. Patients on the small group ward spent significantly fewer days in hospital.

## Semi or Intermediate Institutions

If, for one reason or another, people are not to live in their own homes, need they live in large institutions at all? The logical next step, beyond reforming the institution or part of it, is to create new facilities which are planned in such a way that they avoid the worst features of the large institution. Small informal autonomous units, located in reasonably well-populated areas and encouraging their residents to work and have recreation in the community, might manage to provide for some of the freedom, activity and responsibility which we associate with independent home life, whilst at the same time continuing to provide residential care for people who require it or who have been committed to it. Thus it is not surprising to find that the movement towards reform within institutions has been accompanied by a growing movement towards setting up 'intermediate' or semi-institutional facilities.

In their survey, Raush and Raush (1968) located 40 halfway houses, as they have come to be known in the U.S., for people who were or had been psychiatrically ill, and which were established by 1963. All but 13 had been established in the previous 5 years, since 1958, and only 3 had been established before 1953. Ten years later a survey of U.S. halfway houses primarily serving the mentally ill revealed 209 houses (National Institute of Mental Health, 1975). There has been a parallel movement in Britain towards the setting up of hostels (as they tend to be called in the U.K.) for the mentally ill (Apte, 1968; Hewett et al, 1975).

In both countries there have been similar movements, during the same period of time, in the offender field (Keller and Alper, 1970; Sinclair, 1971). In addition there is now a wide variety of hostels, halfway houses, homes or centres which make residential provision for categories of people many of whom might at one time have lived instead in a large institution. This variety is illustrated by a report (1973) of a working party of the Central Council for Education and Training in Social Work (a British Organization) which considered education for residential social work. It considered 25 types of centre which came within its remit. These included facilities for children, such as children's homes, reception centres and approved schools; facilities mainly for adults, such as hostels for unmarried mothers, probation hostels, prison after-care hostels, hostels for drug addicts and those for alcoholics; facilities for families, including family rehabilitiation units; facilities for the handicapped such as homes for the deaf and for the epileptic, hostels for the mentally ill, and homes for the mentally handicapped; and facilities for the elderly. Similar types of residential community seem likely to proliferate in the future - mention would now have to be made of refuges for battered wives, a rapid recent development in the U.K., and even of specialist hostels for compulsive gamblers, of which at least one exists in Britain. Other residential settings, such as foster homes, and nursing or convalescent homes, boarding schools and hotels used as permanent homes by retired people, were thought to lie only just beyond the working party's remit. Quite apart from this broad range of residential provisions, there now exists a variety of non-residential facilities, such as day hospitals, day centres, sheltered work-shops and therapeutic social clubs, which are intermediate or 'transitional' in the sense that they cater for people who have come from, or who might otherwise have been in, institutions. As in other particulars, terminology in this field is confusing even over the basic matter of the distinction between residential and non-residential facilities - for example, Keller and Alper use the term halfway house to refer to, "...any relatively small facility, either residential or non-residential..." (1970, p.10). However, we shall be concerned in this book exclusively with residential provision.

## SMALL RESIDENTIAL HOSTELS

What are small hostels or halfway houses like, and what gives them their intermediate or non-institutional quality? To answer this question we shall draw particularly upon the thorough survey of hostels for the mentally ill in the U.S. carried out by Raush and Raush (1968). Not only does their book, The Halfway House Movement: a Search for Sanity, raise most of the major issues to do with the organization of small hostels, but also the general description they provide and the diversity they found is a very fair reflection of residential communities for alcoholics and others with which we are familiar in the U.K. Reference will also be made to studies of hostels for the mentally ill in Britain (Apte, 1968; Hewett et al, 1975), and an account of American halfway houses in the field of corrections (Keller and Alper, 1970).

### Size

Firstly, most hostels or halfway houses are small organizations. Of the 40 houses they surveyed, Raush and Raush found none housing more than 30 residents; the average number was 12. Most held between 6 and 15 residents, but 5 held 5 or fewer and 7 held more than 20. However, some had potentially higher capacities, and two of the houses with the smallest number of mentally ill residents had in addition places for people who had not been ill. In Britain, the Royal Commission which lead to the Mental Health Act of 1959 - an Act which instructed all local authorities in the country to set up after-care hostels for the mentally ill - recommended that hostels should have between 20 and 30 residents, with a maximum of 50 (Apte, 1968, p.15). Apte himself found an average of 18 residents in the 39 hostels which he studied, the two largest serving 35 and 53 residents. Keller and Alper (1970) have stated, "...a small population is an essential characteristic of the halfway house idea and is found almost universally" (p.12). They indicated that most probation or parole hostels accommodated between 10 and 30 residents, but that one of the earliest and best-known halfway houses (Dismas House) could accommodate 60, although it was seldom fully occupied.

### Location

Consistent with the intention that small hostels be intermediate in nature and consistent with the rehabilitation ideology of many of them (about which we shall have more to say in Chapter 4), is the urban or suburban location of most houses. They are intentionally 'in the community' rather than placed at a distance from it. The building may be purpose-built, as with some of the probation and parole hostels described by Keller and Alper, but is more likely to have formerly been a private home or to have been used for some unrelated purpose. There is certainly no set format. Of the houses Raush and Raush studied, half were in large former private residencies ('big old places' as they call them) but 3 occupied ex-hospitals or convalescent homes and 4 ex-hotels or motels. Three were exceptional in being in rural farm settings and one was in the grounds of an existing hospital.

The size, location and architecture of the hostel are its basic structural features which give it its non-institutional quality, and which serve many organizational purposes. Privacy is one such function. It exists in the ideal home but is lacking in many institutions. Of the 40 American halfway houses, most had single or double rooms for residents; 6 had dormitories but only one had dormitories containing 5 or more beds (Raush and Raush, p.69). In hostels for the mentally ill in London standards of privacy varied from a high level offered by one local authority hostel where each resident had a single bed-sitting room, to that offered by several voluntary hostels occupying large Victorian mansions with enormous bedrooms shared by up to 5 or 6 residents (Hewett et al, 1975, p.399).

A major function which the location of the typical hostel serves is the opportunity it provides for residents to obtain paid employment in the outside community. The daily involvement of residents in the real world, and the practising of normal roles, especially that of employee, are amongst the most vital elements of any 'open' facility, and hence encouragement to take outside work is a principal feature of hostels that distinguishes them from large institutions. Furthermore, in Goffman's terms, it is impossible for the hostel to become a total institution if residents spend much of their time away from the hostel and under a different authority, that of an outside employer.

Raush and Raush found that almost all halfway houses encouraged their residents to get paying jobs. Indeed:

> ...the ability of the resident to hold a self-sustaining
> job is seen as one major, if not the major criterion of
> the halfway houses' success in integrating the resident to
> the broader social community (p.139).

Thirty-four of the 40 houses contained at least some residents who were in part or full-time work, although the percentage of current residents working was often less than 25% and no house had more than two-thirds of its residents in work. In fact the ability, or at least willingness, of the potential resident to obtain employment is often made a requirement for residence in a hostel or halfway house, especially in those that intend that residents should only remain for a matter of months rather than years (Apte, 1968, p.33; Hewett et al, 1975, p.398). However, like Raush and Raush, Apte found that even hostels with explicit policies requiring employment had large numbers of unemployed, or partly employed, residents even when they were located in areas which had full employment at the time (Apte, p.56). Hostel residents are expected to pay for their board

and lodging out of their earnings or social security or welfare
payments, as if they were making their own way in the community.
Raush and Raush refer to these payments as 'fees' (pp.75-81), whereas
in British hostels they would normally be referred to as 'rent'.
Fees varied greatly in the houses surveyed by Raush and Raush (a
factor of 20 separating the lowest and highest rates) and many of the
houses covered the bulk of their costs from this source. Most hostels
for the mentally ill in Britain charge a modest rent (around £7.50 in
1973) and would not expect to cover more than about a third of their
costs in this way.

Staffing

Just as staffing arrangements are crucial in the large institution,
so too do they reflect the ideology of the typical hostel or halfway
house. Firstly, there have emerged no fixed ideas on the professional
training necessary to be a staff member, or indeed about whether
professional training is needed at all. Raush and Raush found that
two-thirds of mental illness halfway houses had non-professional
supervisors or managers who were the functional heads of houses,
although they were often subordinate to an outside professional
consultant or director. The degree of actual involvement of the
latter varied widely. One in 3 did have professionally trained
directors involved on the premises day-to-day, but their training
varied: 6 were social workers, 2 psychologists, and they included
an occupational therapist, a vocational guidance counsellor, a
physician, a clergyman and a registered nurse. They concluded:

> ...there is no specific professionally based training
> presently directed towards the management of a halfway
> house. Nor has there been any investigation of the type
> of training which would best serve the needs of halfway
> houses (p.95).

All but 4 of the houses had a managing body - in some cases part
of a parent organization (usually the Veterans Administration) and
sometimes formed on an ad hoc basis mainly from local professional
people, business men and civic leaders.

In Britain, Apte has pointed to the lack of recognized training
for the position of warden in hostels for the mentally ill, the lack
of established standards, and the range of vocations from which staff
are recruited. Approximately half of all staff had a background in
nursing, whilst many had no relevant training at all beyond secondary
school: for instance, 2 wardens had done missionary work abroad and
3 had worked as foremen in industry (Apte, 1968, p.44).

Whilst Apte viewed the diversity of staff as a reflection of
lack of standards, Keller and Alper welcomed the range of backgrounds
to be found among staff in parole and probation hostels in the U.S.
There is, however, obviously a contrast between types of staff to be
found in such halfway houses and those to be found, for instance, in
English hostels for the mentally ill. The contrast perhaps reflects
the relative status of the two types of house in the two different
countries, and the greater availability of University graduates in
the U.S.:

> Directors and other personnel in halfway house work are
> recruited from various sources - holders of the Master's

degree in social work, psychology or sociology. Others
came from education, bringing such skills as music
appreciation, athletic coaching, counselling and guidance.
Many of the earliest halfway house directors were clergy-
men: several came from probation or parole work. Some
directors have come from maximum-security institutions,
finding themselves drawn by the challenge of an open comm-
unity-based facility. Others have abandoned careers in
business. Nor is there any likelihood that this range of
recruitment resources will diminish...all possible sources
of recruitment must be continually tapped (Keller and
Alper, pp.125-6).

They also argue for the employment of ex-offenders, and for the
use of non-professional volunteers.

Not only does the non-institutional ideology of the small hostel
allow for flexibility in the background of staff members, but it also
allows (although by no means guarantees) a much reduced staff presence. Keller and Alper quote from a survey of 28 youth-serving
residential centres: 10 had no staff living on the premises, and in
some no adult staff members were on duty at night (p.13). With
evident approval, they cite the Los Angeles Manhattan Project for
adult and adolescent probationers, parolees and ex-psychiatric
patients which operated largely without 'staff' at all. A number of
highly publicized drug rehabilitation programs in the U.S., such as
Synanon, Day Top Village and Phoenix House (e.g. Yablonsky, 1965),
have sometimes operated in a similar way, with professionals involved
in planning, policy and publicity, but little in evidence in day-to-
day operations.

Nevertheless, when outlining a typical halfway house budget,
Keller and Alper refer to the likelihood of an average house, serving between 20 and 30 residents, having a staff of between 6 and 8 -
director, assistant director, work supervisor, house father, secretary and cook. In practice many small hostels are evidently extremely
well staffed in numerical terms. The 1973 NIMH Survey found an average of 7 full-time and 3 part-time paid staff and a volunteer in
psychiatric halfway houses; in size the median hostel had 17 places
(NIMH, 1975). Apte cites an average staff-to-resident ratio of 1:
$10\frac{1}{2}$, with a wide range from 1:4 to 1:33(p.46). However, these figures excluded 'non-supervisory staff' such as domestic housekeepers,
cooks, gardeners and maintenance staff.

Terminology

The intermediate, or hybrid, character of the small hostel, as
well as its relative recency and absence of laws governing its operation (Raush and Raush, p.73), makes for an absence of rigidity not
only about organizational matters such as staffing patterns, but
even about the appropriate terms to be used to describe the people
who live there, the staff, and even the places themselves. Although
the term 'residents' seems to be most widely used, expressions such
as 'clients', 'members', 'guests', and 'patients' are also found to
describe people who live in small hostels. The staff member in
overall charge may be referred to as a 'director' or a 'warden' -
perhaps a clear indication of the status of the person concerned and
of the project - but a variety of other terms are used including

'manager', 'administrator' and 'house parent'. To describe the place itself the term halfway house has never been widely used in Britain, and Keller and Alper point out that the term is avoided by some people in the U.S. who prefer expressions such as 'residential treatment centre' or 'rehabilitation residence' (p.13). The term 'hostel' is most widely used in Britain but many are concerned to distinguish their facility from the relatively large, institution-like, 'hostel' run for profit and without a rehabilitation or treatment purpose. A wide variety of other terms have been used, including 'rehabilit- ation centre', 'group home', 'home', 'residential community', 'comm- unity' and many others. As will already be clear, the terms 'halfway house', 'hostel' and 'residential community' are used synonymously in the present book, although the expression 'small hostel' seems to us the most general and least ambiguous, and is the term we prefer.

## Informal Atmosphere

If there is any one word that captures the spirit of most small hostels, and which distinguishes them from the large institutions against which they are a reaction, it is probably the word 'inform- ality'. Size, location, architecture, the involvement of residents in the outside community, and the possibility of staffing arrange- ments quite distinct from those of the institution, all make it possible for the hostel to achieve an atmosphere that approaches that of the ideal home. Keller and Alper make a telling point when they say:

> One feature common to most halfway houses is that they post
> no special sign or plaque that might identify their purpose,
> or otherwise make them distinguishable (p.13).

Thus, on the outside at least, many halfway houses are indistin- guishable from ordinary residencies. Inside the houses, according to Raush and Raush, "...all contrast greatly with the hospital where schedules, rituals and rules are fixed" (p.167). They follow Redl (1959), who wrote about the therapeutic milieu in residential work with children, in emphasizing the way in which space, time, and objects are used in the halfway house. They stress the freedom of movement between rooms, and the flexible organization of time in keeping with the needs of the individual and other members of the community rather than in accordance with arbitrary rules. But in particular they mention the flexible use of 'objects': use of the kitchen and laundry equipment, the carrying out of household tasks and the use of objects for recreation such as televisions and record players, as well as the organization of shopping and other trips necessary for the maintenance of the house, may all be organized on a flexible basis with both residents and staff contributing. This ordinary, informal, way of going about things provides residents with much more practice in relevant skills than they would get in the typical institution, prevents distance developing between residents and staff, and can also provide a succession of shared tasks in the setting of which important discussions can take place both amongst residents and between residents and staff (Raush and Raush, pp.167-70).

Tizard et al (1975),whose collection of writings, Varieties of Residential Experience, mainly concerns facilities for children, have focused upon unit autonomy as a crucial variable in organization. They believe that research evidence shows that where a residential unit is autonomous, and where the head of the unit has freedom to take important decisions, there is both a higher quality of interaction between staff and residents and an all-round higher level of morale (pp.8-10). The autonomy of halfway house staff is one of the main factors which Raush and Raush had in mind when they cited, with approval, an incident described in Rothwell and Doniger's (1963) account of Woodley House. The incident concerned a dispute between pro and anti-T.V. factions in the house. The former decided to convert part of the basement for their use, hence leaving the living room to the others. A staff member took them in her car to buy paint and other materials and later the same day the newly decorated television room was in use. Such an incident could not easily happen in a large institution and Raush and Raush list the following 8 factors to do with the organization of a halfway house that made the event possible:

1) The group is small enough to enable discussion and decision; 2) it is located in a house with living room and basement, etc., and with which the residents are sufficiently identified to be concerned with decoration; 3) the ecological setting is such that resources - in this case, paint and decorating materials - are easily available, but they must be sought outside the house and through contact with the community; 4) the problem is a practical one of comfort and convenience, not a matter of formal rules and regulations; 5) communication is direct and simple; 6) a staff member who had decision-making power is immediately involved; 7) the staff member is not limited by the prescribed definition of 'professional' role; 8) action can be direct and immediate (p.162).

The contrast with the typical large institution described earlier in this chapter is clear. There have, however, been few detailed and direct comparisons of life in institutions and hostels. One interesting, and direct, comparison, made by King et al (1971) and summarized by Tizard (1975), was made between 5 hospitals and 8 hostels for mentally subnormal children. All hostel unit heads were more autonomous than all of their counterparts in the hospitals. Although in fact they had more domestic and administrative work to do, they were able to organize their time in their own way and were thus able to spend more time in actions that brought them into contact with the children. Careful and reliable observations showed that they interacted more frequently with children than was the case for heads in the hospital settings, and showed more warmth and acceptance and less rejection in their behaviour towards children. There was less of a status hierarchy amongst staff in the hostels, and junior staff also spent more time talking with children and were more accepting and less rejecting of them.

So far in this chapter we have sketched a global, and rather congratulatory, picture of the ideology behind much of the small hostel movement, and have described something of the social organ-

ization of a hypothetical small hostel. Just as the large institution has come to have a stereotyped, and bad, image, so it is perhaps inevitable that small hostels should acquire a favourable, but
equally stereotyped, image. What is lacking is a more detailed
examination of the aims and methods of small hostels, a consideration of variation and degrees of departure from the stereotype
that are to be found amongst real small hostels, and a critical
evaluation of their work. These issues will be taken up in the following three Chapters. But first we turn to look at one special
variety of small hostel - the subject of the research which is reported in detail in the second part of this book - namely small
hostels for people whose major problem has been identified as one of
excessive drinking or alcoholism.

## SMALL ALCOHOLISM HOSTELS

### Views of Alcoholism

Most hostels which are for the mentally ill, or for offenders,
find it difficult to cope with 'the alcoholic', and many have admission rules which specifically exclude people with that particular
problem. Furthermore the view has come to be held, rightly or
wrongly, that the processes of recovery from, and rehabilitation
after, alcoholism require group interaction amongst people who share
the problem. Hence the need for specialist facilities and groups
such as Alcoholics Anonymous and in-patient Alcoholism Treatment
Units. Also the problem is one of sufficient scale, and is sufficiently often accompanied by separation from family and by temporary
or chronic homelessness, to have created a large specialist need for
accommodation and rehabilitation.
There is more to it than that however. Chronic drunkenness,
excessive drinking, or alcoholism, have long been widespread problems
in many countries; as, for example, was particularly the case in
Britain during much of the 18th and 19th centuries and in the early
part of the present century up until the first World War. Such
behaviour, which is in the nature of an excessive indulgence in something which for many people has pleasurable accompaniments, is not
easily seen as solely a problem of illness, or alternatively solely
a problem of immorality or crime. It has generally been regarded in
the latter light, although there have been sporadic arguments in
favour of viewing it as illness for at least 100 years and probably
for far longer (e.g. Rush, c1785). It is however only in the last
20 or so years that there has been a massive professional and public
acceptance of the idea that 'alcoholism is a disease'. The growing
popularity of Alcoholics Anonymous is one of the main sources of
this acceptance but there are undoubtedly others. A major role is
frequently attributed to E.M. Jellinek's book, The Disease Concept of
Alcoholism, published in 1960 at the beginning of a decade which saw
a rapid growth in the number of small hostels both generally and for
alcoholism in particular. There was growing scientific and professional focus on the possibility that many people on 'Skid Row',
many members of the prison population, and many people who were regularly paraded in front of the courts on minor drunkenness charges
were really alcoholics and therefore ill rather than intentionally
delinquent (e.g. Pittman and Gordon, 1962; Edwards et al, 1966).
The view of alcoholism as a disease, coupled with the general move

against institutions and towards hostels gave great impetus to the
movement for the setting up of small specialist, therapeutically-
oriented, alcoholism hostels. At the same time there has been recognition that a lengthy period of in-patient psychiatric hospital
treatment can only ever be offered to a small minority of people with
alcoholism and in any case may not itself be of great therapeutic
advantage (Edwards and Guthrie, 1966; Orford and Edwards, 1977).
Hostel residence may be more appropriate as an alternative to hospitalization, or following a brief period in hospital, for many people
whose problems are as much social as they are medical.

## Recent Growth

The recent boom in alcoholism halfway houses in the U.S. is un-
questionable. The NIMH survey of halfway houses for the mentally
ill and alcoholics, which was referred to earlier when discussing
hostels for the mentally ill, found no fewer than 597 halfway houses
primarily serving alcoholics (NIMH, 1975). Comparative figures for
psychiatric and alcoholism houses showed how much better served the
U.S. is with the latter type of specialist facility than with the
former. Overall, nearly three times as many alcoholism hostels were
located than were psychiatric hostels and the country was better
covered by the first. Eleven states were without psychiatric halfway
houses but only one was without an alcoholism hostel.

The large majority of alcoholism halfway houses had been established since 1960: In fact the numbers of houses figuring in an
NIMH directory prepared in 1971 which were established in successive
5 year periods between 1945 and 1969 were: 1945/49 - 11, 1950/54 - 11,
1955/59 - 41, 1960/64 - 70, and 1965/69 - 121 (NIMH, 1972). Although
some houses may have gone out of existence in the meantime, it appears
that the growth of alcoholism halfway houses was almost exponential
during the 1950's and 1960's.

On a much smaller scale there has been a similar boom in the
U.K. A directory of alcoholism facilities in England and Wales produced by the Camberwell Council on Alcoholism in 1974 listed between
30 and 40 small residential communities making special provision for
alcoholics: almost all are of very recent foundation. Of the 11 such
hostels in the London area, which took part in our own survey, 10
were established in 1960 or more recently.

## Role of the Voluntary Body and Government

Understandably, on account of the innovative nature of small
hostels, it has been a combination of highly motivated individual
pioneers and voluntary (non-statutory) bodies, rather than statutory
authorities, who have taken the lead in their establishment. This
was true in the early years of development of hostels for the mentally
ill both in the U.S. (Raush and Raush, 1968, pp.50-2) and in Britain.
More recently, organizations such as the Veterans Administration in
the U.S., and Local Government Authorities in Britain, have inaugurated
their own hostels. But even when there is an obligation upon an
authority to supply such facilities, as there has been upon Local
Government Authorities in Britain in the case of psychiatric hostels
since 1959, such obligations have not always been fulfilled and
voluntary bodies still play a major role.

In the case of the more specialized field of alcoholism hostels, in Britain at least, individual initiative and the voluntary body have certainly been predominant. As well as having a long tradition of catering for single homeless people, voluntary bodies had the advantage of being much more free to innovate in an area where neither the scale of need nor the value of the new facilities had been established. On the other hand, voluntary agencies undoubtedly have organizational demerits by way of smallness, competitiveness and a tendency to isolation (Owen, 1965, p.321), and it is perhaps to these demerits that the alcoholism hostel field owes much of its fragmented character.

It was only in the late 1960's and the early 1970's that there was evidence of growing Government interest in hostel provision for alcoholics in Britain. A Home Office Working Party was set up to consider the treatment of 'Offenders who habitually commit offences involving drunkenness', and its report in 1971 included the following fairly confident statement about small hostels:

> We believe that it is the relatively small, therapeutically-oriented hostel which at present affords the most hopeful prospect of successful treatment of the habitual drunken offender, and on which a major proportion of available resources of money and effort should be expended in the immediate future (Home Office, 1971, para. 10.13).

It was recognized that not everyone who might benefit from a place in an alcoholism hostel was an offender, and Government responsibility for hostel provision then passed to the Department of Health and Social Security who issued a circular (DHSS Circular 21 of 1973) on 'Community services for alcoholics'. The case for further expansion of hostel facilities was argued and the hope was expressed that Local Government Authorities would begin to play their part. Nonetheless it was recognized that voluntary bodies would continue to be the prime movers for some time to come:

> Many alcoholics however find it easier to accept the type of help most often found at present in a non-statutory setting. Statutory authorities will need to take account of this in planning services: they may need to look to voluntary sources to provide some of the specialized facilities that will be needed and for indications of the approach most likely to be successful (p.2).

A very small number of Local Government Authorities are now taking the initiative in establishing small alcoholism hostels in the U.K. - these authors know of two such Authorities in the country - but the large majority of such hostels are still under the auspices of voluntary agencies. In the U.S. too, according to the 1973 NIMH survey (NIMH, 1975), 90% of alcoholism halfway houses are owned by non-profit, non-Government organizations.

A positive sign of the recent growth in alcoholism hostels in Britain, and an indication of a lessening of the fragmentation of effort which characterized the early years of the movement, has been the recent formation of the Federation of Alcoholic Residential Establishments (FARE) which is open to people who work in, or have an interest in, alcoholism hostels. The Federation was formed at the first National Symposium on Hostels for Alcoholics held in March 1974, and there have been two National Annual Symposia, as well as several regional Symposia since then. The aims of the Federation, to quote from its own publicity, are:

> Providing a communication link between all staff working with alcoholics in residential settings, and collecting and collating their views, experience and expertise. Presenting the views and experience of federation members to statutory services and relevant national and local voluntary agencies, and promoting closer links with these agencies. Working with relevant national and local coordinating agencies to improve and extend residential facilities for alcoholics and the agencies necessary to support the work of these facilities. Stimulating training and discussion seminars and groups...

## Alcoholism Hostels in London

The final section of this first chapter draws upon the results of the authors' own survey, carried out in Summer 1972, of all small alcoholism hostels located in the London area. This exercise was a relatively rapid and superficial one, and was designed to complement the much more lengthy and detailed study of two of the houses - the investigation which is reported in Part II of this book.

### Definitions

The interview administered to staff at the 11 houses which took part in the survey was partly modelled upon that used by Raush and Raush in their survey of hostels for the mentally ill in America (1968, pp.213-22) and the questions asked are reproduced in Appendix E. The 11 hostels involved are those described briefly in tabular form in Table 1. There is immediately a problem of definition in deciding what facilities to include, and which to exclude, when making such a survey. Whilst all of the houses shown in Table 1 probably qualify as undisputed examples of the small alcoholism hostel (although some are not so small, and two also admitted residents other than alcoholics), others were omitted which might have qualified. Facilities were not included, for example, that were described as 'short-term', 'assessment centres', 'first-stage houses' or 'shelters', even though these might have been exclusively for 'alcoholics'. Hence, had we been conducting a survey in the U.S., we would have excluded the occasional alcoholism halfway house, covered in the NIMH survey, which stipulates a maximum length of stay of, for instance, 10, 14 or 30 days (NIMH, 1972). Also excluded were 'three-quarter way houses' which consisted of fairly independent living units; also hostels which claimed to 'accept' alcoholics, unless it was known that some special provision was made for alcoholics there, or that a substantial proportion of residents fell in that category. On the other hand we saw no logical reason for excluding, as was done in the 1973 NIMH survey (NIMH, 1975), facilities without 'round the clock' supervision or facilities which only took referrals from one mental health source.

Table 1: Small hostels for alcoholics in London, 1972.

| House Yr. Estd. | Established by | Capacity | Sex | % Ex-Prisoners | Staff Ratio[b] (Staff: Resident Capacity) | Number Resident |
|---|---|---|---|---|---|---|
| A 1964 | Psychiatrist & Vol. Org. | 12 | M | 50 | 1:12 | 0 |
| B 1966 | Psychiatrist & Alc. Council | 10 | M | 100 | 1:15[c] | 0 |
| C 1960[a] | Christian Mission | 46 | M+F | 70 | 1:6 | 6 |
| D 1964 | Ex-Prisoners' Aid Society | 20 | M | 100 | 1:10 | 1 |
| E 1969 | Christian Mission | 18 | M | 90 | 1:9 | 2 |
| F 1967 | Psychiatrist & Vol. Org. | 12 | M+F | 25 | 1:12 | 0 |
| G 1968 | Spec. Vol. Alc. Org. | 8 | M | 75 | 1:24[c] | 0 |
| H 1971 | Christian Group | 7 | F | 60 | $1:3\frac{1}{2}$ | 1 |
| I 1879 | Priv. Indiv. & Christ.Order | 45[d] | F | 25 | 1:3 | 5 |
| J 1968 | Psychiatrist & Vol. Org. | 15 | M+F | 30 | 1:4 | 1 |
| K 1961 | Christian Society | 40[d] | M | 60 | 1:7 | 2 |

[a] Accommodation for female residents opened 1965.

[b] Based on no. of full-time equivalent staff, excluding domestic and secretarial staff.

[c] One member of staff covered these two hostels.

[d] These houses admitted residents other than alcoholics.

Origins and Purposes

The origins of the hostels in this small sample are of interest and they undoubtedly exert a major influence on the way they operate. There appeared to be two major routes whereby they had been set up, although both involved non-statutory bodies. Five had their origins in a religious mission or society, whilst a further four had been set up at least partly at the instigation of someone in a specialist psychiatric treatment service, usually in conjunction with a voluntary body active in the residential social work field. Of the remaining two hostels, House G could be said to belong in this sec-

ond group of hostels of medical origin as it was set up by a voluntary body whose own origin lay in the psychiatric field. This leaves
House D started by a Discharged Prisoners' Aid Society. Any such
cursory description of origins is bound to be much over-simplified -
for example in some instances people working in the Probation Service
had been as influential as psychiatrists in establishing the hostel -
but there remains a fairly clear distinction between hostels with a
religious background and those with origins in modern, secular,
concern with 'treatment'. It may be noted that the three longest
established hostels were all in the religious group and are the three
with the largest capacities. Those with roots in psychiatry tend to
be much smaller and tend to operate without residential staff.

The origins of alcoholism hostels are related (but in no very
simple way) to the group of people for whom they cater, and hence to
their most frequently used sources of referral of potential residents.
In two instances (Houses F and J) the specific purpose of the house
was to serve as an after-care facility following treatment in a hospital alcoholism treatment unit. In a third case (House A) it was
expected that a special, but not exclusive, referral relationship
would exist with such a hospital unit. At least three of the remaining hostels (Houses B, D and E) set out with the intention of
specializing in the rehabilitation of ex-offenders, and for that
purpose received per capita grants from the Home Office (a system of
financing later taken over by the Department of Health & Social
Security in the case of alcoholic ex-offenders). These were hostels
for 'Skid Row' or 'vagrant' alcoholics. All, or almost all, of their
residents had been in prison at one time or another, whilst a variable
and smaller proportion of residents at the other houses were ex-
prisoners.

There were two major groups of sources of referral to the hostels.
Doctors and social workers working in psychiatric hospitals constituted one principal source, particularly to those hostels set up with
such a referral link in mind. The second group of sources, particularly used by hostels set up to deal with ex-offender alcoholics,
consisted of staff of the Prison and Probation and After-Care Services, along with staff of Department of Health and Society Security
reception centres (providing mostly over-night accommodation for
homeless single people in a large institutional setting). Besides
these two groups of sources, other referral agents such as general
hospitals, general medical practitioners, voluntary social service
agencies, clergy and Alcoholics Anonymous,provided relatively very few
referrals.

Size and Structure

Of the 5 hostels with a religious foundation, 2 were housed, at
least partly, in converted chapels, and the other 3 were housed,
respectively, in a 100 year old Council doss house, a large Georgian
country manor house with extensive grounds, and an East End tenement
house. The rest of the hostels were housed in unremarkable buildings,
mostly between 50 and 100 years old, easily passing for ordinary
dwellings in residential districts. Three of the 5 of religious
foundation had names of Christian Saints incorporated into their
titles, whilst the remainder were named after the roads in which they
stood, or after an individual of national or local, historical or recent, importance. There were no examples of the use of evocative

41620

words or phrases, commonly found in the titles of halfway houses in the U.S., such as 'Serenity', 'Friendship', 'Phoenix', and 'Stepping Stones'.

In speaking of the size of a hostel, the word 'small' clearly has no absolute meaning. Three of the houses were considerably larger than the rest, having a capacity of between 40 and 50. However, two were hostels making special but not exclusive provision for alcoholics, so the group of alcoholics was considerably smaller than the total group, and in any case one stated a preference for operating with around 30 residents.

At the time of the survey, resident occupancy varied between 33% and 90% of capacity. Two of the 11 were less than half full (both had extensive repairs or decorations going on at the time), and only 3 were more than three-quarters full. However, it is probably misleading to speak of 'under-occupancy' in a small hostel or to argue that such figures indicate an absence of need for all the places provided. In the following Chapters (particularly Chapters 2 and 8) we shall discuss a number of good reasons, to do with the dynamics of residency in small hostels, for most alcoholism hostels operating between half and three-quarters full much of the time whatever their size.

House C was unusual in having substantial numbers of both sexes amongst its residents. The male and female parts had been established at different dates and had for some years existed side by side as separate hostels with separate staffs. Recently they had been at least partly integrated. Other than this one hostel, 2 were exclusively for women and 6 exclusively for men, leaving 2 others that advertized themselves as catering for both sexes. These were the same 2 small hostels (F and J) exclusively taking from hospital units (at least when they were first set up). Neither had more than a very small number of women residents at any one time. Since 1972 another of the medically-originating hostels (House A) has started to admit women residents in addition to men. All maleness is a feature of North American alcoholism hostels also. The NIMH survey found 65% of such hostels admitting only men and a mere 22½% admitting both sexes. In contrast, the comparable figures for psychiatric halfway houses were 15% men only and 67% mixed sexes (NIMH, 1975).

Sleeping accommodation, and hence privacy, is variable. Whereas nearly all were able to accommodate their residents in single, double or occasionally treble bedrooms (the 2 female hostels but only one of the male hostels accommodated all their residents in single bedrooms), there were 2 hostels (one large and one smaller) where all, or the majority, of residents were accommodated in cubicles without fixed doors. Both these houses had their origins in a religious organization; one was housed in a converted chapel and the other in a converted doss house; and staff at neither were satisfied with this type of accommodation.

Specialism

Both in Britain and the U.S. the large majority of hostels making special provision for alcoholics do so to the exclusion of other categories of people. A small proportion, however, do not: some admit other offenders, others cater for the mentally ill but make special mention of alcoholism, and others mix people whose problem is with alcohol with others whose problem concerns other drugs. Of the 2 larger hostels in the present sample which were not exclusively for alcoholics, both accepted people with a wide variety of problems, but the male hostel (K) included specific sub-groups of men with gambling problems and with sexual problems, and staff at the female hostel (I) referred specifically to drug addiction and prostitution.

On this question of specialism the Government circular favoured hostels specifically for alcoholics (DHSS, 1973, para. 16), and indeed DHSS grants for the setting up of new hostels have been made contingent upon this specialism. The purpose of this may have been to give support to hostels that made special provision for alcoholics but its effect is to give particular encouragement to hostels that make not only special, but also exclusive, provision. One of the staff members of one of the larger non-exclusive hostels was fairly outspoken on this matter, stating:

> Our policy is positive and does not support 'ghetto' type
> units that specialize in a particular category of problem
> such as alcoholics or gamblers.

We know of a further project in the London area, not included in this survey for this very reason, which is aware of serious drinking problems in a proportion of its residents but self-consciously makes no special provision for this group, arguing that the 'labelling' of people as 'alcoholics' is counter-productive. Nor was questioning of the need for specialism limited to staff at already non-specialist hostels. Staff at one of the small specialist houses stated:

> I would like alcoholism not to be the admission criterion.
> I don't believe in houses for a single category of need.
> There is nothing here which is special to alcoholism. It
> could be applied to all sorts of need.

Staffing

As Table 1 shows, there was considerable variation in staffing arrangements. Most of the smaller houses referred to their senior staff member as a 'warden', although there was considerable ambivalence about the use of that particular term. Staff at one hostel stated adamantly that the term should not be used and that the term 'social worker' would be better. Others preferred the term 'administrator'. It was only at the larger establishments that terms such as 'director', 'sister superior', 'deputy director' and 'senior assistant administrator' were used. Three staff members in charge of hostels had no assistants other than domestic and secretarial assistants, whilst all others had at least one assistant and sometimes many more. Staff-to-resident ratios varied from 1:3 to 1:24. The median ratio was 1:9.

Despite the small numbers of hostels involved, Table 1 also shows quite a definite relationship between the staff-to-resident ratio and the size of the hostel. All 3 of the larger hostels with capacities of more than 40 had a favourable staff ratio of 1:8 residents or less. On the other hand, of the 5 smallest hostels with 12 residents or fewer all but one had a relatively unfavourable staff ratio of 1:12 residents or more. The single exception (H) was already exceptional in being exclusively for female residents.

Also apparent in Table 1 is a fairly clear relationship between

staffing ratios and the existence, or not, of residential staff.
Again it is the 4 small, exclusively or mainly male, hostels, with
at best a single staff member, which are the ones without any staff
in residence at the hostel (A, B, F, G). All others have at least
one residential member of staff, and sometimes as many as 5 or 6 in
the larger hostels.

The relationships between hostel size and numbers of staff, and
whether the staff are resident, are almost certainly to be attributed
to differences in origin and ideology. Although there are exceptions,
the smallest hostels, without residential staff, tend to be those that
derive most directly from the movement towards non-institutional
treatment of offenders and the mentally ill. They represent the
clearest examples of reaction against the large institution, and they
are most likely to identify with the general therapeutic community
approach. The larger, usually older, Christian, hostels less
obviously share this ideology.

The question of staff training was touched upon lightly in the
survey. The training of those working in residential social work is
often said to be unsatisfactory in general (e.g. Central Council for
Education and Training in Social Work, 1973) and the state of affairs
in specialized alcoholism hostels is probably no exception. Of the
staff at these 11 hostels nearly all were quite untrained or had some
non-social work qualification. In fact only at 2 houses did a staff
member have a relevant social work qualification, both were larger
hostels, and in both cases it was an assistant or deputy only who
had the qualification. At one of the smaller hostels the staff member
in charge was an experienced probation officer. Otherwise qualifications included nursing, teaching, theology, art and catering, whilst
others had obtained degrees of no particular relevance or had come
from jobs in industry. At least 3 staff members in charge of hostels
had themselves suffered from alcoholism. The NIMH survey of alcoholism
halfway houses in the U.S. (1975) found no fewer than 60% of all staff
to be 'recovering alcoholics'.

Staff specifically appointed to work in a hostel do not of course
exhaust the range of professional and other supports available to it.
All but one of the hostels surveyed made some use of trained, specialist, visiting staff. Seven hostels mentioned a visiting psychiatrist although the frequency of his visiting varied from 'regular' to
'occasional' or 'hasn't been for 4 months'. The psychiatrist's function varied: sometimes the emphasis was on seeing individual residents
when necessary, sometimes on selection of new residents, and sometimes
on advising staff. The next largest category of visiting specialist
staff was that of 'social worker' including senior staff or colleagues
employed by the parent organization. The other fairly frequently
mentioned category, mentioned by 5 hostels, was that of 'probation
officers'. At least 2 of the houses liaised with a psychiatric out-
patient department so that residents would be assured of extra specialist help if necessary. The importance of a link with Alcoholics
Anonymous was mentioned by only 3 hostels out of the 11. This may be
an important difference between alcoholism hostels in Britain and the
U.S. where most are quite strongly affiliated to AA (NIMH, 1972).
Finally, a general practitioner was mentioned as a regular visitor by
3 hostels. Only one hostel (D) was quite without specialist professional visiting staff. It's permanent staff were also without
training.

All but the larger women's hostel (House I) had a committee, although titles other than the word 'committee' were preferred in some cases. In one instance the group was called an 'advisory body' although it seemed to be a conventional committee in all but name. In some other cases (including Houses A and B) where the house was part of a larger organization, there was no committee for the hostel itself (although the larger organization had committees dealing with matters such as staffing and finance that affected the house) but the staff member in charge had available to him the advice of a relatively small (3 to 5 people) 'support group'.

Hostel Programs

All but one of the hostels in the survey had some form of weekly group meeting, the exception being House D. Nearly all the rest had a single meeting a week which they called a 'house meeting' or a 'group meeting'. However, one house called its meeting 'group therapy', one had a single group therapy meeting in addition to a house meeting, one had an 'individual group' in addition to a house meeting, and House A had a 'group therapy and business meeting' as well as a 'visitors meeting'.

Thus, although some form of group meeting was almost universal, none of the hostels made use of anything like an intensive group work program. Partly because of the expectation that at least some residents would obtain employment outside the hostel, nearly all had no more than one or two group meetings a week, held in the evenings. There was no representative of a type of program (which we know to exist in at least one English alcoholism hostel outside London) involving at least one day-time or evening group meeting on almost every day of the week.

All 11 hostels allowed for the possibility of residents obtaining work outside the house during their stay there. With possibly one exception, none of the hostels aimed to cover their running costs from charges made on residents. All charged a rent of between £5 and £7 per week, which was certainly no more than the resident would have to have paid for accommodation and part board elsewhere at the time. If a resident was not working he or she was required to contribute all but a small proportion of the weekly Social Security payment. The larger women's hostel (House I) was exceptional in charging between £12 and £20 weekly depending upon individual resources.

In practice the proportion of current residents in work at the time of the survey ranged from none at all to 100%. At 5 houses less than a third of the residents were in work at the time; at the remaining 6, two-thirds or more were in work. Staff were also asked whether working outside was compulsory, encouraged, or not particularly emphasized. Only at one hostel out of the 11 (House D) was outside work compulsory. The remainder were roughly equally divided between those that actively encouraged working and those that stated that they did not particularly emphasize it. However, whether staff said they encouraged or did not particularly emphasize working outside appeared to have no relationship with the actual proportion of current residents working at the time.

Staff at several hostels recognized that it would be wrong to pressure men into obtaining outside work if they were not ready for it, particularly in the early stages of their residence. Nonetheless at all these 11 hostels the expectation was that fit residents would attempt to obtain employment, and not one of them discouraged outside work or disallowed it, or provided a program of events in the house which would preclude it. This of course is an extremely important fact in understanding the nature of these small hostels. The program of events in the house is relatively non-intensive and geared to the possibility of residents obtaining work. There were no examples, in the survey sample, of houses providing their own work program or where the program of events in the hostel was so intensive that work would have interfered with it.

The very word 'program' is in fact misleading in relation to these small hostels. Whatever influence is brought to bear upon the residents during their stay, it is undoubtedly brought to bear principally by the sheer experience of living in a community of people with a common purpose. Indeed one might expect this common living experience to be more socially influencial than a whole variety of 'therapies' or specially engineered events. The emphasis is undoubtedly on non-institutional informality. Residents can get work outside the house; they come and go more or less as they please; there are certainly no uniformed staff and sometimes no residential staff at all; residents at all houses were involved in some domestic tasks, and there were virtually no rules other than those concerning the consumption of alcohol.

However, there are undoubtedly degrees of informality. The larger hostels emerged, perhaps understandably, as being decidedly less informal. They had cooks and domestic staff which left residents little scope for anything other than small voluntary chores, and they were likely to stipulate times for breakfast, times after which residents should be in at night and bedtimes. Some of the smaller hostels, on the other hand, as well as having a relatively large number of residents to a staff member and no residential staff, were quite likely to require that residents cook their own meals at least at weekends and had no particular rules about such things as the timing of meals. The larger female hostel (House I) was clearly more institutional than most in many ways, referring on occasions to its residents as 'patients' and exercising a fairly high degree of control over residents to the point of 'discouraging them from going to each others rooms'. Whereas it is difficult for the larger hostel to be very informal, the small hostel clearly has a choice, and not all smaller hostels were very informal. In particular one medium-sized hostel (House D), already referred to as the only one making outside work compulsory, and the only one without any professional hostel or visiting staff, was again the only smaller hostel to share with the larger hostels the making of rules about times for such things as meals and bed.

The degree to which residents are involved in making major or minor decisions about the day-to-day running of the hostel is a variable of major importance, and is of course crucial in deciding what degree of contrast with the large institution the hostel provides. The hostels in the survey were by no means uniform in this matter, but a lengthier discussion of this topic is reserved for Chapter 3 where we consider varieties of residential hostel experience.

Although staff stress that sobriety alone is not enough, the
control of drinking behaviour in small hostels for alcoholics is a
major preoccupation. Without exception, all these hostels had a 'no
drinking' rule for their alcoholic residents. They shared with
Alcoholics Anonymous and most hospital treatment services an almost
total allegiance to the belief that all alcoholics must abstain
totally from drinking.

In actual practice the 'no drinking' rule was exercised variably both between houses and within houses. For most, the no drinking rule referred to drinking both inside and outside the house. Any
reported instance of drinking made the individual concerned a candidate for discharge. On the other hand, at least one house, the
small hostel for women (House H), had a.rule that no drinking was
allowed in the house. If residents drank outside they would not be
admitted to the house in a state of intoxication but if they came
back sober their 'case would be reviewed'. Here there was a clear
distinction between drinking on and off the premises. Most houses,
though, subscribed to the view that controlled drinking for their
residents was impossible, that drinking away from the house would
inevitably come to light and would inevitably be associated sooner
or later with uncontrolled drinking or intoxication or disruptive
behaviour, and that to make a distinction between drinking in the
house and away from it was therefore academic.

Although known drinking made the individual concerned a candidate
for discharge, this ultimate penalty, whether enforced by staff,
residents, or staff and residents jointly, was variably enforced at
some hostels depending upon the individual case. A staff member of
one of the larger hostels stated: "You may give one man 5 chances
because you believe he's really trying and another none because you
think he is a con man".

Although the issue of drinking gives small alcoholism hostels a
special character, this chapter must conclude by returning to its
general starting point. Alcoholism hostels are part of the movement
away from institutional care and towards community care and self-
help. It takes but little to see that the features they share with
other types of small hostel are more fundamental than their unique
characteristics.

# Chapter 2
# The Aims of Small Hostels

The official goals of an organization are invariably general
and vague.  Stated at a high level of abstraction they must
be translated into operative goals before they can be used
as the basis of policy (Smith, 1970, p.6).

The present authors are not alone in observing a lack of clarity
that exists over the very basic issue of what small hostels are for.
Other research workers have pointed to the lack of a coherent model
of what hostels are trying to do, and have noted the consequent
confusion in the minds of all concerned, and a dearth of guiding
principles upon which to base actual practice inside hostels (Apte,
1968; Sinclair, 1971).  If hostels are to make a more incisive
contribution, and if they are to become more than a fashion of just 2
or 3 decades, they must, as a priority, develop a more coherent set
of ideas about their means and ends.

## A SOCIAL INFLUENCE MODEL OF HOSTELS

Apte has considered various theories which attempt to explain
the operation of halfway houses for the mentally ill (1968, pp.18-
25).  These include social role theory, socialization theory,
acculturation theory, a grading of stress theory, and finally a
social milieu or therapeutic environment theory.  Each of these view-
points has much to commend it.  Indeed the number of models which
have some appropriateness argues for the many functions which the
hostel or halfway house could perform.  It may be misleading to
search for a single model within which to understand what the many
different types of hostels can do for the many types of people who at
one time or another live in them.  The hostel's overall purpose is
well summarized by the phrase, similar to ones which hostel residents
frequently use spontaneously, 'The place is helping me get on my own
two feet'.  Hence its precise functions are as difficult to pin down
as are those of the family, which serves a similar type of general
purpose for its young, dependent, members.

## Socialization

Subsumed under this very general caring function are at least
two sub-functions shared by all care-givers.  Firstly, there is the
need for the care-giving person, group or organization to train its

members (its children, trainees, novices, or residents)in attitudes and behaviours which it considers to be appropriate. This is the soc- ialization function, and it involves the control element of human relationships. Staff members, as well as the rest of the resident community, are in a powerful position to influence a resident, and they use this position of influence to encourage what is believed to be right thinking and conduct. As Keller and Alper (1970) write of halfway houses for delinquents in North America:

> ... ⟨they⟩ attempt to change the attitudes and consequent behaviour of such boys by manipulating the peer group so that it endorses, rather than opposes, acceptable standards (p.39).

This model is most obviously applicable when the consumers (res- idents, inmates, pupils etc.) are youthful or in need of behavioural 'correction'. Hence the model is particularly apt for hostels for juvenile delinquents, but is not a complete formulation when applied to hostels for the adult mentally ill, for example.

Providing Skills and Resources

The second care-giving function might be termed 'providing access to skills and resources'. Most adults make their way without the need for professional, or other special, care because they have acc- umulated personal and social resources that enable them to do so. People who come to hostels or halfway houses have usually lost many of the skills and resources they had, as a result of illness or long periods of institutionalization. Hewett et al (1975), in their study of residents of psychiatric hostels in England, noted that in add- ition to personal handicaps (almost all had suffered with severe mental illnesses):

> The majority of the people studied were without significant family support. They were a special group of single, home- less people who had particular accommodation problems. They earned low incomes and were competing for accommodation in a situation of severe housing shortage (p.402).

As will be apparent in Chapter 6, residents of alcoholism hostels are likely to have little or no recent contact with family, may have had much experience of mental hospital or prison, and may have few educational or occupational resources. A main task in helping someone 'get on his feet' is that of easing his access to material, social and personal resources that will increase his competence or ability to cope with everyday life outside an institution. As is the case with any care-giving, this is probably done in a whole host of different ways ranging from improving a person's personal social skills (which, if successful, may amount to nothing less than 'personality change'), all the way to giving a person an address from which he can look for employment. It includes both the provision of a new peer group for friendship and support, as well as the availability of staff who may be able to offer both counselling and practical assistance.

If the socialization function of a residential hostel corresponds to the control dimension of human relationships, then the 'resources' function corresponds to the acceptance or support dimension. It is not too much of an over-simplification to say that good care-giving (in this case provided by hostel staff and resident group) consists of a careful mixture of control and acceptance. As we shall see, the mixture is difficult to achieve in practice.

## Cohesiveness and Atmosphere

Whether it's task is principally that of socializing it's residents through social control, or improving its residents' skills and resources through social support, beneficial social influence is intended. Our purpose now is to argue that social influence will be maximized in the hostel when conditions of <u>cohesiveness</u> exist there. Processes of social influence, such as reward and punishment training, imitation, social comparison, and contagion, are encouraged by mutual liking and respect, by frequent and accurate communication, and by spending time together and sharing activities. According to The Handbook of Social Psychology (Collins and Raven, 1969), the following are amongst the characteristics of the highly cohesive group:

1 A high level of 'responsible activity' - members voluntarily take on tasks for the group, there is a high level of participation and attendance at group meetings, members persist in working towards group goals.
2 A relatively high level of satisfaction and morale.
3 Members not only judge other members' behaviour favourably but also perceive other members as being similar to themselves and as having mutual feelings to themselves.
4 Fuller and more accurate communication amongst members.
5 Relatively much interpersonal influence.

The small hostel aims to develop what Keller and Alper (1970, p.43) call a 'positive group culture' characterized by an esprit de corps and an atmosphere of mutual concern. We would state the conditions which small hostels aim for, and which would in theory produce the most social influence, as follows: <u>Cohesiveness around a coherent ethic approved publicly and privately by all staff and most residents.</u>
For a whole variety of reasons these conditions do not always pertain in care-giving residential settings. Furthermore, small hostels may be particularly vulnerable to variations in social atmosphere, for two separate reasons: their smallness, and their non-institutional informality. Paradoxically, their high ideals and their principal virtues expose them to special risks.
There are two sides to the problem which may be thought of separately - the problem of initial creation of a cohesive atmosphere, and the problem of maintaining such a social climate once established. Keller and Alper have much to say about the first of these problems under the heading 'building the culture'. "All agree...", they state, "...that the initial stages in the creation of the group culture are fraught with difficulties" (p.59). At an early stage the predominant resident attitude is contrary to the spirit that staff would like to engender - problems are denied, there is the feeling that individuals should not be involved with others' problems, and a belief that the halfway house is aiming for an environment which is too permissive in comparison with the more institutional environments that many residents have known.

Oscillations in Stability and Atmosphere

Once a satisfactory climate (or cohesiveness around a satisfactory ethic, as we would call it) is established, there is then the problem of maintaining it. In fact, in our experience, small hostels rarely succeed in maintaining a highly satisfactory culture for very long; their history is characterized, rather, by more or less marked fluctuations, or oscillations, in atmosphere. Ups and downs appear to be endemic to these small communities, as they are, according to Rapoport, to any therapeutic or rehabilitation unit oriented towards 'community therapy'. In his book, Community as Doctor (1960), Rapoport describes such 'oscillations' in the climate and social organization of the therapeutic community at the Henderson Hospital. At times of greatest equilibrium, tension was low and patients' behaviour on the whole conforming. More frequent deviant behaviour was shown at other times, when the social climate was characterized by tension, defensiveness, aggression and withdrawal. Indices of participation, such as group attendance, showed a decline, and there were corresponding changes in attitudes. Staff and patients were in agreement at times of equilibrium, but at other times anti-unit values were more openly expressed. At such times individuals who expressed negative attitudes were the most prestigeful amongst the patient group. Staff-patient communication was impaired as a result (Rapoport, 1960, pp.135-142, 155-8).

We have observed similar fluctuations in stability and atmosphere at a small hostel for 'compulsive gamblers'. The hostel's smallness (capacity for 7 men), coupled with the relatively high turnover of residents which seems to be a fact of life in hostels for people with habit or behaviour problems, made it extremely difficult to build up and maintain a stable group. As one relatively long-staying resident put it, there were "constant comings and goings" of residents. Almost every month someone new came or an existing resident left, and the stability of the house depended upon a small handful of residents who were relatively constant figures. Once a stable group was established, there was the constant threat of disintegration, which had in fact occurred three times in the first three-and-a-half years of the hostel's existence.

Minutes of committee meetings held around the time of such crises showed that staff were demoralized, and committee members were prompted at these times to ask fundamental questions about the purpose of the house itself. As might be expected at times of crisis, the committee looked for ways out, such as converting the house into something quite different (such as an office for Gamblers' Anonymous) or by making radical alterations to selection procedures.

Elements of Atmosphere

Although stability in numerical terms is of vital importance to such a small organization, it may be less important in larger units, and is in any case only part of the business of 'building up a good group'. The social climate or atmosphere of a stable group may or may not be favourable, and the values and attitudes expressed by members of a stable group may or may not be consistent with staff-approved goals. Again the small hostel for gamblers is illustrative. There appeared to be at least two separate elements of 'good atmosphere'.

The first was social, and would be applicable to almost any residential group including a nuclear family. Residents were able to describe definite signs of 'togetherness' and 'friendliness'. They described entering the house and seeing fellow residents talking together, and enquiring after each other, rather than sitting solemnly watching television. The atmosphere could also be gauged from the number and range of joint shared activities.

The second criterion of good atmosphere was more ideological than social, and in this instance had to do with the attitudes of residents towards the control of their gambling. Committee minutes displayed continuing concern felt about the difficulty in meeting this criterion. It was reported at one meeting that all residents were gambling, and the administrator and his assistant wanted to know 'how long gambling should be tolerated?' By way of contrast, residents of a later period spoke warmly of the high level of mutual concern, and the seriousness which everyone felt about giving up gambling.

Selection-In of Residents

How do small hostels foster the group cohesiveness which our model views as an essential condition for the social influence task upon which the hostel is engaged? Apart from inducing conformity by the application of rules and sanctions and the operation of a variety of informal pressures, hence increasing cohesiveness and creating the circumstances for further social influence, there are at least two other general means which are used virtually universally for bringing about relative conformity in the values and behaviours of members of groups and organizations. Both are concerned with selection of members, and may be termed 'selection-in' and 'selection-out'.

The avoidance of residents who might cause disruption, and the desire for residents who will mix amicably with others, are obviously major considerations in small, relatively informal, non-institutional, residential communities. Hence hostels are frequently preoccupied with the selection of new members in terms of criteria, some of which are relatively clear cut, others of which are more vague and indefinite. Many general hostels for the mentally ill or for offenders have admission rules excluding such categories as alcoholics, drug addicts, people with organic brain damage, the subnormal, people of known homosexual orientation, and people with a history of violent anti-social conduct.

One of the most regularly recurring criteria of selection, understandably in view of the central place of work in rehabilitation, is employability. Likely ability to find and hold gainful employment shortly after admission to the hostel, or even in some cases possession of a job prior to selection, is very often a condition of admission to a small hostel. However, as will emerge more clearly in the following Chapter, it is important not to generalize too widely about small hostels. As in other matters, there are wide variations to be found in selection criteria and stringency. American halfway houses for the mentally ill, for instance, include many with strict employability selection criteria, but there are others which view getting and holding a job as one of the end results of successful rehabilitation and not as an initial selection criterion (Raush and Raush, 1968, p.87). There are similar contrasts in hostel policies regarding severity of mental disturbance as indicated by years of prior psychiatric hospitalizations. Raush and Raush contrast Conard House in San Francisco where the average amount of hospitalization was 14 months, with Wellmet House in Boston where the average was 12 years (p.88).

As well as differences between different hostels, the need for stringency in selection varies from time to time at the same house. Many houses aim principally for a mixed but balanced group of residents with a sufficient number of 'better risks' or residents whose rehabilitation is relatively advanced, to provide a strong enough peer group culture to support and influence others. It is a delicate business maintaining such a balance whilst allowing for a steady, but not too fast, throughput of resident members. As Keller and Alper write:

> Major problems relate to intake and departure. If too many newcomers are received at any one time, the group culture, which may have been painstakingly developed over many weeks, may be completely disrupted in very short order (1970, p.66).

Problems inevitably develop in relationships between hostels on the one hand, and individuals and organizations who refer prospective residents or who are themselves prospective residents on the other. The very difficulty of specifying precisely the criteria upon which selection is based, and the evident fact that the criteria change somewhat from time to time depending on the occupancy and internal social dynamics of the house, are bound to make for misunderstanding. The whole procedure may appear very logical and necessary from the inside looking out, but to the outsider trying to get in, or trying to get a client in, the procedure may appear distinctly illogical and counter-productive. Referral agents accuse small therapeutic hostels of guarding their facility too jealously, and of never giving their clients a fair hearing, whilst hostel staff often accuse referral agents of 'dumping' people on them, of making 'bad referrals', and of having insufficient knowledge of their house and how it works.

Selection-Out of Residents

Apart from selection-in, selection-out is a major means of maintaining an appropriate value climate, or atmosphere, so that members, especially new members, may be influenced for good rather than for ill. Just as it can be demonstrated in conformity experiments that 'norms' can be transmitted across several 'generations' of new experimental subjects, provided there is some continuity of membership from one period of the experiment to the next (Jacob and Campbell, 1961), so staff are naturally concerned with preserving some continuity of membership over time, or with fostering an established nuclear, 'culture carrying', group. These 'older' members should have status with, and hence influence over, newer members, and should hold to the values and display the behaviours of which staff approve, and which are consistent with the hostel's goals. The process of selection-out is vital here. The lengths of stay of residents in halfway houses is highly variable; hence the membership at any one time is a select representation of former new entrants, and relatively long-stayers potentially wield an influence disproportionate to their initial status as the few amongst all former newcomers.

Hence the process of selection-out is as crucial as that of selection-in, although the former may be a process over which staff have relatively little control. Hostels for offenders who have been referred by the courts or who are on probation may have the power to recommend return to court. Indeed Keller and Alper state that, at a certain stage in the development of a satisfactory hostel culture, this sanction may have to be used a number of times, "...until a small nucleus for the creation of a positive group finally remains ..." (1970, p.43). Other types of hostel with close referral links with a psychiatric hospital may be in a position to recommend re-hospitalization, and other hostels may discharge a resident for breaking a specific rule - as is frequently the case when the no-drinking rule is broken in alcoholism hostels. Otherwise, selection-out is a naturally occurring process only partially within the control of hostel staff and residents.

Staff Behaviour

Much of the evidence of the research to be reported in the second part of this book points to the importance of staff as key figures in small alcoholism hostels, and the same is almost certainly true in other types of hostel. It is scarcely surprising that staff should make a disproportionately major contribution to group cohesiveness. They have a specialized role and have greater 'social power' than other members. In many hostels:

> The warden can give or withold privileges which are intensely important to the resident, such as allowing or withholding privacy, lengthening or curtailing a resident's stay, taking a flexible attitude in the interpretation of rules and regulations, and seeing that an unemployed resident is cared for (Apte, 1968, p.53).

Even with greater democratization, the staff member in charge retains a definite managerial role, and hence staff characteristics that make for popularity are at a premium. There are, for example, strong hints from the research to be reported later (Chapter 8) that the amount of time staff members spend with their residents is an important variable. This is scarcely surprising in view of the large social psychological literature attesting to the importance, for interpersonal attraction, of the sheer volume of interaction between persons (e.g. Secord and Backman, 1974, p.221).

Nevertheless, there are undoubtedly staff characteristics that make for an improved quality, quite apart from quantity, of interaction with residents. As is the case with most of the issues to do with the organization of small hostels that we touch upon in Part I, there has been relatively little good research on the subject. On this issue, however, there is one piece of research, on English probation hostels, which is of particular interest and which should be replicated in other types of hostel. This is the research, from which we have already quoted, carried out at the Home Office Research Unit by Sinclair and his colleagues. They examined the relationship between failure rates (based on the percentage of residents leaving as a result of absconding or being reconvicted) and wardens' attitudes in 16 different hostel regimes (i.e. periods of tenure of individual wardens). They identified two components of attitude which were positively associated with success: strictness as opposed to permissiveness; and emotional closeness - which included warmth and willingness to discuss residents' problems with them - versus emotional distance. Particularly salutary was the finding that these two attitude components, each separately associated with success, were negatively associated with one another. Hence wardens who displayed warmth and willingness to discuss problems were also likely to be over-permissive, whilst those who were relatively strict tended to be lacking in behaviour making for emotional closeness. The ideal combination of warmth and firmness was a combination relatively rarely encountered (Sinclair, 1971, pp.112-14).

There is in fact much evidence that it is such a combination of warmth and firmness which is most likely to make socializing agents popular with those they are in a position to influence, whether these agents be parents, teachers, husbands and wives or psychotherapists. It is however important to appreciate that Sinclair's research concerned hostels for young probationers - a setting in which the socialization function may be presumed to be of paramount importance. It might reasonably be supposed that the relationship between strictness-permissiveness and popularity or effectiveness is different in settings where residents are older, more mature, or suffer from mental health rather than conduct problems, and where the 'providing access to skills and resources' function may be more important.

Keller and Alper (1970) have described in some detail what they consider to be the ideal leader of a probation or parole halfway house. Although they present no research evidence to back up their claims, their ideas are consistent with some of our own and those of Sinclair. They stress, for instance, the need for staff to involve themselves and spend time with residents. They write of the need for staff to make themselves readily available, to take meals with residents, to take part in recreation with residents, and to invite informal contacts through keeping the office door open. Warmth and closeness are indicated by showing genuine regard for residents, permitting residents to express feelings on all subjects, being able to talk, joke, and communicate in person-to-person fashion with residents, and generally reducing status differences between staff and residents. By analogy with the classic social psychology experiments on leadership of boys clubs (Lewin et al, 1939), staff should, according to Keller and Alper, avoid authoritarian leadership. On the other hand, they should display definite leadership qualities and avoid the laissez-faire approach. They must in fact display what Sinclair showed to be the relatively rare, "ability to walk the very thin line between friendship and authority..." (Keller and Alper, 1970, p.53).

## Hostels as Complex Systems

When discussing these, or indeed almost any other, facet of hostel social organization, it is important to bear in mind the complex inter-reacting nature of social events. Simple relationships between staff, resident or outcome variables, let alone ones that can be unambiguously interpreted in terms of cause and effect, are scarcely to be expected when such a complex organization with so many separate inputs and processes is the subject of study. Further results from Sinclair's study of probation hostels illustrates this complexity well. The permissiveness of the warden's attitude was not only correlated with failure rate, but was also correlated with the size of the dis-

crepancy in attitude between the warden and the matron (most of the
probation hostels were run by married couples, the husband serving as
warden and the wife as matron). In other words, matrons were rarely
as permissive as their wardens and hence in practice it was rare to
find a warden and matron who presented a unified permissive view.
When the effect of this discrepancy was partialled out, the warden's
permissiveness was no longer significantly correlated with failure
rate. It was therefore possible that permissiveness was not a bad
thing in itself, but appeared bad because it created strain between
warden and matron.

In his analysis of social disorganization in a hostel community
Sinclair came to essentially the same conclusion that the present
authors reached (Chapters 8 and 9) concerning the causes of disorganization in an alcoholism hostel. The conclusion was that breakdown was normally the result of a 'combination of misfortunes' and
could never be attributed to a single cause. However, he noted how
events became simplified in people's minds as time passed so that a
whole complex train of events might well be attributed to a single
cause, not infrequently the warden's personality or behaviour. Only
if events were analyzed whilst they were occurring was it easy to
appreciate their truly interdependent nature (1971, p.94).

Organizational Factors

Staff behaviour will undoubtedly be affected, not only by individual predilection and temperament, but also by aspects of the social
structure within which staff have to work. Like many features of
social structure, one which should in general operate in favour of
the small hostel in contrast to larger institutions is that of staff
autonomy. This is a factor which Tizard et al (1975) have singled out
as being of particular importance in residential provision for children. They believe there is good evidence that where a unit is relatively autonomous and the head of the unit has relative freedom to
take decisions, this leads to a higher quality of interaction between
staff and residents and to better morale.

Some of the best evidence for the importance of autonomy comes
from 13 residential nurseries studied by Barbara Tizard (1975). These
nurseries were chosen to represent the extremes of autonomy: at one
extreme were those relatively like hospitals, which were run by the
supervising matron and which gave junior staff relatively little
decision-making freedom; whilst at the other extreme were those approximating to foster-care, organized into separate flats or cottages,
and where individual members of staff had relatively great autonomy.
Detailed observational study of both types showed significant differences in quality of staff-child interaction. In the latter, more
autonomous, units staff spoke to children using longer and more complex sentences, passed more informative remarks to children, provided
more explanations when giving children commands, and answered more
questions. They spent more time reading and playing with children,
and the children were more often observed to be active rather than
passive in what they were doing. Not only were there these differences in observed behaviour of staff and children, but when the
children were given intelligence tests, significant differences
emerged in verbal (but not non-verbal) aspects of intelligence, with
children in the autonomous units achieving the higher scores.
Tizard's explanation of these findings concerns the way in which

relationships between superordinate and subordinate members of staff might prevent the relatively junior members of staff, who have the greatest day-to-day contact with residents, from being as stimulating as they might otherwise be.

## Staff-Resident Consensus

Where the residents of small hostels are adults or adolescents rather than young children, then much of the quality of the environment will be reflected in the degree of consensus between staff and residents about attitudes and values relevant to rehabilitation. Numerous accounts exist of the presence within organizations for the treatment of deviants, of influential groups whose values are other than those of the staff. The notion of an 'inmate code' in prisons is well known (e.g. Glaser, 1964, Chs. 5 and 6), and there are accounts of similar difficulties in controlling the influence of delinquent values in probation and parole hostels (Keller and Alper, 1970, Ch. 4; Sinclair, 1971, Ch. 4). There are, however, similar accounts from quite different settings.

One of the best in our view is that provided by Polansky et al (1957). They described how aspects of the informal social structure of the patient group in a small private psychiatric hospital interfered with staff efforts. Staff became aware of a particular 'nucleus' of patients who came to be known to the staff as the 'problem clique'. Of particular importance was the fact that this group was of relatively high prestige, and their opinions were likely to be seen by other patients as representing 'the norm':

> ...we had reason to believe that the informal group structure
> consisted of this core of patients who were 'in', and an
> actual majority of others who were more or less peripheral.
> Several patients interviewed at discharge were still smarting
> over never having made the grade with that exclusive, sophis-
> ticated, and socially prestigeful friendship circle. This
> state of affairs, too, was indicated in an analysis of the
> sociometric data. Not only did the clique show a large
> number of intertwined mutual choices ... but members of the
> core clique also received disproportionately more choices
> from persons outside the clique than they gave (p.390).

Unless staff can maintain a community whose leaders stand for the same virtues, the same activities, and the same aims of which staff approve, then a struggle is bound to ensue and the socializing influence which staff can wield will be in opposition to that exerted by the peer group. It is this feature of social organization which Grygier (1975) has attempted to quantify in the context of training schools and centres for delinquents in Canada. The technique he has developed is known as the Measure of Treatment Potential (MTP) and its rationale is based on the assumption that a greater potential for treatment exists in a residential unit that is free of elements of an anti-treatment culture, and where a single unified normative system exists rather than separate and opposed staff and inmate systems. The technique is based upon a comparison of sociometric choices (likes and dislikes) made by residents from amongst fellow residents, and behaviour ratings made of all residents by staff who are closely in touch with those they are rating. Wherever a relatively high positive correlation exists between favourable staff ratings and

acceptance by fellow residents, then a relatively high level of treatment potential is assumed to exist. It is not yet clear from the
research that has been carried out whether the relatively higher
treatment potential of some units is in fact realized, but in the
meantime there is evidence that MTP scores are related to structural
features, such as unit size and staffing levels, as well as to
characteristics of residents and staff:

> The high MTP units are small, and the staff/pupil ratio is
> high. The staff are well selected, imaginative and self
> reliant; the children are young, relatively less aggressive
> and respond readily to staff leadership (Grygier, 1975,
> p.162).

Once again this short quotation captures the complexity of the
matters under discussion. Quality of environment is determined by a
multitude of factors of very different kinds, and sources of
variation are themselves inter-related.

Summary

Figure 1 is a summary of the argument of this chapter so far.
The task of the small hostel, it has been argued, is that of social
influence. Depending upon the age of residents, and the nature of
their problems, this task may be best construed as one of socialization, or alternatively as one of providing improved skills and
resources. In either case the key concern is that of creating a
hostel social environment characterized by cohesiveness around a
shared philosophy. The creation and maintenance of such an atmosphere is not an easy or simple matter and in small hostels social
climate and organizational stability are particularly liable to
swings or oscillations. The atmosphere at any one moment is a
complex function of the processes of selection-in and selection-out
of residents, the style and personality of staff as well as the
nature of the organizational constraints within which they have to
work, and of the degree of consensus between staff and residents
regarding the attitudes and values that make up the hostel's
philosophy. It is in the context of our research on small hostels
for alcoholics that the present authors have developed this model of
the way in which a small hostel works, and it is to a more detailed
consideration of the specialized alcoholism hostel that this chapter
now turns.

## THE AIMS OF SMALL ALCOHOLISM HOSTELS

Reference has already been made in the previous chapter to the
intermediate nature of a behaviour disorder like alcoholism. Histor-
ically the attempt to view alcoholism as illness has met with much
resistance and has never been fully accepted. It contains elements of
delinquent non-conformity as well as elements of psychological disorder, and this is reflected in the purposes for which alcoholism
hostels were set up, their sources of referral, and the background
histories of their residents. Both psychiatric hospitalization and
imprisonment are to be found in the histories of many alcoholism
hostel residents, and the proportions who have these experiences vary
from house to house.

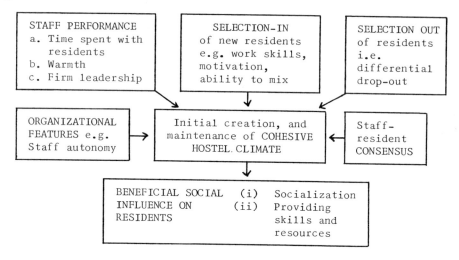

Figure 1: A model of the social influence task of a small hostel.

Stated Aims

A small hostel for alcoholics is therefore likely to share some
of the features of hostels for offenders and some of the features of
hostels for the mentally ill. Hence its social influence task is
partly that of behavioural reform and socialization, and partly that
of providing the means of acquiring greater skills and improved resources. It is not surprising to find, therefore, that the aims of
small alcoholism hostels, as stated by staff members interviewed at
each of the 11 houses in our survey of hostels in the London area,
were all-encompassing, as well as somewhat vague and difficult to pin
down. Emphasis was usually put upon a wide concept of rehabilitation
expressed in terms such as the following:

> Being back on the right road; Realizing he can do everything
> he wants to without drinking; Thinking constructively; Going
> out for recreation and meeting people; Learning about them-
> selves as individuals; Total rehabilitation of the individual -
> physical, mental, emotional and spiritual recovery; Learning
> trust and mutual respect; The opportunity to learn through
> interpersonal situations; Radical change in life style.

It was noticeable that the use of the word 'spiritual' was not
confined to staff members working in organizations set up by religious bodies. The ideology most commonly expressed by staff was
similar to that expressed in a schematized form in Figure 2. The
ultimate end of the hostel social influence process is the achievement of personal fulfilment, the realization of potential or 'self
actualization', but these are perhaps the goals of all socialization
and it is with the acquisition, or reacquisition, of an integrated
social status, via stability in accommodation, work, and contacts with
family and peers, that alcoholism hostels are principally concerned.

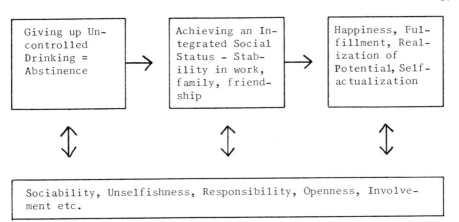

Figure 2:    The ideology of small alcoholism hostels.

In practice this becomes the 'ends' of the hostel's work.

Drinking Goals

Abstinence from alcohol, or 'sobriety' to use the preferred term, although referred to by staff at most hostels, was usually mentioned only in passing and received no mention at all at three houses, two of which were exclusively for alcoholics. The rest implied strongly that sobriety or abstinence was merely a means to an end. As one staff member put it, "Just to stop drinking is not enough". Even so, the belief in the connection between abstinence and higher order goals, at least for alcoholics, is so strong that it has become the sine qua non of alcoholism rehabilitation, an 'end' in itself. The control of drinking behaviour is in fact a major preoccupation. On the matter of abstinence all 11 houses in the survey were firm, and all had a 'no drinking' rule for their alcoholic residents. All the houses were committed to the idea, held by Alcoholics Anonymous and throughout most of the hospital treatment services, that rehabilitation required total abstinence.

Just as a serious shared commitment to giving up gambling activities was a crucial part of the cohesiveness that characterized good times in the hostel for compulsive gamblers described earlier in this chapter, so too was a shared ethos about the importance of giving up drinking a main ingredient of the positive hostel culture which many alcoholism hostel staff fought hard to establish and to maintain. There are in fact several accounts documenting the early difficulties experienced in setting up new alcoholism hostels with relatively permissive rules about drinking behaviour. In all instances an atmosphere with which staff were satisfied was only achieved with the introduction of stricter 'no drinking' rules which were developed to cope with an apparently uncontrollable situation. One of these accounts (of House A) contains the following description:

We have since been given vivid accounts of the drinking that
went on and the bottles of wine being kicked under the table;
men looking for sobriety were likely to find nothing much
more than a drinking party in progress. At this stage, there
were 5 residents left, and no warden. This was the turning
point, for the 5 remaining residents were very genuinely concerned in trying to find sobriety, and these men, almost accid-
entally, formed themselves into a nucleus of a true therapeutic
community, and taught us all over a period of 6 months what
a therapeutic community for alcoholics can be, its possibilities,
and its limitations (Edwards et al, 1966, p.1407).

Staff at another house in the survey sample recounted a similar
experience. As the staff member put it: "With drinking in the house
there was a lot of trouble and the house got a bad name. The warden
was changed and the house became one for sobriety". This type of
experience appears to be fairly common, and to many the operation of
a house with fairly strict rules about drinking appears to be the
only feasible option.

In yet another written account, of an alcoholism hostel recently
set up in the English Midlands, Corden et al have described the staff's
reluctance to initiate stricter rules themselves, and their eventual
relief when residents took the initiative:

...for the resident worker this period (before the change) res-
embled a nightmare, full of conflicts and some dreadful incidents. But the temptation to take on an authoritarian or paternalistic role was resisted. After about 5 months a small
nucleus of residents gained a majority in a meeting for a
rule that everyone should abstain from alcohol while living
there. Anyone who did not adhere to that rule, it was agreed,
must leave (1974, p.258).

In the light of this experience, so common to those who have
tried to set up alcoholism hostels, and in view of the abstinence
philosophy that has prevailed in alcoholism treatment circles for the
past several years, it is not surprising that 'giving up uncontrolled
or alcoholic drinking' has been interpreted almost universally to
mean total abstinence from alcohol. It is true that whilst the concept 'alcoholism' has currency, and as long as specialized alcoholism
agencies exist, the control of drinking will be bound to be an aim of
these agencies in practice. Nevertheless, the universality of total
abstinence as the goal seems likely to change over the years to come.
For one thing, there is a growing realization, in the context of
hospital treatment services, that abstinence is only one of the leg-
itimate ways of ceasing to be an uncontrolled drinker (for example,
see Sobell and Sobell, 1973; Orford et al, 1976). In view of this
steadily accumulating evidence that some 'alcoholics' can learn to
control their drinking, it is to be expected, indeed hoped, that some
small hostels with an orientation towards 'controlled drinking' will
be attempted in the near future. There is at least one well-documented
experiment of this kind (Collier et al, 1970; Oki, 1974; Ogborne and
Collier, 1975). In this experiment, being carried out in a Canadian
farm community, residents are free, after an initial probationary
period of abstinence, to choose between abstinence or drinking controlled by a graded series of fines which depend upon level of intoxication and amount of associated disturbance. It is only by

setting up hostels which allow a degree of drinking, but which at the same time incorporate careful control over drinking, that a real alternative to the total abstinence hostel will be attempted.

The Canadian controlled drinking hostel experiment is, however, by no means free of problems, such as early drop-out and relapse, which are probably endemic to any alcoholism treatment or rehabilitation programme (Ogborne and Coller, 1975). This particular halfway house is also considerably larger than many of those in the London survey, and considerably larger than Houses A and B which were studied intensively, and it remains to be seen whether the degree of structure which may be necessary to maintain the fine distinction between controlled and uncontrolled drinking is compatible with the desire for non-institutional informality which underlies the philosophy of many smaller hostels.

## Oscillations in Stability and Atmosphere

There is plenty of evidence, both from our own research and from accounts given by others, that small alcoholism hostels experience the same difficulties of building and maintaining a satisfactory culture as do other types of small hostel or halfway house. There is, for instance, a most illuminating published account of fundamental changes which occurred during the first 2 or 3 years of operation of one of the houses which we later studied in detail (House B). In his book, Vagrant Alcoholics, Tim Cook, who was the first staff member at House B, writes:

> The first 2 years show clearly the chaos and turmoil of a house unsure of what it was doing or where it was going... the 3rd year was clearly the breakthrough, and the low turnover and high rate of residence show this. Since that time, there has never been a return to the chaos of the earlier years (1975, pp.16-17).

He clearly views the 3rd and subsequent years as a new era, and sees the house before and after the 3rd year as having had two quite distinct identities. Doubtless he would argue that it would do great injustice to the ongoing, developmental, nature of such a community to think of the house in its early years as being the same place, or as having the same potential for influencing residents as in its later years. Amongst the changes that occurred were the withdrawal from group meetings of the psychiatrist who was an important figure at the house early on; the moving out of the one, formerly residential, member of staff; and most importantly, the increasing task and decision-making involvement of residents. The following quotation from the same book illustrates this change:

> ...two incidents must serve to illustrate the difference in house atmosphere and dependency on staff, when a staff-dominated house is in operation and when it is not. In 1967 /year 2_7 I was woken early one morning by an irate resident wanting to know why there was no tea (though clearly residents using the tea should have foreseen the need for more as the current supply dwindled). But then that was not their job, it was the staff's! In 1969 /year 4_7, while away on holiday, I was rung up to be told that everything was fine and that, as the roads were icy, would I please not come back for a few

more days, there being no need for me (p.25).

Once a satisfactory state of affairs exists in the hostel, the problem of maintenance remains. In terms of stability, neither House A nor B has done so well in the last few years. At House A, the resident group built up to a period of unrivalled stability between the 4th and 5th years. The same stability was not achieved at any time in the subsequent 6 years, and on three occasions, at roughly 2-year intervals, turnover increased and stability declined markedly. The most serious of these declines occurred during the period of our intensive study at the house and is described in much greater detail later (Chapter 9). Each 'low point' appears to have been the culmination of 9 to 10 months of steady decline, and in each case the subsequent build-up of a resident group has been more gradual, and has scarcely been achieved after 12 months, when the next decline has set in.

House B also took as much as 3 years to establish a stable resident group which was then maintained for fully 2 years before declining. As at House A, this stability has scarcely been achieved in the subsequent years. There have not been the dramatic declines that have been part of the recent history of House A, but nor has there been the establishment and maintenance of the type of stable group that characterized both houses in earlier times.

These data concern numerical stability only, and have nothing to say about the quality of life that prevailed from time to time in the hostels themselves. It was possible to study the latter during the 18 months of intensive study at Houses A and B and the data showed clearly that stability need not be the same thing as a good atmosphere (Chapter 8). It may, however, be the case that at least a moderate level of stability is a necessary, although not sufficient, condition for good atmosphere in a small hostel community with relatively high resident turnover. Certainly the period of rapidly declining stability at House A (during the Spring and early Summer of year 9) saw an increase in staff and resident tension and rapidly diminishing morale. In such small groups, with rapid comings and goings of members, oscillations which may have therapeutic value in a larger, more institutional, setting (Rapoport, 1956, p.358), can bring the enterprise to a low point from which it may take many months to recover, and which can even pose a serious threat to its continued existence.

## Contributions of Staff to Atmosphere

The staff role in hostel communities is a special one and we believe, on the basis of evidence from our own studies as well as research such as that of Sinclair (1971) on other types of hostel, that their role is a vital one. At Houses A and B, residents' opinions regarding atmosphere varied systematically, both with the favourability of their perceptions of staff, and with the amount of time they had with staff. When staff were in more frequent contact with residents, the latter liked staff better and had a more favourable view of the atmosphere in the house (Chapter 8). These relationships were most dramatically seen when there was a change of staff member, as there was at both houses in the middle of the period of study. As Sinclair has noted in hostels of quite a different type, there is little pressure for uniform practice by hostel staff and hence,

"Hostels change sharply with a change of warden" (1971, p.44). There is a similar absence of clear directives to staff in alcoholism hostels and, accordingly, staff members make widely differing interpretations of their role. For example, our data suggest that the time a staff member spends in face to face contact with residents can vary by as much as a factor of 10 (Chapter 8).

The data on contact time are based on a total sample of only 4 staff members at alcoholism hostels. Furthermore they are descriptive only, and hence cause and effect relationships cannot be established. Nevertheless, the results are at least consistent with the hypothesis that more time spent by staff with residents will lead to greater liking of staff, and that greater resident-staff liking will contribute to cohesion and a sense of positive atmosphere. Although the exact nature of a relationship must be taken into account, and there must be circumstances when reducing the amount of contact between a particular member of staff and particular residents would be beneficial, in the setting of a small hostel which allows such latitude in this respect volume of contact itself may be important. The time which staff are prepared to spend with residents may be a fairly unequivocal indication of 'sustained concern' (Glaser, 1964) or 'doing more than the minimum the job requires' (Blumberg et al, 1973) on the part of staff, and may therefore be expected to be related to residents' liking for staff.

Although our data on staff reputations are less clear in respects other than contact time, it does appear that individual staff members acquire individual reputations consistent with their background and training, their attitudes, and their style and manner of working. For example, that one staff member at House A should be frequently charged with, 'not letting the men get to know him', might have been anticipated from a knowledge of his formal training and manner. The reputation of another staff member for 'letting the men get to know him' and for not 'treating them like children' was consistent with his youth, his lack of previous training, and the emphasis on informality in his avowed intentions and in his evident manner.

## Selection-In of Residents

All the houses surveyed, without exception, were selective in some degree in their choice of new residents. There was no way of ascertaining the true ratio of admissions to total referrals for most of the houses in the survey, but during the 18 months of the more intensive study at Houses A and B 29% of referrals resulted in admission at House A, and 27% resulted in admission at House B (Chapter 6). These figures are remarkably similar and, possibly, fairly typical.

Data from the survey gave the impression that entry to a small hostel community for alcoholics was guarded very carefully. A personal interview was involved in the selection routine at all houses, sometimes more than one interview, sometimes separate interviews with staff and with existing residents. In addition, a 'survival period' was sometimes required prior to admission, for example after coming out of prison. Sometimes a number of visits to the house were required over a period of some days or more prior to admission, and sometimes it was required that entry to the house be preceded by regular attendance at a 'shop front', at an assessment centre or 'quarter-way house', or by a period spent as an in-patient in a specialized hospital alcoholism treatment unit.

In some cases the referral-selection chain was quite lengthy (Chapter 6). At House C for example, the final decision was only made after fairly detailed referral information had been provided, and assessed by two staff members, after a subsequent interview with the same staff members, and finally after visits by the prospective resident to the house over a period of one week. The involvement of existing residents undoubtedly lengthens and complicates the procedure. The shortest referral-selection procedure was in operation at House D where existing residents were not consulted. One house (House F) operated a 3-week 'probationary period' after admission. Residents and staff would consider a man's suitability after this time and full resident status would not be conferred until after this period was over.

## Selection Criteria

Two selection criteria were mentioned in one form or another at nearly every house in the survey. The regularity with which they were mentioned and the emphasis they were given indicates their importance in setting the stage for the type of hostel communities which staff intended to create and maintain, using 'Selection-in' as a major means of bringing about the desired state of affairs.

At the smaller, totally specialist, hostels it was stated without exception that the prospective resident's desire or motivation for 'sobriety' was a major selection requirement. They all operated on the principle that they were dealing with 'alcoholics' and that total abstinence from alcohol was a sine qua non of rehabilitation. Indeed some houses required a period of abstinence prior to admission. In one case a period of one week's abstinence was required, in another case four weeks. Part of this notion of 'motivation', which appears to be the major selection factor, is the recognition on the part of the prospective resident that he is an 'alcoholic', a factor mentioned by several. Notably, the two hostels making special, but not exclusive, provision for alcoholics made no mention, in answers to questions about selection, of desire or motivation for abstinence or sobriety (they did nonetheless have a 'no-drink' rule at least for the alcoholics amongst their residents).

The second factor, again almost unanimously mentioned as a selection criterion, was the ability to mix amicably with other residents. This is obviously of paramount importance in such small, relatively informal, non-institutional, residential communities. What appeared to be essentially the same factor was mentioned in a variety of different ways. For example:

> He should be able to mix with other men; Rejected if the majority don't like him, and putting up with him would be too much, or if he did not accept group standards; Rejected if he wouldn't attend meetings or help in running the house, or if there was some deep personal dispute between him and an existing resident; Requires communication ability with regard to participation in group discussion - must indicate that he is prepared to cooperate.

Only at 3 hostels did staff fail to mention some factor of this type. All 3 were houses with a relatively large complement of staff or with emphasis on the authority of the warden.

Staff at small hostels for alcoholics appear to be united in their concern about these matters. However, what is equally clear is the highly subjective nature of both the main selection criteria - motivation for sobriety and ability to mix - and the evaluative, near-judgemental, nature of these criteria. The feeling was often expressed that the business of selection was a subtle one, that the "wool could easily be pulled over one's eyes", and that motivation, in particular, could easily be "put on". It was not necessary just to determine whether there was a desire to stop drinking, but also whether it was "genuine", "honest" or "very strong". There was suspicion of a prospective resident who was "...full of promise and who is conning you". "Someone just wanting a home", was not suitable at House F (a very revealing remark the implications of which we shall return to in Chapter 4).

The detailed examination of Houses A and B made the reasons for staff preoccupation with selection abundantly clear. Nearly everyone who stayed for longer than a few weeks acquired some sort of reputation, either as someone who contributed to the house, or as someone who was a preferred social partner, or as someone who was particularly understanding, or else as the opposite of one of these (Chapter 8). There were instances that appeared to demonstrate interaction of individual temperament and the social environment of the hostel, but in other cases it seemed that residents brought with them qualities that had implications, sometimes quite profound, for the hostel culture or atmosphere. Some residents bring with them long-standing reputations for sociability or active involvement for example. Others are more 'passive', or come with reputations as 'loners'. Small communities need enough of the right material and their needs are greater or lesser at different times.

From time to time there is apparent confirmation of the worst fears held by those who run small hostels about the potentially disruptive influence of the type of person which careful selection procedures are designed to try and keep away. (Chapter 9 contains descriptions of at least one such occasion). Occasionally, at the other extreme, the various elements of residents' approval, as well as staff approval, come together to invest a particular resident with true 'star' or leadership status. This was observed in particular in the case of one man at House B (Chapter 9), but it is not often that the right combination of qualities exists in one person. Similarity to most other residents in terms of values and social history must confer a great advantage, and to be already known to several residents before coming to the house is an added advantage. If these advantages are combined with a willingness to become fully involved in what is going on in the house, with intelligence and a capacity for insight and openness, and with a degree of sociability and an absence of disruptive behaviours, then favour is likely to be found with staff as well as with fellow residents (particularly if, in addition, the person's history shows him to have all the hallmarks of having been deviant in the past - drunkenness offences numbering in the hundreds, for example, in the case of hostels for offenders). Whilst a combination of virtues may be necessary for all-round popularity, a single stigma, such as unwillingness to become involved, or a tendency to unreasonable argumentativeness, may be enough to provoke unpopularity and even to prompt staff into outright pessimism about 'getting a group going' at all in the presence of the individual concerned.

Staff-Resident Consensus

Staff and residents sharing a philosophy and avoiding the development of a 'contra-culture' are matters of much relevance to specialized alcoholism hostels. In our experience of Houses A and B, it
would often have been the case that 'treatment potential', in the
sense used by Grygier (1975) in his Canadian studies, would be at a
relatively low level. It was relatively rarely that the different
elements of residents' approval, as well as staff approval, came
together to invest someone with true leadership status. At House B
especially it was not infrequently the case that the same resident
who had a reputation as a preferred social partner had a simultaneously held reputation as someone who made relatively little contribution to the running of the house. Furthermore, at both houses,
staff and residents were as often in disagreement, as in agreement,
about which residents deserved approval. Lack of consensus was
particularly evident with men who were socially popular with others.
At both houses staff were more likely to make disapproving comments
about these residents, and at House A they were, if anything, relatively under-involved in group meetings (Chapter 8).
The threat that staff's efforts will be sabotaged by the influence of a countervailing resident culture is most pertinent in alcoholism hostels such as House B which were intentionally set up to try
and influence 'skid row' or 'vagrant' alcoholics or chronic drunkenness offenders. The social influence task is then far more like
that to be found in hostels for probationers or prison parolees, than
like that of a hostel for ex-psychiatric patients. The social backgrounds of staff and residents are particularly likely to diverge
widely, and residents may well continue to share in a culture which
is alien to rehabilitation workers. For example, Cook et al's account
of the 1st year at House B includes the following statement:

> ...it is perhaps not surprising that it was difficult to help
> these men. Almost without exception they showed a profound
> apathy which severely impaired their ability to follow a
> constructive rehabilitative programme. They were afraid to
> take the most elementary steps in establishing contact with
> normal society ... during the first year it was left to the
> hostel staff to decide on the standards of behaviour to be
> expected of the residents (1968, p.241).

Different expectations about how residents should behave in the
hostel, and over what constituted the rehabilitation process, were
apparent during the intensive study of House B. To staff there were
many things, other than drinking and purely domestic events, which
mattered. They had in mind a community which was 'therapeutic' in a
variety of other ways. They expected residents to show a high level
of interest in fellow residents, and to want to take responsibility
for, and to be willing to discuss, each other's social and interpersonal problems. Residents, on the other hand, were likely to see such
matters as non-problematic or beyond their competence to discuss. For
example, personal misconduct involving 'difficult' or disturbing social behaviour, was likely to be seen as reflecting personality, or
even psychiatric, problems, and was accordingly seen as being more in
the province of the professional helper (Chapter 7). Other matters
were simply considered matters for personal decision and not subject
to control by others. Gambling activities provided perhaps the best

example of staff-resident strain of this kind.

A stronger norm of communal responsibility for members' conduct prevailed at House A but again, as at House B, not all residents shared the staff's preference for a community which had widespread controlling powers in the interests of personal change (Chapter 7). A particularly forthright complaint about the influence of a contra-culture comes from Blumberg et al's report of the halfway house (HWH) which was part of their comparative experiment:

...men continued to be 'contaminated' by the skid row ethos. This influence was rarely absent from HWH. ...the men brought skid row into HWH, with its secretiveness, lack of real involvements, disdain for do-gooders, and the need to con in order to demonstrate to themselves and others their indifference to their need for trust... When such feelings were strong, there was a high rate of turnover in HWH (1973, pp.185-6).

Under these circumstances staff often feel there to exist an antithesis between a genuinely 'therapeutic' atmosphere or milieu, on the one hand, and mere 'support' on the other. Staff may feel that residents are 'using' the hostel for accommodation purposes rather than for genuine rehabilitation. Wiseman, in her book, Stations of the Lost, noticed how certain 'stations on the rehab route' may become relatively desirable, often by default, on account of the quality of accommodation, food, recreation, and sometimes medication, which they provide (1970, p.165). Also relevant here are some data from the prior study carried out at House C. A survey of residents' opinions suggested that the majority valued the security the hostel provided, and the relative protection from the temptation to drink which was afforded by the no-drinking rule, rather than the 'therapeutic' ingredients of group meetings and other opportunities to discuss personal problems (Orford et al, 1975b).

Summary

As in Chapter 1 we have argued in this chapter that alcoholism hostels are more like than unlike other types of halfway house or hostel. Their task may be more easily construed as one of socialization than is the case for some other hostels, because of the emphasis on drinking-related attitude and behaviour change. But this task is pursued in a way fundamentally similar to that of other hostels: by maximizing the social cohesion of the collective group of residents and staff.

# Chapter 3
# Variations in Hostel Organization

The previous two chapters proceeded on the assumption that it is reasonable to discuss small hostels in the round as if one hostel was like another. Indeed, in terms of the contrast which most provide with the large institution, and in terms of the social influence task upon which they are engaged and their consequent need to develop a cohesive group culture, the things that almost all small hostels have in common are as apparent as their differences. Already, however, it is clear that hostels differ in many ways: for example, in the types of problem that their residents have been troubled with, their sizes and the relative numbers of staff and residents. The purpose of this chapter is to demonstrate that small hostels, despite the qualities they share, can be organized to fulfil their task in very different ways.

## The Comparative Study of Institutions

In the introductory chapter to their book, Varieties of Residential Experience, Tizard et al (1975) criticize single case studies of residential institutions, and argue for a comparative approach. Descriptions of individual mental hospitals and correctional institutions (such as those provided by Goffman, 1961, and Polsky, 1967), they say, ignore much variation that exists between institutions, and hence can lead to a misleading stereotype. The same is true when it comes to a consideration of facilities that have developed as a reaction against large institutions. They themselves recommend that attention be paid to three sources of variation; namely ideological variation (which itself affects the other two types), organizational variation (they focus especially upon unit autonomy), and staffing variations.

Variation in the social climates of mental hospital wards containing a large proportion of people with chronic schizophrenia has been best described by Wing and Brown (1970) in their report, Institutionalism and Schizophrenia. They demonstrated major differences between 3 mental hospitals, for example in the degree of ward restrictiveness, which were related to the patient's clinical condition (in particular to the degree of social withdrawal). Although it is impossible to be certain, they argued that measurable changes in nurses' attitudes over a period of 8 years were attributable to policy changes and were truly causative of changes in social withdrawal in patients who remained in the hospitals during that period. The fact that Wing and Brown's ward restrictiveness scale was found to be a useful means of detecting differences between mental hospital wards, itself demonstrates the scope that exists for exercising restrictive control, or alternatively for allowing responsible freedom, in an institutional setting.

In quite a different setting, Bartak and Rutter (1975) have demonstrated differences in adult staff behaviour in 3 separate units for autistic children. They made careful and reliable time-sampled observations of staff behaviour, and event-sampled observations of child behaviour and staff reactions to it. On most measures Unit A was contrasted with Unit C. There were, for instance, more than twice as many staff acts of educational instruction at Unit C than at Unit A (although such staff behaviour was frequent in both). In contrast, whereas playing with children, and staff demonstrations of physical affection or approval towards a child, were common at A, they were scarcely observed to occur at all at C. The tone of voice used by staff members was rated and again these two units were sharply contrasted, staff at A regularly using a warm tone of voice but never a very critical tone, and staff at C showing the reverse pattern. When sequences of behaviour were examined to see how staff behaved contingently upon good or bad child behaviour, it was found that staff at A displayed, "...indiscriminate warmly expressed approval...", whilst those at C used "...approval and disapproval...usually contingent upon the child's behaviour, but ... warmth was infrequently expressed through tone of voice" (pp.189-90). In this sense, staff at Unit B, who occupied an intermediate position on most of Bartak and Rutter's measures, were the most discriminating in their response to child behaviour. Barbara Tizard's (1975) study of residential nurseries where unit staff were relatively more or less autonomous in their work (already described in Chapter 2) is another demonstration of differences in the quality of interaction between staff and children in institutions.

## VARIETIES OF SMALL HOSTEL

These illustrations of a comparative approach to the study of residential institutions and facilities are taken from settings rather different from small hostels for adolescents or adults, but they serve to demonstrate the fact that differences in social environment are to be found when they are looked for, even though the facilities concerned may appear uniform on superficial examination. They also suggest some of the directions in which we might look to discover variation. It is in fact towards the area of decision-making that most of the rest of this chapter is oriented. Previous studies of hostels, such as that of Apte (1968) and that of Sinclair (1971), have found that the amount of decision-making allowed hostel residents is a variable quantity, and our own research confirms that this is the case in small hostels for alcoholics. It is obviously similar to the variable of ward restrictiveness considered by Wing and Brown (1970) and others who have studied large mental institutions. Furthermore, it occupies a central place in most philosophies of rehabilitation, and it is of major importance to those who set out to design an environment for the handicapped or distressed which avoids the social ills of the large institution.

## Hostel Practices

In his study of hostels for the psychiatrically ill, and of the hospital wards from which the hostel residents came, Apte (1968) developed a hostel-hospital practice profile (HHPP), partly based upon the ward restrictiveness scale used by Wing and Brown. Answers given by staff to 65 items contributed to two separate scales ('restrictive vs. permissive practices' and 'responsibility expectations'), although it is clear from the results that scores on these two scales were correlated. The first scale contained questions about the control of residents' physical movement, of their food and drink intake, over privacy, over a resident's physical state, over dress, over personal belongings, over everyday activities and over social relations. The scale of 'responsibility expectations' included questions on responsibility for personal property, for starting one's own day, for personal appearance, for medical care and finally for participation in hospital or hostel management. A sample question from each of these 13 areas is shown in Table 2. The number of restrictive practices varied in the 25 hostels which Apte studied, across a broad range from a low of 4 to a high of 28 out of a possible 44 (the median number of restrictive practices retained in the hostels was 18). Thus many hostels, whilst operating within a structure which would allow departure from an institutional regime, continued to operate what Apte called 'institutional practices'. Hostel staff were particularly likely to maintain control over everyday activities such as smoking, television watching and resting on the bed during the day, and also over social relations such as having visitors and mixing with the opposite sex, which was only very infrequently encouraged. Similarly, in terms of the 'responsibility expectations' scale, hostels varied from one that expected responsibility of its residents in 19 out of 21 areas, to one that expected responsibility in only 8 areas (median 13). The single question about participation of residents in the operation and management of the hostel revealed that only 4 out of 25 hostels fostered this kind of responsibility. As Apte put it:

> It is important to note that the halfway house as yet has not chosen to use the concept of resident participation or self-help as a way of encouraging greater responsibility (p.74).

It must of course be borne in mind that that statement was made a whole decade ago and the position may have changed somewhat since then.

Sinclair's (1971) is another study which demonstrates that hostels, this time for boys between the ages of 15 and 20 who were on probation, can vary greatly in the degree to which they afford their residents freedom to make responsible decisions about the conduct of their own personal lives and about the operation of the hostel in which they live. He assessed the degree of a hostel's permissiveness in each of 4 areas: allowing boys to decide for themselves about their manner of dress, allowing boys to stay out late on different nights of the week, allowing boys to change jobs if they found their present work disagreeable or were offered a better one, and leisure time freedom within the hostel (this latter area Sinclair calls 'hostel customs').

Table 2: Items from the Hostel Hospital Practices Profile (Reproduced
with permission from Apte, 1968, pp.123-5).

---

In the evening, after 7.00 p.m., can the resident leave the hostel or
hospital alone, or is it expected that they be accompanied by another
resident, friend, or relative?

Do residents have a choice in planning the menu for the main meal?

Is bathing allowed unsupervised?

Are there any specific precautions taken against the residents harming
themselves or others? (Knives, medicines, tools locked, and steps
shielded).

Are there any items of required dress during the day?

Resident's belongings are catalogued upon admission to hostel or ward?

During weekdays may residents use their bed to rest whenever they wish?

Are residents allowed visitors of the opposite sex in their sleeping
areas during the evening after 8.00 p.m.?

The policy regarding the resident's money is that all of it is retained
by the resident for his own handling?

The residents are awakened in the morning by staff going around to
arouse them, or sounding of a gong or bell?

The staff makes arrangements for the patients or residents to obtain
haircuts?

Does the staff keep the medicine for the residents?

Are meetings held at least once a month between staff and residents
for the purpose of discussing and working out problems in regard to
rules, regulations and services at the hostel or ward, with the intention of giving residents or patients a greater degree of responsibility in its operation and management?

---

Hostels that were permissive in one area tended to be permissive in
each of the others.

Degree of Contrast with the Institution

Raush and Raush, in their study of hostels for the mentally ill in
the U.S., give some interesting examples of freedoms which residents may
be surprised to find, having come from a hospital setting. One woman,
for example, expected that others might object that she cooked herself
2 eggs for breakfast, and was surprised to learn that she was free to
come into the kitchen to cook herself a cake. Another resident commented that no one seemed to mind if she came down stairs when she was
unable to sleep during the night. On the other hand they note that

rules vary greatly. For example, some houses set standards on personal appearance and cleanliness whilst others left these matters to the individual. One insisted that bathroom doors remain unlocked at all times, and the number of showers or baths to be had each week, and the hours during which they were to be taken, were stipulated. At some houses residents had their own keys and could come and go as they wished, whilst at others coming-in times were specified. Although Raush and Raush made no attempt to measure decision-making freedom or restrictiveness, they stated:

> Thus, the distance of the halfway house from the hospital
> model is not invariably great. ... If we measure halfway
> houses' approaches to rules against the hospital standard,
> we find them ranging from 'quarter-way' to more than 'three-
> quarter-way' in the nature and extent of their rules and
> in the formality or informality with which these are pres-
> ented to the resident (p.126).

The degree to which the hostel was truly 'halfway' or intermediate between the hospital on the one hand, and total personal responsibility in the community on the other, was a matter with which Apte was especially concerned. He sought to find out whether the individual hostels which he studied really formed 'logical bridges' or transitions between the hospital and the world outside, by comparing individual hostels with individual hospital wards from each of which a number of hostel residents had come. This comparison was possible for 13 hostel-hospital ward pairs. Although on average the number of institutional practices was fewer in the hostels than on the hospital wards - most halfway houses had between $\frac{2}{3}$ and $\frac{1}{2}$ the number of restrictive practices found on the average ward - there was little evidence of the individual matching which might have been expected if a serious attempt had been made to grade the degree of responsibility expected of residents in the two environments. At one extreme was a house where patients were expected to leave a highly traditional hospital ward to enter the least institutional of the 13 halfway houses. This house retained only 16% of the institutional practices of the ward from which patients had come. At the other extreme was a halfway house with very slightly more institutional practices than the hospital rehabilitation ward from which most of its residents came.

Paternalistic Hostels

Although direct evidence on this crucial point is lacking, there seems no reason to suppose that the successful pursuit of a cohesive hostel culture, and successful progress in the rehabilitation of residents, will be related in any simple way to the degree of permissiveness or absence of institutional practices in hostels. The complexity of the issues involved in deciding what is best is well brought out in the published account of Norman House which, according to Turner, the first warden and the author of the account, was the first halfway house in Britain for ex-offenders (it was established in 1954). He wrote:

> ...neither in its origins nor in its development was it a
> therapeutic community as the term is commonly understood.
> It was paternalistic. The rules, such as they were, were imposed
> on the residents, and the community had no authority over

their selection, nor over their departure. On the other
hand the organization of life within the community was
simple, and the degree of participation was high. ...what
was important was not where authority rested but how it
was used. It had to be seen to be fair, but in that sense
it had something of the quality of the authority that is
vested in the true therapeutic community. It meant close
involvement by the staff in the life of the community
(Turner, 1972, pp.188-90).

Turner was able to reconcile paternalistic control with a belief
in a high quality of staff-resident interaction, and with the sort of
staff behaviour which we argued (Chapter 2) was likely to contribute
to a positive social climate:

...what they ⟨the residents⟩ were saying, it seemed to me,
was that they had failed in freedom because they lacked
support, and supervision, and a strong, positive leadership.
...what ⟨he⟩ needed was the protection and support of
the substitute family which would direct his coming and
his going, praise him for his success, and admonish him for
his failures. It would notice his existence, listen to
his tales of woe, laugh at his jokes, and respect his points
of view. He could grow in such a climate whilst previously
his experience of life diminished him (pp.184-5, 192).

The small hostel for compulsive gamblers which was described in
Chapter 2 could fairly be described as paternalistic, although publicity referred to the house as a therapeutic community and the non-
authoritarian contrast with large institutions was stressed. There
were no guidelines dictating exactly how authority was to be exercised
in the house, and in practice it appeared that there was a large
measure of control by the full-time administrator and his full-time
assistant who between them looked after a group of residents which
varied in size from 4 to 7 at different times.

Many examples of staff control could be given. A whole variety of
matters which can merit disciplinary action arise in the day-to-day
running of a hostel and have to be dealt with in some way or another.
However, the retention of staff control was particularly apparent over
the recruitment of new members and the occasional disciplinary discharging of old members. The rather uncertain, middle-of-the-road,
position taken at the house over these matters was reflected in the
statement in committee minutes that, "Before any new member is
admitted the members of the house are consulted". 'Consultation' can
of course take a variety of different forms but the statement at
least seems to imply that residents do not have formal voting or veto
powers in the matter, and on the one occasion on which it was possible
to ask residents in detail about this consultation process, it
appeared that the process was a rather uncertain one and by no means
bound to enable residents to express their feelings openly.

When staff take responsibility for exercising authority they do
of course lay themselves open to the charge of interference or
authoritarianism, particularly when the limits of resident responsibility are not clearly laid down or understood. There were, for
example, misunderstandings and tensions over whether staff should
have access to, and should periodically inspect, residents' bedrooms,
and over the advisability of working overtime or of working other

than a normal morning and afternoon shift. From time to time residents expressed fear of "regimentation" and felt that the administrator was "keeping an eye on them". Residents were likely to complain that staff were "harsh" or "inconsistent". One resident described a "token democracy" and another thought the administrator had "a touch of governor-mania".

Many residents, on the other hand, welcome a degree of paternalistic control. On more than one occasion residents were brought into line by the administrator's firm handling, and subsequently appreciated it. They felt that it was the administrator's place to wield authority and without it they would "not have survived". In any case democracy and self-determination are relative and at least one resident expressed his appreciation of the freedom which the house offered in comparison with prison or some other large institution. For example, he enjoyed having his own front door key and being able to come and go as he liked.

Institutional Hostels

Despite what they have in common, therefore, it is quite possible to discern differences in the social organization of small hostels or halfway houses. In some cases these seem to represent quite different degrees of reaction to the large institution. For example, Raush and Raush (1968) noted a distinction, which others have also made, between halfway houses on the one hand and 'work camp houses' on the other. The latter were situated in rural settings, and functioned as small communities providing employment and social activities on the grounds. Thus, in terms of their location and the range of activities provided in the one setting, these were much more like traditional mental hospitals and would probably even qualify as 'total institutions'. In their own survey, Raush and Raush discovered only 3 houses that had been established before the mid 1950's which was roughly the time that the small, urban, hostel movement began and the term 'halfway house' came into popular usage. All 3 were in rural settings and had been established through the individual pioneering spirit of concerned non-professionals. Their very ideology was distinct from that of many of the more recently established small hostels:

> Although it is doubtful that their founders were conscious
> of this, each of the facilities harped back to that enlight-
> ened, early 19th century period of 'moral treatment'. All
> were, in a sense, spiritual retreats. The orientation was
> less psychiatric, or even psychological, than humanistic.
> A return to the virtues of a simpler, more natural, more
> loving life was emphasized. Two of the institutions...
> emphasized and continue to emphasize religious motives.
> All stress the spiritual benefits to be found in work and
> in cooperative living. All 3 facilities are active to this
> day (pp.49-50).

The distinction which Raush and Raush are making is not unlike distinctions between certain types of commune described by Rigby (1974). Amongst the types he describes are 'therapeutic', 'activist' (set up with a deliberate political or other social purpose), 'religious' and 'self-actualizing' communes. The examples which he provides of therapeutic and activist communes are urban in location, whilst examples of the other two types are rural.

## The Importance of Size

Variation in the exact size of small hostels has already been
referred to in Chapter 1. Some are very small, even of average
family size, whilst others are much larger with up to 30 or even 100
or more residents at a time. The extreme smallness of the smallest
hostels allows intimacy and yet privacy, features that are difficult
to arrange and which are often quite lacking in large institutions.
It also allows the informality, and the varied, personal, and immediate reaction to individuals' needs which Raush and Raush describe
as the hallmarks of good quality of social life in a residential
setting (Chapter 1). However, these same authors confirm our impressions when they state that smallness of size is not an unmitigated
blessing. They touch on the crucial matter of oscillation in social
climate and the danger of social disorganization when they write:

> In very small groups much is demanded of individual members,
> and the demands may be too great for a particular resident.
> The addition of a new member is more likely to precipitate
> a crisis in a very small group. ...the small group is more
> likely to face permanent total disorganization if it does
> not exercise careful selection of new members (1968, p.83).

They suggest, as a compromise, the 'double house' of which they
found 6 examples in their survey. In each case 2 small houses
existed close to one another, and operating under a single administration. In any event the exact size of a hostel is clearly a
characteristic of major importance and is one which we will discuss
again in the specific context of alcoholism hostels later in this
chapter.

## Selection and Social Organization

Although the social organization and climate of a place are
partly determined by pre-arranged purposes and structures, social
life depends as much upon who happens to come to live there. It does
insufficient justice to the reciprocal nature of human interaction to
think of children being solely at the mercy of their parents rather
than the other way about, or as residents being the only ones who are
influenced in a small hostel. To some degree or other, parents adjust
their behaviour to accommodate their children, and hostel staff undoubtedly do the same with their residents. Apte puts the point the
following way in writing of hostels for the mentally ill:

> Not only can the social environment influence the resident,
> but the resident can also influence the formation of the
> social environment. Halfway houses that deal more with one
> type of mental illness than another, for example, will
> invariably be affected by the various manifestations of the
> ex-patients' emotional condition and behaviour. Either
> purposely or knowingly staff will adjust the milieu to
> accommodate the problems arising out of the most demanding
> problems and severe behaviour. In consequence, certain
> types of social control will be used... (1968, p.101).

It is therefore not surprising to find that a hostel like Norman House, described above, which was self-styled paternalistic, and perceived "supervision and the provision of good leadership" as being amongst the major forms of social control required, had in mind a particular type of resident. Using terminology which is still widely employed, although it looks strangely out-dated in print, Turner describes different "prison types": Although the, "...aggressive type of psychopath is always more stimulating company than the passive, inadequate psychopath", it was nonetheless the latter for whom he felt Norman House was most suitable (1972, p.181). There is a complementariness, or reciprocity, between the childlike behaviour of the "passive, inadequate psychopath" and the parent-like type of social control which Turner describes.

In their sample, Raush and Raush found selection policies which required potential residents to meet differing criteria in terms of years of hospitalization, age and sex, for example. In many cases it was evident that selection and social organization were mutually dependent upon one another. For example, whilst most houses accepted residents of very mixed ages, and most were for males only or for males and females together, there was one house in their sample which was designed exclusively for young women under the age of 25. This house was, "...as might be expected, closely supervised, and it has a more than usual number of formal mechanisms for control" (1968, p.89).

There are several studies of patient social organization in mental hospital wards (e.g. Murray and Cohen, 1959; Brown, 1965) which suggest that, quite apart from the deliberately engineered structure of the ward, the amount of friendly interaction is inversely related to the average degree of mental disturbance of ward patients. Fairweather's study (1964), whilst showing that a reorganized small-group ward brought about a much higher level of social exchange between patients than occurred on a traditional ward, nevertheless showed that social interaction was limited by severity of disorder even in the small-group environment. All types of patient benefited from being on the ward but non-psychotic patients showed the highest levels of social interaction and psychotic patients who had been in hospital the longest showed the least. Rapoport (1960) refers to the disturbing and destructive influence of new patients in a therapeutic community who are "...of exceptionally disruptive or psychotic personality" (p.144). The community could only accommodate a certain proportion of such people, he argued, and discharge or transfer to more traditional wards of the mental hospital had on occasions to be used to restore a satisfactory climate. Hewett et al (1975) noted that the most permissive hostel in their preliminary sample (in terms of Apte's measure of restrictiveness-permissiveness) was run by a voluntary organization which admitted that they tended to accept fewer people who had suffered long-term psychotic illnesses than did other hostels.

## Staffing and Social Organization

Nevertheless it cannot be gainsaid that organizations and the people who set them up have certain assumptions about the way they will operate, and may deliberately engineer the envrionment to work in a particular way. Organizational assumptions and constraints are often indicated by the type of training that is thought suitable for people who will hold key positions. There are a number of examples

of this in the case of facilities for children in, Varieties of
Residential Experience (Tizard et al, 1975). One example comes from
the child welfare project (King et al, 1971) which studied hostels,
voluntary homes and hospitals for subnormal children. Each unit
received a score on a 30-item child management scale which assessed
the degree to which the unit operated a pattern of care that was
'child oriented' or 'institutionally oriented'. As Figure 3 shows,
there was no overlap in scores between hostels and hospitals. But
what is more, within the group of hostels and voluntary homes the
type of training that the unit head had received was related to child
management, with nurse trained or untrained heads being responsible
for units with the larger child management scores (indicating a more
institutional orientation). Heads trained in child care (C.C.)
tended to be responsible for units with lower scores.

Similarly, Heal and Cawson (1975) describe the change from an
educational to a child care model implied by the transfer of responsibility for residential treatment for juvenile delinquents from
the Home Office to local authority Social Service Departments which
followed the 1969 Children and Young Persons Act. Approved Schools
became Community Homes and as the relevance of teacher training
declined so the relevance of child care training increased.

In the study of 3 units for autistic children carried out by
Bartak and Rutter (1975), types of staff-child interaction were consistent with each unit's rationale. Unit A where, it will be recalled,
staff displayed a far higher level of warmth and physical affection,
deliberately set out to use 'regressive techniques', and the staff
(a head child psychotherapist and lay workers) believed in a permissive environment and the fostering of close relationships with
adults rather than providing a structure for learning specific skills.
Unit C, at the other extreme as far as staff behaviour was concerned,
was intentionally a school and emphasized a structured learning environment.

Raush and Raush refer to the different orientations of professional and non-professional staff in American halfway houses for the
mentally ill. Professional training, they say, on the whole goes
with a belief that living conditions can be explicitly designed to
effect change. They find that such staff are much more likely to be
innovative, for example by instituting programs of self-management,
introducing people who have not been psychiatrically ill to live with
those who have, and mixing sexes in the same house. Non-professional
staff on the other hand, although more likely to be psychiatrically
oriented and to refer to residents as 'patients' for example, made a
separation between treatment and social organization. Typically, in
houses run by such staff:

> ...the structural arrangements of the house and the processes
> of life within it are not subject to continuous thought and
> review. The halfway house itself is not emphasized as a
> major agent for significant change in people's lives (1968,
> p.98).

Part of Apte's conclusions about halfway houses for the mentally
ill in England was that their effectiveness had often been extremely
limited owing to the failure of administrators to develop a cadre
of suitable staff. He points out that $\frac{3}{4}$ of halfway house wardens
had the bulk of their experience in an institutional setting and
hence, "...brought into the halfway houses values and modes of

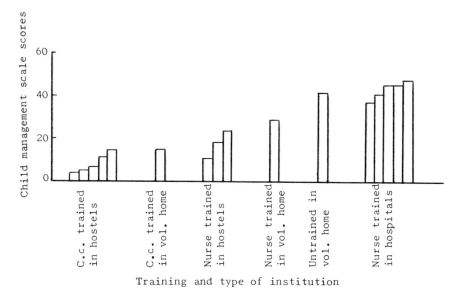

Figure 3: Training of unit heads and child management scale scores. (Reproduced with permission from Tizard, 1975, p.62).

behaviour towards the mentally ill typical of institutional environments" (1968, p.113).

Inter-Staff Strain

In practical terms this chapter has tried to make the point that there is a variety of distinctive ways in which small hostels can be run, even though their aims may be basically the same. The terms 'hostel', 'small hostel' and 'halfway house' are generic ones sub-suming a variety of types. There seems however, and our observations of alcoholism hostels bear this out, to be a strong tendency on the part of hostel planners, committee and staff to pay insufficient regard to these differences. There are many important issues to do with the design, organization and operation of a halfway house. These issues are inter-related but they require advance consideration if they are to be worked through consciously and deliberately rather than haphazardly. Unless there is clarity on these issues there is likely to be confusion and misunderstanding, and hence conflict amongst all concerned - staff, previous staff, senior staff, committee members, residents and even ex-residents.

Caudill (1958) described in detail a conflict between nurses and junior doctors in a mental hospital. The hospital was at the time going through a period of change, moving from a traditional, cus-todial, orientation to a more psychodynamic one. At the same time nurses remained responsible for day-to-day control of patients, whilst doctors were largely engaged in psychotherapy. Nurses tended to think that doctors were too permissive with patients, and the doctors in turn felt that nurses were too authoritarian. A very similar clash of values in community homes for juvenile offenders is

described by Heal and Cawson (1975). Staff cohesion and cooperation
was made difficult, they believe, by the different orientations and
training of the two main groups of staff, namely teachers and child
care staff. The former were likely to perceive the latter as insufficiently 'professional' and as being unable to discipline prop-
erly; whilst the latter charged the former with having a 'typical
school-master attitude', and were likely to complain that the place
was 'teacher dominated'. Similarly, Sinclair (1971) describes strain
that can easily occur between the warden of a hostel for young probationers and the liaison probation officer under whose supervision
a boy remains whilst he is a resident. Sinclair found that most
liaison probation officers thought the warden more authoritarian than
they considered ideal, but that the wardens considered themselves less
authoritarian than the probation officers thought them (p.48). Apte
(1968) also describes a lack of concensus between the different occupational groups (wardens, mental welfare officers, and medical officers of health) involved in halfway houses for ex-psychiatric patients,
about the most important functions which the halfway house served. He
concludes that, "...the training, experiences and professional roles
of these three groups constitute a major influence on how they perceive the community role of the halfway house" (p.48).

Even when staff share similar training, there are likely to be
differences in age, outlook and temperament and these can give rise
to a difference in orientation to the work, and hence to tension.
Inter-staff tensions are perhaps particularly likely in small hostel
communities on account of the very personal, and intense, nature of
the work, and because of the absence of a blue-print or agreed 'technology' for running a house. Times when senior staff change are
probably of particular importance. When staff change the house does
indeed seem to enter a new 'regime', and not necessarily one with
which former members of staff or other interested observers may feel
in sympathy.

## VARIETIES OF SMALL ALCOHOLISM HOSTEL

After the foregoing it must come as no surprise to discover variety amongst those specialized hostels which make provision for people
in the category 'alcoholic'. Hints have already been given in Chapter
1 of important differences between the alcoholism hostels that took
part in the small survey of alcoholism hostels in London. There were
variations in exact size, in whether provision was exclusively for
alcoholics or not, what types of organization set them up (mainly
religious or mainly treatment-oriented), the category of client for
whom they were designed (mainly ex-psychiatric patients or mainly ex-
prisoners), and their relative formality or informality. Resident
decision-making is, however, the factor to which we wish to give
greatest attention.

### Resident Decision-Making

This matter was explored in greater detail at 8 of the hostels in
the London survey by asking about the way in which each of 16 everyday decisions were taken. At each hostel, between 1 and 3 members of
staff and between 2 and 3 residents were asked these 16 questions.
Replies were categorized as indicating either that the decision was
made (i) solely by staff, (ii) jointly by staff and resident(s) (or

sometimes by staff and sometimes by resident(s)) or (iii) solely by a
resident or residents. Figure 4 shows the 16 decision-making items
and the frequency with which each of the 33 respondents (14 staff members and 19 residents from the 8 houses) indicated resident only or
mixed staff and resident participation.

## Different Decisions

First of all it can be seen, towards the top of Figure 4, that
there is no single item for which all informants indicated resident
involvement. Even with those items at the very top, those with most
residents involvement, there were still at least 1 or 2 houses out of
the 8 where residents were said to be not involved. Items with most
resident involvement (and usually resident(s) only rather than mixed
resident and staff involvement) concerned domestic decisions like
deciding what to have for breakfast, deciding what time to get up in
the morning, deciding when to make beds, and deciding to initiate
entertainment within the house. Other items about which residents
were mostly involved, but usually jointly with staff, concerned social
support and discipline. Most of the other items were on the whole the
province of staff decision-makers. Right at the bottom of the Figure
are items representing those decisions in which residents are rarely
involved. These include policy (deciding to issue a new rule), and
particularly financial matters (deciding how bills were to be paid
and deciding to take action over failure to pay rent). In these
cases residents were never thought to be exclusively the decision-
makers. In fact there was no single house where there was agreement
amongst all the informants that residents were even partly the decision-makers on these matters.
Decision-making which provided a particularly clear division between houses with a high level of overall resident involvement and
other houses, had to do with membership. It is a sure indication that
one is not living in 'one's own place' if someone else makes decisions
about who one's fellow residents are to be. Hence it is a particularly
radical step away from institutional organization for staff to re-
linquish to residents some of their rights to decide on matters of
selection and discharge.
As Figure 4 shows, the item 'deciding to discharge a member' was
9th in the list of 16 and was in fact one of the best discriminators
between houses that allowed much resident involvement and the others.
The matter of selection of new residents was enquired about separately.
The degree of involvement of existing residents in the selection process varied greatly. At the no-involvement extreme was a hostel
(House D) where the warden received referrals, considered this information, decided whether to interview the prospective resident, carried
out the interview himself and made his own decision - all without
reference to the existing resident body. Incidentally, this procedure
did have the advantage that it constituted the simplest, and hence
possibily the swiftest, referral-admission procedure of all. Some
degree of resident involvement was represented by other houses (e.g.
House F) which required that the prospective resident be interviewed
by the existing resident group as well as by staff, but where it was
clearly stated that staff made the final decision. At the resident-
involved extreme was House G, where it was stated that the staff
screened prospective residents, but where the final stage consisted
of an interview with existing residents who had the power to accept

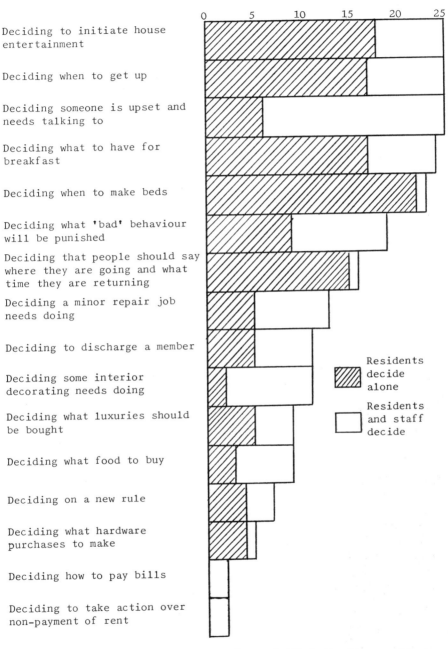

Figure 4: Number of informants (out of 33) indicating resident involvement in decision-making at 8 alcoholism hostels.

or reject. Data from our more intensive study of Houses A and B
(where the same policy officially held) showed that this resident
power may sometimes be more evident in theory than in practice. In
the event the power to reject at this final stage of the procedure
was relatively rarely used. The large bulk of applications which did
not result in an admission to the hostel were accounted for by failure of the prospective resident to proceed with his application, or
by a rejection by staff at relatively early stages of the process
(Chapter 6).

Different Houses

Taking all 16 items shown in Figure 4 together, and reordering
the data in terms of separate houses in order to show up differences
between houses more clearly, produces the results shown in Figure 5.
It can be seen that, with a few exceptions, there is a large measure
of agreement between the different informants from the same house
about the general level of resident involvement to be found in their
particular hostel.

The two larger hostels for which we have data of this sort
(Houses C and K) both turn out to be relatively staff-dominated. The
smaller houses, on the other hand, are strung out along a dimension
of staff versus resident-dominance. The most common pattern (Houses
E, H and J) is one of a moderate degree of staff dominance similar to
that displayed by the two larger houses. However, some of the smaller
houses depart one way or the other from this most common pattern. For
example House D (20 residents) was almost totally and exclusively
staff-dominated. This house was also exceptional by the absence of
visiting professional staff or group meetings and by its rule making
outside work compulsory. This was also the house with the simplest
referral-selection procedure, totally controlled by the staff member
in charge. This staff member stated that residents could lead independent lives but that he observed them closely: he would invite
them into his room to talk with them individually if he felt something was wrong. He also stated that the front door to the house was
kept shut in order that a resident had to ring to be let in, hence
giving the staff opportunity to see whether he had been drinking. If
a resident had been drinking staff would immediately tell him to leave.
This clearly represents one way of running a small hostel for alcoholics.

Deviating from the average house, but in the other direction, were
two small houses (F and G) with a clearly greater-than-average degree
of resident participation in decision-making. House F was set up at
the instigation of a psychiatric treatment unit and subscribed to the
'therapeutic community' ideal. It had a capacity of 12 residents and
a single, non-residential, social work member of staff. Unlike most
other houses, residents were responsible for deciding about the internal upkeep of the house, for disciplining and ultimately discharging fellow residents if necessary. They were involved too in
policy-making. However, in all of these areas the emphasis was on
joint staff and resident decision-making, and residents were rarely
autonomous decision-makers except in regard to their own day-to-day
lives. They were not involved in financial matters nor, according to
the 2 residents interviewed, were they involved in deciding what food
should be ordered. Significantly, on the other hand, the staff member
interviewed  thought that residents were involved in this latter

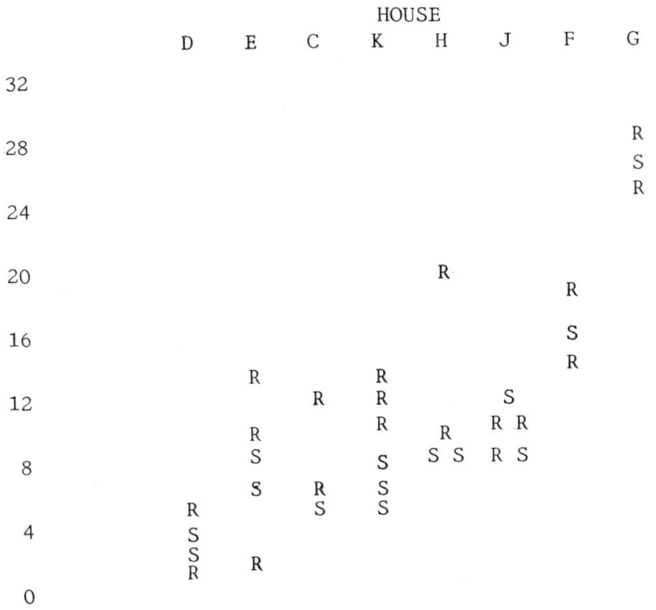

```
                              HOUSE
              D     E     C     K     H     J     F     G

 32
                                                         R
 28                                                      S
                                                         R
 24

 20                                R           R
                                                 S
 16                                              R
                    R           R
 12               R     R           S
                  R           R   R R
  8               S           S  S S  R S
                  S     R     S
            R           S     S
  4         S
            S
            R     R
  0
```

Key: R indicates the report of a single resident; S indicates the report of a single staff member. In each case 2 points were given if the reporter indicated decision-making by residents above, and 1 point for joint resident and staff decision-making. 16 items gave a range of scores from 0 to 32

Figure 5: Different degrees of resident involvement in decision-making at 8 alcoholism hostels.

activity.

The most extremely resident-dominated house was House G, however. This was a very small house, with a capacity for only 8 men, which shared a single non-residential staff member with House B. It had no particular expectations of how long residents would stay (see Chapter 4 for a fuller discussion of length of stay) and was therefore almost in the nature of a 'group home' or 'three-quarter way house'. As at House F, just described, residents were involved in almost the full range of activities asked about, but the difference was the non-involvement of staff. Residents at House G were unusual in being autonomous in their decision-making regarding the upkeep of the house, the disciplining and even discharging of fellow residents, and the forming of new rules. Even here, however, the staff member acted as rent collector and was responsible for initiating action if anyone failed to pay their rent.

Houses F and G therefore represent two other ways in which small hostels can be run, one involving residents fairly fully in all manner of decisions but retaining shared staff and resident responsibility, the other approximating a near-autonomous self-running community.

Disagreement and Dissatisfaction

Informants, both staff and residents, were also asked whether they felt there was disagreement about who should decide things, and whether they personally were satisfied or dissatisfied with the way things were decided. Figure 6 shows the results for 7 houses for which these data are available, ordered, from left to right, from those with relatively little resident participation to those with most resident participation. There is a strong suggestion of relatively little <u>disagreement</u> about who should make decisions in the relatively staff-dominated houses. As soon as resident participation rises above even a fairly modest level, disagreement rises and remains high for all houses which have at least that level of resident participation or more. The relationship between <u>dissatisfaction</u> and resident involvement appears rather different. There is relatively little dissatisfaction with the way decisions are made in the staff-dominated houses and even less dissatisfaction in the extremely resident-dominated houses. Dissatisfaction is at its highest in the intermediate area where there is a measure of resident involvement but still a large measure of staff-domination.

It is not difficult to make sense of these data in terms of a preliminary explanation, complicated though they may seem at first glance. The system of decision-making in the very staff-dominated houses is clear cut, there is virtually no room for disagreement and satisfaction is reasonably high. At the other extreme, when resident participation is high satisfaction is very high, but there remains

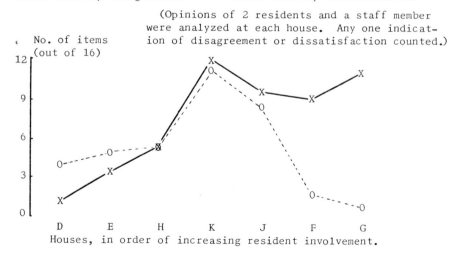

——Items with any disagreement    --- Items with any dissatisfaction

(Opinions of 2 residents and a staff member were analyzed at each house. Any one indication of disagreement or dissatisfaction counted.)

No. of items (out of 16)

Houses, in order of increasing resident involvement.

Figure 6:  Disagreement and dissatisfaction over decision-making related to resident involvement at 7 alcoholism hostels.

quite a large measure of disagreement. We would interpret this as
meaning that a fairly clear cut ethic of self-determination exists in
these houses which produces a relatively high level of satisfaction.
On the other hand, as we have already noted, staff are still involved
in some highly important areas and the community is by no means fully
autonomous, even in the most extreme case. Under these conditions
there is bound to be debate about the boundary between staff and resident roles and disagreement is bound to remain. It is the hostels
in the middle of the range, where residents have a degree, but only a
degree, of responsibility, that appear to produce a combination of
disagreement and dissatisfaction. The number of houses involved in
this analysis is very small and it would be dangerous to base any
firm conclusions upon them, but it is worrying to think that the
commonest pattern of hostel decision-making organization might be the
one most clearly associated with disagreement and dissatisfaction.

## Size of House and Staffing

There is almost certainly some relationship between the exact
size of an alcoholism hostel and its position on the dimension of
greater to lesser resident participation in decision-making. The
exact nature of the relationship is not entirely clear from the small
number of instances which we have gathered, but it may be that a
hostel is unlikely to achieve a combination of informality and resident involvement if the size of the resident group is much larger
than around 10 to 15. Houses F and G were small (capacities of 12
and 8 residents respectively), as were Houses A and B (which would
undoubtedly have fallen towards the top end of this scale had it
been possible to include them). The two larger houses included in
Figure 5 (Houses C and K with 46 and 40 residents respectively) were
both 'average' houses with only a certain amount of resident involvement.
Whether or not a staff presence is maintained at night times and
during weekends is probably a good indication of whether staff intend
that residents should take a large measure of responsibility. In our
small sample, Houses F and G (along with A and B) were the only
houses without residential staff.
With a dozen residents or fewer living in a house that looks, at
least from the outside, like an ordinary family dwelling, and with a
single non-resident member of staff, informality and resident self-
determination may be relatively easily achieved. With larger numbers
of residents, and with the inevitable increase in numbers of staff
which that entails, these qualities are less easily attained. The
published account of the first few years at House C describes how
numbers of residents grew in the first few months from only 4, to 12,
to 20, and finally to 30. As the report succinctly puts it, "As the
number of residents increased, so did the rules..." (Ingram-Smith,
1967, p.296). Whilst it may be difficult for the larger hostel to
achieve the greatest degree of reaction to the large institution, it
is of course possible for a hostel to retain an institutional quality
in a whole host of ways even though it is, in terms of sheer numbers,
relatively small. House D, and to a lesser extent E, were the best
examples of this in our sample. Neither was established by an
organization or an individual with a modern treatment orientation.

Examples of Contrasting Philosophies

Although there appears to be no very telling evidence to suggest that one degree of resident participation or another is best overall, nonetheless those who organize and operate small hostels often espouse one particular model strongly and champion its virtues over those of other types. Different workers are equally enthusiastic about quite different approaches. For example, Corden et al (1974), writing of the establishment of the alcoholism hostel in the English Midlands, are amongst those who argue for 'participation'. Under the title, Teetotal Democracy, they write:

> ...former alcoholics can, in running their own self-governing community, help themselves to conquer their problems. ...our bias was towards a democratic and therapeutic community. We believed that the community would only be of value to individuals if they had a direct influence on its growth, and we wished to avoid substituting dependence on a structured institution, for alcohol (p.258).

Similarly, from the account of setting up one of the few alcoholism hostels in Britain to be run under local government auspices, in Scotland:

> ...it should be apparent that the project team believe that rehabilitation in its broadest sense ... can only take place when collective group responsibility and participation occur, both in decision-making and the daily running of the hostel. ...probably the most crucial $\int$ example of this$\overline{\phantom{J}}$ for both prospective, and indeed for existing residents is the power to decide who comes into $\int$ the hostel $\overline{\phantom{J}}$ and under what conditions residents leave (Edinburgh Corporation, 1974, pp.45-6).

By way of contrast, Ingram-Smith, writing about House C, was of the view that:

> It is usual that alcoholics have to undergo a reversal of their previous life. This is most easily done in a mildly authoritarian environment. In accepting their inter-dependence upon the community, they have to acquire an independence in such things as the organization of their leisure time activities, choice of friends and personal behaviour. At the centre we have a quite firm framework of rules which give a sense of security and yet are not obtrusive (1967, pp.304-5).

A published account of observations made by an independent research worker at House K depicts well the semi-institutional atmosphere of this larger hostel. For example, the account contains a description of offices and interview rooms, of the self-service cafeteria-style dining arrangements, of the expectation that all men will be "up and about" by 7 a.m. each morning whether they are working or not, of the need to get special permission to stay out after 11 p.m. at night, and of the sleeping facilities consisting (as they did at House C) of partitioned-off cubicles offering a bare minimum of privacy (Leissner, 1971, pp.111-2). Concerning the sleeping arrangements:

Most of the men seemed to be quite satisfied with this, but quite a few have expressed the wish for more privacy. Some of the men feel that the living arrangements maintain the 'institutional' or 'hospital' like atmosphere. While several of the men, especially ex-prisoners, feel that their living arrangments at ⌐House K⌐ are 'only slightly different from what it's like in an institution..', it is perhaps more significant that a number of men say that they like the present arrangements 'because it's not too different from what we're used to, but cleaner and more comfortable' (p.126).

The following remarks about the 6-member house committee which is "responsible for the overall running of the house and plays a leading role in organizing and leading group activities", are very telling, and provide a marked contrast with reported developments at House B (see Cook, 1975, Chapter 2, and also Chapter 2 above):

This committee was originally supposed to be elected by the men. This, however, led to considerable difficulties and friction due to the men's inability to make use of the 'democratic process' and their lack of judgement in electing men with sufficient ability and authority. The staff, therefore, decided to appoint the committee (p.128).

## Selection and Social Organization

There were illustrations amongst this small sample of alcoholism hostels of the complementarity of social organization and membership. It was, for instance, noticeable that the admission criteria for House G (where residents were given a large measure of autonomy) included the requirement that potential residents should have had a 'considerable period of abstinence' in the past, possibly in a small hostel environment (whether this period of abstinence should have been in the very recent past was a matter about which staff of the project disagreed). House G was therefore specializing in the further rehabilitation of men who were by no means naive about the ways of small alcoholism hostels and who could be said to have progressed considerably in their rehabilitation already. No house whose selection criteria were less strict allowed as much resident autonomy.

The best illustration of this complementariness comes from the more detailed study of Houses A and B, and here we anticipate results which will be described in much greater detail in the second part of this book (Chapters 6 and 7). Many of the differences that emerged between these two houses could be interpreted in terms of the stated intention of concentrating on 'skid row' or 'vagrant' alcoholics at House B. As a result many more residents at House B, than at House A, were multiple drunkenness offenders, or had multiple offences of other types; more were crude spirit drinkers and had been on or near 'skid row' in recent years; and many more at House B had had a deviant social status throughout their adult life. Staff at House B were much more likely to share the complaints of Blumberg et al (1973, Chapter 11), and the writers of the recent Scottish hostel report (Edinburgh Corporation, 1974, pp.12-3), about the apathy and passivity of residents and of the difficulty of stimulating resident participation in group meetings and in general decision-making in the hostel. During the time of the research, group meetings were indeed less emotional

at House B than at House A, and meetings, as well as the referral
and selection process, were more dominated by staff at House B.
Residents at House A were more in favour of the house taking action
over a variety of undesirable resident behaviours, and were more in
favour of residents themselves being involved in this action.  There
was always more evidence of an ideological clash between staff and
many residents at House B.  At House A residents held as strong, if
not a stronger, belief in 'democracy' than did the staff, whilst at
House B the staff belief in resident participation generally ran well
ahead of residents' views on the subject.

In many ways then, the particular biases, intentional or otherwise,
in the selection process operated by a hostel may make it relatively
easier or more difficult to put particular methods into operation.
On the other hand, it is of course impossible to know with certainty
to what extent differences in hostel routine, such as those found
between houses A and B, are really to be attributed to the differing
characteristics of residents.  An argument could be made out attributing the rather greater degree of democracy and 'therapeutic'
orientation of House A to the higher level of educational attainment,
higher job status, and higher level of social stability of its residents, or to their more frequent intensive experience of specialized
hospital treatment.  Staff dominance, the relative placidity of house
meetings, and the less pervasive 'therapeutic' orientation at House B
might be attributable to the norm of non-interference in others' personal affairs prevailing in public 'bottle gangs' of which many residents of House B had been members.  On the other hand, changes of
orientation over time do occur in hostels, and it is impossible from
a single investigation to know to what extent resident characteristics
are really major constraining factors.

Whatever their origins, there are measurable differences between
the social environments of different hostels as this chapter has
tried to show.  Not only should we be cautious in making general
statements about hostels, therefore, but those involved in their
planning and management would do well to appreciate the alternatives
open to them and to make a rational and planned choice from amongst
them.

# Chapter 4

# Problems and Prospects for Small Hostels

Doubts ... are beginning to create an atmosphere of disen-
chantment with the hostel idea ... We can continue with
the present haphazard and uncoordinated development of
hostels up and down the country, or we can assess the
strengths of residential care and concentrate on developing these to the best of our ability (Hinton, 1970,
p.2).

Not surprisingly, the euphoria that was felt about small hostels in
the late 1950's and early 1960's has given way to a more objective
appraisal. There is much less willingness now to accept on trust the
claims of those who run small hostels, or of those who would run them,
and there is a new demand for 'program evaluation' and even for
'controlled experiments'. There are in fact next to no studies, known
to the present authors, which employ the objective measures, controls
or comparisons, and follow-ups which would be necessary for a strict
evaluation of small hostels in terms of their proven ability to
achieve medium or long-term goals for their residents. Sinclair's
Home Office study of probation hostels (1971) is a notable exception,
and we shall refer later in this chapter to studies by Myerson and
Mayer (1966) and Blumberg et al (1973) which, for all their shortcomings, at least attempt to reach this research standard in the case
of alcoholism hostels. There are, however, problems in the interpretation of such research quite apart from the technical difficulties
of carrying it out.

## LOCATING PROBLEM AREAS FOR HOSTELS

Our own approach to researching alcoholism hostels, and to
summarizing research and writings on small hostels in general, has
not been in this 'evaluation by objectives' (Larkin, 1974) or 'outcome'
research tradition. What seems more useful at present is to identify
problem areas in the operation of small hostels; to locate the 'bugs
in the system'. There seems no doubt that identifiable problem areas
exist for hostels, and the best thing for now may be to spell these
out in the hope that this will lead to improvements. Outcome research
may more usefully proceed when some of the biggest faults have been
identified and corrected, and when hostels are working in such a way
that there can be a real expectation of meeting objectives. We shall
concentrate on just two main problem areas here.

Halfway House or Home?

There has been a tendency on the part of those involved with small hostels to subscribe to an idealized account of what hostels do. This version supposes that residents, once admitted, make rapid rehabilit- ative progress along a smooth upward path towards a planned and orderly departure, followed by re-entry to the approved, non-marginal, world of social and occupational stability. This corresponds to what Durkin (1971) has called 'the policy of rehabilitation'. It stresses the need to encourage the individual to conform to the values of the community and to achieve full re-integration and 'normality'. It was the philosophy of rehabilitation which underlay the transition from institutional care to community care and which supported the idea of hostels as transitional establishments, or 'halfway houses', through which individuals passed relatively quickly en route for a normal life of complete autonomy in the community.

There is a failure, Durkin argues, to appreciate when a hostel is appropriately operating with a policy of rehabilitation, and when it should operate within an alternative philosphy, that of 'the maintenance of the deviant within the community':

> In an industrial society based on competition, some individuals will always fail to achieve the high standards of community norms. The mentally ill are an example of such failures. According to this concept they are accepted within the comm- unity in the role of the mentally ill person, without being expected to conform to community norms (Durkin, 1971, p.1).

Fletcher (1970) is also critical of the assumptions contained in the term 'rehabilitation', although he evidently does not think it possible to make such a clear distinction between just two philosophies, and two types of hostel, as does Durkin. Rather he emphasizes a flexible approach in which a hostel is seen as providing merely 'a stable and helpful environment', to which people may come and from which people may go at various times and for various reasons, bringing with them a variety of different needs. Whether or not clear dis- tinctions can be made, it does now appear to be the case that hostels inappropriately run with a strict transitional philosophy may merely help to perpetuate instability.

Many hostels make the assumption that residency there will be temporary: residents are thought of as being halfway from one place to another. Sinclair (1971) discusses this matter in relation to probation hostels. He notes the illogicality of viewing such hostels as short-term training institutions, whilst at the same time selecting boys from bad homes (or from no home at all) to which they could not be returned in the short term. He cites other critics, such as Grygier, who wrote:

> The greatest weakness of hostels seems to be the strictly limited length of stay. To suggest that 6 or even 12 months' stay in a hostel would solve their problems permanently is not realistic (Spencer and Grygier, 1951, p.9).

Apte (1968) points out that the term 'hostel' is generic and covers 'transitional hostels', or halfway houses, on the one hand, and permanent residencies or 'non-transitional hostels' on the other hand (pp.9-10), and recalls that the British Mental Health Act of

1959 referred to the need for both short-stay and long-stay hostels. In practice, however, Apte found that although "...the majority $\angle$of hostels_7 started with the expectation and objective of providing a time-limited service...early experience with patients with chronic disabilities required a change in their aims..." (p.31-32). Rather than questioning the appropriateness of the 'transitional' model as a blanket model for all hostels, Apte clearly regards long-stay as inefficient. He refers to the 'blocking' of places, and the 'silting up' of bed space occupied by residents remaining for one year or more, and goes on to point out that this is an "ubiquitous problem" not limited to halfway houses, and that the core of the problem is, "...the frequently encountered problem of the emotionally dependent and unresourceful mental patient or inmate" (p.91).

Other studies of hostels for the mentally ill in England (e.g. Fletcher, 1970; Hewett et al, 1975) have found that even short-stay hostels, "...where the intention of the sponsoring body...is that residents should not make permanent homes there but should become sufficiently independent to leave" (Hewett et al, 1975, p.396), contain substantial numbers of residents who have been resident at the hostel for more than 1 or 2 years. Hewett et al state:

> It has sometimes been assumed that 'social treatment' would enable sufferers to recover completely from their illness or at least to compensate completely for any residual handicap. Our pilot study suggests that it is more likely that they reach a plateau in recovery, beyond which they are unlikely to progress, in spite of further 'social treatment'. More significantly, it suggests that they may continue to need special environments simply in order to maintain the degree of recovery achieved. If this is the case, the question then arises of where and how to create such 'maintenance' environments, both for the people with the low level of impairment described here and for the more impaired 'new long-stay' patients still living in hospital (1975, p.402).

Durkin (1971) has proposed the term 'compensatory hostel' as the long-term counterpart to the short-term halfway house:

> It provides a permanent home for certain categories of mentally ill who because of the nature of their illness could never be rehabilitated. Such a hostel compensates for the inability of the community in an industrial society to tolerate those unable to keep up with its demands. A compensatory hostel avoids the otherwise inevitable results of such illness, either social isolation within the community or non-identity within a large institution (p.7).

Such a hostel would be expected to place far greater emphasis on its function in providing for the housing needs of its residents, and would also be much more likely than transitional hostels to provide sheltered work or training facilities.

Creating and Maintaining a Favourable Hostel Atmosphere

The second major problem area concerns hostel culture. Anyone who knows much about small hostels at first hand would be likely to endorse the view that:

> ...to create and run a hostel ... which is a real halfway house, a part of the community rather than an extension of the hospital system, is a very difficult operation. It requires a great deal of thought, effort and enthusiasm, and a high level of skill particularly in the field of human relationships... (Fletcher, 1970, p.7).

In fact, whether what is intended is a transitional halfway house, a compensatory maintenance environment, or a small hostel with some hybrid or quite other philosophy, a central problem in the operation of small hostels is that of creating a culture, or atmosphere, which can exert an influence on residents consistent with the hostel's goals. Much has already been said in Chapter 2 about the difficulty of maintaining a continuously satisfactory social environment in hostels, and about the way in which the climate may oscillate and on occasions plummet to levels of chaos and disorganization. There is a need for residents and different levels of staff to be cohesive around the set of beliefs and values which constitutes the hostel philosophy, and a need to minimize, by means of selection and inter-personal influence, social behaviour which is abrasive and disruptive. The smallness and relative informality of the hostel makes it part-icularly difficult to contain people whose social behaviour is un-popular or difficult. Fletcher refers particularly to people who receive psychiatric diagnoses of 'hysteria', 'psychopathy' or 'per-sonality disorder', who may be most likely to be rejected by treat-ment organizations:

> The hostel may be on the whole less able to contain such persons than a hospital although they show just those problems for which hostels exist, namely, a failure of social adaptation and a need for a more than usually tolerant or helpful home environment (Fletcher, 1970,p.3).

The limited tolerance of disturbed behaviour in hostels comes as a disappointment to many, particularly to those who would refer prospective residents. The needs of the small hostel, which must put a high value on cohesiveness and atmosphere, are for careful and often time-consuming selection. Tension and misunderstanding frequently arise between those outside the hostel who may see it as an available service for all those in a particular category of need, and staff and existing residents inside the hostel who may see it as a group of people living together whose equilibrium must be closely guarded. Apte notes conflict over selection for local authority mental after-care hostels in Britain:

> When unsatisfactory candidates are referred, the local authority complains that the hospital is trying to send patients that no one else will accept. The hospital then complains that the local authority's admission policies are 'too rigid' and that they will only take those who do not need the halfway house in the first place (1968, p.51).

Several writers refer to the dangers of admitting long-stay hospital patients to hostels as the result of both misunderstandings between hostel and referral agent and to administrative pressures to keep hostels full (Durkin, 1971; Fletcher, 1970; Mountney, 1965). In these circumstances it is not surprising that hostel staff often

prefer to establish a close working relationship with a very small
number of referral agents, perhaps even with just one referral agent,
who can be relied upon to 'understand' the hostel, to appreciate its
'balanced aquarium' nature, and not to 'dump' unsuitable people on it.

## Prospects - Varieties, Adjuncts and Alternatives

Many of the problems that have arisen over small hostels derive
from the assumption that there is one type of hostel which can do all
things for all people, and that a hostel can stand alone, sufficient
in itself. The folly of these assumptions has slowly become clear as
experience in running hostels has been gained, and the future lies in
clearer planning for varieties of type of hostel, and in setting
hostels within a more comprehensive system of care.

### The Need for Variety

For one thing, in research on social treatment of all kinds it
is relatively rare to find simple 'main effects' whereby one 'treatment' shows clear gains over others. Samples of subjects, residents,
patients, or pupils turn out to be heterogenous with regard to many
variables. Under these conditions it is far more likely that one
'treatment' will do good things for some subjects, and that another
'treatment' will do good things (not necessarily the same kinds of
good things) for others.

Durkin (1971) gives examples of categories and types of person
who might be more suited to the compensatory hostel than to a transitional halfway house. These include large numbers of the mentally
handicapped at present in hospitals but who could reside in hostels;
the elderly mentally ill who tend to block places in transitional
rehabilitation hostels; the homeless or vagrant chronically mentally
ill; as well as many drug addicts and chronic alcoholics. The
important point is that the needs of people selected for residence
in a hostel, the goals of that hostel, its social organization, and
the behaviour of its staff should be designed to match more satisfactorily than is often the case:

> If rehabilitative and compensatory hostels are to fulfil
> different functions they must contain different types of
> social organization... A rehabilitative hostel should be
> permissive in character, leaving the individual as much
> freedom and responsibility as possible in areas such as
> social relationships, dress, personal belongings and leisure
> activities. Wherever possible, residents should be
> encouraged to participate in the administration of the
> hostel by choosing their own menus, making their own rules
> and selecting new residents. ...a greater amount of
> imposed organization would be expected in compensatory
> hostels (Durkin, 1971, p.4-5).

Durkin cites Apte's (1968) finding that many hostel wardens held
restrictive attitudes and employed restrictive practices in their
hostels even when the hostel was intentionally transitional and rehabilitative, and argues, quite rightly, that the roles of hostel staff
should be, "...clearly defined according to the type of hostel in
which they work..." (p.7). Yet another hostel variable (discussed in
Chapter 3), namely whether staff are residential or not, should be

matched to hostel goals. Having staff in residence is more suited to the compensatory type of hostel: non-residential staff might be more appropriate for a rehabilitative hostel.

Although he avoids the simple distinction favoured by Durkin, Fletcher (1970) makes a very similar point, arguing that a distinction should be made between the relatively severely handicapped who will require a relatively protective hostel, and the relatively mildly handicapped who would find such a hostel too authoritarian and paternalistic. Hence:

> Any kind of residential accommodation ought to encourage independence in its residents as far as possible. No person should be compelled to live in a more protective situation than he needs. Accommodation available should be as varied as possible, from very protective hostels to unsupervized group homes, flatlets, and boarding out schemes in areas where lodgings are to be found (p.16.).

## Hostels as Part of a Comprehensive Service

Not only is there a need for a variety of hostels, differing in terms of internal organization, but there is equally a need, now widely recognized, for a variety of adjunctive services. With experience of running hostels has come the realization that they cannot stand in isolation, that rehabilitation is a continuing process and cannot be conducted within the confines of a few weeks stay in a hostel, and that thought has to be given to the creation of a variety of environments facilitative of this process. Already, in 1968, Apte was writing:

> ...it is important to note that the hostel is only one of a group of transitional institutions that have been developed, mostly in the last two decades, to care for, treat, and rehabilitate the mentally ill. ...there has been a proliferation in the variety and number of these institutions. The major types can be classified as follows: (1) day hospital, (2) night hospital, (3) transitional hostel, (4) foster care home, (5) sheltered rehabilitation workshop, (6) therapeutic social club, (7) out-patient psychiatric clinic (p.26).

To these might be added assessment units, shop-front offices, day centres, information and advice centres, night shelters, three-quarter way houses, group homes, and houses consisting of relatively independent bed-sitters or flatlets. These are amongst the variety of additional facilities which it has been necessary to create in order to provide the continuity of care which it seems the hostel alone is insufficient to provide.

## The Need for Further Innovation

One of the sources of variation in hostel provision, and one direction in which further innovation might take place, lies in the degree to which provision is specialized. The trend to develop highly specialized facilities for one category of person ('alcoholics' are one such category) has been criticized - for example by Meacher (1972) who studied facilities for the 'aged mentally infirm'. On the other hand, there are surely mixtures of people of different ages and types of need which are unsatisfactory and lead to a confusion of hostel aims (Durkin, 1970, p.4). An extension of the idea of de-specializing hostels, is that of mixing people who become resident because of some problem or handicap with those without. For example, in their survey of North American halfway houses for the mentally ill, Raush and Raush found:

> Five of the 40 houses have arrangements whereby as part of a deliberate plan, 'normal' subjects live together in the house with ex-patient residents. Such arrangements ... are suited to the halfway house which in its location and physical structure can function simultaneously as a boarding home. ...the possibility of the creative use of college students and other volunteers in the living arrangements for the mentally disturbed has appealed to many halfway house directors, and it is likely that this combination, at present rather rare, will be met more frequently in the future (1968, p.90).

Such arrangements have obvious implications for the sources and forms of social influence prevalent in the hostel environment. The use of college students, for example, introduces a quite new dimen-sion. It might be supposed that the presence of a number of such socially well-integrated individuals might add to the hostel's pot-ential for appropriate influence. On the other hand, dissimilarities in age, educational and occupational attainments and aspirations, and perhaps important values, could make such 'normals' rather ineffective role models in comparison with 'indigenous leaders' amongst residents or ex-residents (Leissner, 1971, pp.113-4).

Implications for Evaluation

The existence of these various problems and limitations in the operation of small hostels makes the application of a systematic outcome evaluation study problematic. The central problem of creating and maintaining a stable hostel culture poses particular problems. As was quite evident from our own research on alcoholism hostels (see Chapters 8 and 9), a small hostel is not the same thing from one year to the next, or even from one month to the next, and statistical indices of functioning such as the proportion of 'irregular discharges' (Davis, 1973; Orford et al, 1974), or the number of abscondings (Sinclair, 1971, 1975) vary both between facilities and from time to time at the same place. There is little purpose in evaluating an unrepresentative hostel, or a hostel at an unrepresentative time. Generalization can only be made from studies which sample several hostels and/or a single hostel at several different points in time. Research is rarely that sophisticated even in other, relatively well researched, areas.

The discovery that small hostels will meet problems that will prevent them realizing their initial aims unless they are backed up by necessary other components of a more comprehensive system, poses additional evaluation problems. To put the same point another way, there seems little to be gained by evaluating the results of the impact on a person of a relatively brief period in a hostel environ-ment, however favourable, if the individual then returns to an unsatisfactory environment. Only if a stay in a hostel is viewed as a 'treatment', analogous to medical treatment, which should have lasting effects irrespective of the subsequent, post-hostel, environ-

ment, will follow-up data be taken as evidence solely of the effectiveness of the hostel, rather than as evidence of the effect of the
hostel and the post-hostel environment taken together. Rehabilitation is a continuous process, and it is impossible to attribute
long-term outcome to the effectiveness of any one intermediate
environment experienced at some stage during the process. The
notion of psychological change as a lengthy continuous process,
rather than as something resulting from a single brief treatment-
like input, is not of course limited in its application to small
hostels. There is a growing appreciation of the need to monitor
short-term, immediate, after treatment changes, and for the need to
assess and modify longer-term family, transitional or institutional
environments in which people subsequently reside (Tizard, 1976;
Tizard et al, 1975, p.13-6; Vaughn and Leff, 1976).

## PROBLEMS AND PROSPECTS FOR SMALL ALCOHOLISM HOSTELS

Growing scepticism and demand for objective evaluation are as
evident in relation to small alcoholism hostels as they are for
other types of hostel. Rubington, writing of halfway houses for
alcoholics in North America, puts the matter particularly succinctly:

> Unless halfway houses give some thought to independent
> studies of their functioning, they are very likely to
> disappear from the rehabilitation scene as fast as they
> appeared (1973, p.29).

Ogborne and Smart (1974) located only 12 reports of alcoholism
hostels, from all over the world, which contained any information at
all which was relevant to evaluation, and only two came near to
matching the criteria which they considered ideal for an evaluation
study (large samples followed up after a consistent and considerable
period of time using some reliable and valid follow-up instrument).
Both had severe limitations. Myerson and Mayer (1966) reported a
10-year follow-up of 100 men admitted to an alcoholism halfway house
located in a hospital setting. Twenty-two percent were classified as
successfully rehabilitated and a further 24% as partially rehabilitated. Unfortunately the very length of the follow-up, exemplary in
one respect, makes it extremely unlikely that the results could be
attributed to the halfway house experience 10 years earlier, and the
results were not compared with those of any comparison or control
sample. Furthermore, very scanty details are provided of the halfway
house itself, so if there had been better results for the halfway
house group than for a control group, it would have been difficult to
know to what the results could be attributed.

The other study concerns a 'halfway house experiment' reported
more recently by Blumberg et al (1973, Ch. 11). The study involved the
random assignment of subjects to a halfway house (HWH) and 2 varieties
of individual counselling. As many subjects as possible were followed
up at least a year after entering the study. Unfortunately follow-up
was far from complete; only just over half of the HWH sample provided
satisfactory, complete, follow-up information. After much heart
searching on the matter it was decided to rely on drinking behaviour
as the main outcome criterion. The outcome for the HWH sample was
not good. There were rather fewer 'successes' (at least one year's
sobriety during the period of the study) in this group than in the
intensively counselled group (12.5% versus 23.3%). There were also

many fewer 'survivors' (demonstrating moderate periods of sobriety) (18.7% versus 44.2%). Partly because follow-up was so incomplete, and partly because the report of the study was insufficiently detailed, Ogborne and Smart conclude that no generalizations can be made on the basis of this one study (1974, pp.13-4).

A more serious limitation, in our view, concerns the nature of the HWH itself. It is obviously impossible to generalize the results of a single program, especially as in this case there is reason to believe that the operation of the house left much to be desired. It is quite evident from Blumberg et al's account that they met the familiar problem of establishing and maintaining a stable house group adhering to appropriate goals and constituting a satisfactory hostel culture. They write of contamination by the skid row ethos, of the large proportion of men who demonstrated 'conning relationships', and of the high rate of turnover. In this regard, therefore, their finding is similar to our own and to those of others who studied hostels; namely, that hostels are not the same things from one year to the next. Hence their evaluation ideally requires a sampling from several points in the project's history. To base an outcome evaluation of HWH on the particular regime they describe seems unwise.

What is abundantly clear, however, is that evidence for the effectiveness of small alcoholism hostels is hard to come by. Indeed Ogborne and Smart state:

No study has been found which adequately shows halfway house treatment to be better than any other treatment or superior to no treatment at all. Recoveries may be as much spontaneous as related to any effects of the halfway house (1974, p.14).

However they correctly point out:

Such a lack of support for the promise of halfway houses is due as much to the shortcomings of present studies as to the results which they present. ...it is clear then, that we cannot draw any firm conclusions as to the role of the halfway house for alcoholics until there has been a substantial upgrading of research efforts (p.16).

The Argument for the Effectiveness of Small Alcoholism Hostels

The first point in any argument for the effectiveness of alco-holism hostels is likely to make mention of 'baseline expectancies'. It is generally assumed that alcoholism hostels cater for people whose prognosis, without a hostel, would be particularly poor. Hence low success rates cannot be judged in any absolute sense, but must be compared with the success of realistic alternatives offered to people with comparable problems.

Hostels as Experiments

A second point concerns the accomplishment of setting up hostels for 'alcoholics' at all. These were experiments, not only to see whether a certain percentage of people could be rehabilitated in the long term, but also to find out whether houses of this type were feasible. They were 'experimental' in a number of ways. In one sense the alcoholism hostel movement has answered questions which were by no means certain 10 to 20 years ago. Doubts and uncertainties that were voiced then, and are perhaps still voiced by those not familiar with recent developments, sound strangely dated now. For example, Ingram-Smith, writing about the setting up of House C, stated:

> The question of housing a number of alcoholics under one
> roof seemed daunting... In the drawingboard stage a good
> deal of drinking on the premises had been envisaged.
> Because of this there was a liberal supply of metal waste-
> paper baskets which would have been useful in an emergency
> should a resident vomit. Chairs were upholstered in vinyl
> plastic material. Both of these arrangements proved to be
> of great value, though not for the reasons for which they
> were planned (1967, pp.295-6).

With hindsight, Cook can now write about House B:

> As the reality of actually having a house for skid row
> alcoholics drew nearer, it should be noted that many of
> the concerns, wishes, hopes of the people demonstrated,
> in some instances at least, a revealing difference
> between the forecast and the actual events. Concern had
> been expressed about neighbours and their children being
> upset by the possible dreadful goings-on. 'Morning
> discipline' was another fear of the committee. Both
> proved to be totally unnecessary fears. This is how the
> expectations of social work projects need to be challenged
> if any progress is to be made... The history of the house
> has been largely one of the abandonment of almost all
> preconceptions (1975, p.14).

The development of House B from paternalism towards 'democracy' has already been referred to, and in its more recent form House B undoubtedly represents a model which has influenced the setting up of similar facilities elsewhere. The greatest gains have perhaps been made, as Cook suggests, in the altering of prejudices about the potential of people who in recent years have come to be the residents of alcoholism hostels (pp.163-5).

Hostels as Humane Alternatives

It is easy to dismiss small alcoholism hostels as ineffective on the basis of outcome statistics. It is more difficult to come by statistics which demonstrate the accomplishment of setting up facilities which provide the great contrast with large institutions which houses like Houses A and B, for example, evidently offer. On ultimate outcome figures alone, these houses might turn out to be difficult to distinguish from the large, institutional, reception centre. It is therefore not surprising to find the occasional writer, who judges the effectiveness of organizations on the basis of outcome statistics alone, expressing admiration of an institutional alternative such as Camp La Guardia:

> The Camp's goals are modest: there is little expectation
> that 'rehabilitation' in any long-term sense will occur,
> and little need to justify its existence by seeking out
> 'success' stories. In a very real sense the Camp has

adjusted to its inmates, rather than the reverse.  ...
compared to the drunk tank or prison, it seems an ideal
institution (Bahr, 1973, p.258).

In terms of their social climates, however, Camp La Guardia and
small alcoholism hostels are in different worlds.  Camp La Guardia
accommodates over 1000 men; men can stay there as long as they wish
and some have been there for a quarter of a century; men can leave
and return with no question asked although the more disruptive
elements are expelled; small amounts of pocket-money are given, work
assignments are carried out in the mornings and there is a range of
recreational facilities available.  According to the description of
the Camp from which Bahr quotes, it seems that personal interaction
between inmates is at a minimum, that men are mostly "at a bit of a
loose end", people are rarely seen "walking purposefully from place
to place", and there is a problem of filling time.
    There is a powerful argument that whilst, "law enforcement
remains the dominant mode by which habitual drunkenness is controlled"
(Cook, 1975, p.146), outcome statistics are not the only criteria by
which the effectiveness of a hostel should be judged.  Early planning
documents for Houses A and B stressed the role of the hostel as a
"humane alternative" to traditional forms of response.  The argument
for the effectiveness of the small hostel may rest not on differences
in "success rates at follow-up" but on differences in the quality of
life offered in different places.

The Economic Argument

    There is also a very real economic argument for the effectiveness
of a small alcoholism hostel, as indeed there is for small rehabilitation hostels of other kinds.  Although the weekly running costs of
hostels, per resident, are likely to vary widely, in some cases perhaps
even approaching the cost of institutional care, many hostels undoubtedly run at a much lower cost.  What is more important is that working
hostel residents make a substantial contribution to running costs out
of their own earnings, and are productive members of the work force
rather than purely receivers of welfare.  An evaluation of hostels
should include a cost-benefit analysis and a comparison with reasonable alternatives.

In-Hostel Success

    There is, furthermore, a major difference in emphasis between the
sceptics, the 'program evaluators', on the one hand, and those who
write accounts of the small hostels with which they are personally
involved, on the other hand.  The former are likely to require evidence of long-term change.  They are more interested in what happens
after a person leaves a hostel than in what transpires during his
stay.  The latter, on the other hand, impressed with the contrast
between the behaviour of residents during their stay and their former
behaviour, are more likely to attribute subsequent failure to the lack
of after-care facilities or suitable accommodation rather than to the
faults of the hostel itself.  For example, the report of the first
year at House B includes a table comparing the average experience
(e.g. months in prison, months in work, longest period sober) in the
'year before admission' and the 'year after admission'.  The latter

period is, of course, partly made up of time spent in the house itself. On the basis of this comparison, the authors concluded:

> The results during the first year at ⟨House B⟩ show that men who had been leading a skid row existence can often maintain quite long periods of sobriety up to several months in duration in a hostel setting with no more than supportive treatment. ...these results are all the more remarkable in view of the fact that the men were usually in regular outside employment during residence at the hostel (Cook et al, 1968, p.241).

Corden et al, in a similar paper, put the argument for 'in-hostel' success particularly succinctly:

> Of 45 alcoholics with extremely poor prognoses, 13 have remained in the house for periods varying from 6 months to 3 years. They have all avoided further offences, and remained sober throughout their stay. Several others have achieved a higher level of functioning than they had previously attained for many years. This success has been achieved without any restrictions on the residents, except their own rule against drinking (1974, p.259).

Whether 'in-hostel' success is felt to be acceptable as a criterion of effectiveness is likely to depend on whether or not our earlier argument is accepted, that a particular environment can be expected to have immediate effects while a person remains in contact with it, but cannot be expected to have many beneficial effects which override a subsequent unsatisfactory environment.

## Locating Problems for Alcoholism Hostels

It is not our present intention to take sides in this dispute about the effectiveness or ineffectiveness of small alcoholism hostels. We have sympathies with the arguments on both sides. Our own studies were not conceived within the outcome statistics model of program evaluation, and no systematic post-hostel follow-up was attempted. They aimed at the more feasible, and to our minds at present more worthwhile task, of providing a relatively more detailed description of the operation of 2 particular small hostels (Houses A and B) plus a much more superficial survey description of 9 others. Equally, however, it is not our intention to avoid judgement. The approach is that adopted more generally in the first part of this chapter, namely the identification of particular operational problems, in the hope that improvements might follow. Some outstanding problems for alcoholism hostels will be discussed under the following six sub-headings.

### Lack of Clarity

From our own observations it is clear that small alcoholism hostels suffer from the same uncertainties about means and ends which are experienced by other types of hostel. Lack of clarity, at times amounting to confusion, surrounds the work expectation, the operation of group or house meetings, the operation of sanctions for a variety of misbehaviours including under certain circumstances drinking itself, and the degree of involvement of residents in taking decisions. Are these houses dry 'working men's hostels' or 'therapeutic communities', 'halfway houses' or 'group homes'? The list of possible designations is almost endless, and the room for uncertainty and variablility of interpretation almost unlimited.

Information on group meetings illustrates this general point about absence of clarity. Despite the lack of an intensive and explicit 'program', and the emphasis on informality and the sheer experience of communal living, all but one house in the survey (House D) felt the need to hold at least one, and sometimes more than one, weekly house or group meeting. There was uncertainty as to what these should be called and what functions they should serve. Were they purely domestic house meetings, an administratively convenient way of making sure that everyone was together in one place at least once a week so that they could be consulted on domestic matters? Or were they group therapy sessions, essential for the working out of personal problems and interpersonal conflicts? Different houses opted for different emphases. Some, like House A, opted for a group psychotherapy emphasis, whilst others, like House B, opted for more of a domestic emphasis. Differences in emotionality and staff dominance, discovered in the more intensive study of Houses A and B (Chapter 7), with meetings at House A more emotional and less staff dominated, were consistent with these different orientations.

However, meetings potentially serve a variety of functions, and they are unlikely in practice to serve all equally well. At House B, for example, the unemotional, staff-dominated, form which meetings took was not universally approved. Staff remarked to the research worker on a number of occasions that meetings were placid and disappointing. Residents, on the other hand, were generally in sympathy with the domestic business orientation of meetings and did not expect them to be more emotional than they were. A chronic lack of congruence between staff and resident expectations of the meetings existed. This difference of opinion was a reflection of the staff-resident strain which existed over the purpose and orientation of the house and has already been referred to in Chapter 2.

Even when a strong ethic of community responsibility exists, as it did at House A during most of the time of our study there, the hostel climate is by no means immune to changes of interpretation at the hands of new groups of residents or new members of staff. For example, one entirely new group of residents (occupying the house in the last few months of the study) was noticeably more concerned about their members' misconduct than were the residents who occupied the house 12 months earlier (Chapter 7). Furthermore, the first staff member resigned during the course of the study and his successor differed in his understanding of where decision-making responsibility in the hostel lay. The first had been in favour of staff responsibility after consultation with residents, rather than in collective responsibility. This attitude did not pass unnoticed, and at least two other professional workers, both closely associated with the house, were highly critical of what they saw as his attempt to 'sabotage' the former 'therapeutic community' orientation of the house. The uncertainty, and room for different interpretations, which surrounds the operation of small alcoholism hostels means there is no guarantee that a particular mode of operation, preferred at one moment in time, will survive to a later period.

Uncertainty over the Control of Drinking

There is even room for differences of interpretation over the rule banning drinking. Variations in the way different alcoholism hostels handle this matter, for example whether the ban includes drinking away from the house, have already been mentioned in Chapter 1. Although it appears that the primary need for such a rule is the prevention of the disturbing and tempting effects of uncontrolled drinking upon other residents, the view that total abstinence is a prerequisite for successful rehabilitation is also widely held, and a 'no drinking' rule therefore serves at least two purposes. The rule is therefore tested when drinking is known to occur but without the disruptive effects that are usually anticipated. Reports from Bon Accord, The Canadian farm community for 'skid row' alcoholics, suggest that such controlled drinking occasions may occur much more frequently than might be expected, especially if legitimized by the philosophy of the hostel program (Oki, 1974; Ogborne and Collier, 1975).

The intensive study at Houses A and B revealed much greater variation in the opinions of different residents, and even different members of staff, than had been anticipated from superficial acquaintance with the houses which had given an impression of a solid concensus behind a strict drinking ban. Overall, residents at the two houses were roughly equally divided between those who thought that the offending residents should be asked to leave after drinking, and those who did not. Only one of the 4 members of staff thought that the offender should be automatically dismissed. A particularly vocal group of residents at House A (during the early part of the study) made it widely known that they disagreed with the prevailing abstinence view and would themselves attempt controlled drinking after leaving (Chapters 8 and 9).

That rules about drinking are by no means fixed once and for all, and are not always absolute, is shown by the following quotation from the account of setting up House A:

> The group's attitude to the resident who drinks is constantly debated ... the practice at present is that if a man drinks the matter will be discussed at the resident's private meeting and if he does not rapidly mend his ways the matter will then be discussed in the full Wednesday evening session. A man is then given one more chance (Edwards et al, 1966, p.1405).

Similarly, the following quotation from the account of the first year at the Scottish hostel:

> The issue of relapse policy has been a continuous subject for discussion in the groups and, although the residents have maintained a fairly hard line on the matter, they continue to view each case individually on its merits. ...sanctions vary, depending on the individual, between being asked to leave the house or staying in the house conditionally. The conditions are usually the restriction of freedom, in that the person does not leave the house unaccompanied for a week or two (Edinburgh Corporation, 1974, pp.25, 15).

Early and Irregular Leaving

Problems surrounding the length of stay of residents loom large in the consideration of all types of small hostel. However, whilst it is the excessively lengthy stay of many residents which appears to cause most concern in hostels for the ex-psychiatrically ill, it is the unsatisfactory and premature leaving of so many residents that is one of the principal causes of concern at small hostels for alcoholics. Our own studies, backed up by what figures are available from elsewhere, showed that many residents of alcoholism hostels leave very quickly, within just a few weeks of coming (Orford et al, 1974; also Chapter 10 of this book). At Houses A and B (and at House C in the pilot study) many others left within 2 to 4 months, leaving only a small minority who remained for a length of time which even began to approach what most staff considered to be ideal. Probably only a minority accumulated a longer continuous period of 'sobriety' than they had achieved previously without the support of a therapeutic hostel. Most staff of alcoholism hostels consider a very short stay to be of little value, and others argue that a short stay may even be harmful because, "...it sets up an expectancy of failure and a tendency, on the part of the alcoholic, to see subsequent programs... as temporary havens between binges..." (Blumberg et al, 1973, p.179).

A breakdown in the rehabilitation process occurs not only because so many departures are premature but because so many, whether premature or not, are irregular. At Houses A and B, during the period of study there, most residents left in a disorderly or unplanned way, often associated with or soon followed by obvious drinking (Chapter 10). Sometimes, but more frequently at House A, departures were stormy and disruptive. Residents might be reluctant to leave after drinking, or else their drinking provoked lengthy group discussions around the time they left. Alternatively, leaving would follow a period of dispute in the house or, most commonly, residents would disappear only to reappear later, drinking. In other instances, more commonly at House B, departures, though unplanned, had a 'matter of fact' quality. Many residents left of their own accord, without a fuss, and phoned or called at the house later to announce that they had been drinking and were leaving, or simply to collect their belongings.

A high rate of less-than-ideal circumstances surrounding the departure of residents from alcoholism hostels or halfway houses seems, in fact, to be a fairly general finding. On the basis of their recent review of the few published accounts of alcoholism hostels which offer any data of this kind, Ogborne and Smart conclude:

Available data shows that only a minority of clients complete the course and leave with approval and the limited data on length of stay shows this to average under 3 months...which seems very short in view of the many years of heavy drinking and social isolation of the skid row population (1974, pp.17-8).

Successful graduates of therapeutic programs for drug addicts also appear to be a minority (Smart, 1974) and departure characteristics are again remarkably similar, despite the very different age group and different drug of abuse, and the very different nature of the therapeutic programs, such as those based on Synanon and Phoenix House (e.g. Yablonsky, 1965). The same problems of early and irregular departure appear to be endemic to hostels for juvenile or adult ex-offenders also (Sinclair, 1971, Sinclair and Snow, 1971).

The Rehab Circuit

Although no systematic follow-up was attempted, the majority of
ex-residents were known to have had contact with some rehabilitation
or penal agency or institution within a few months of leaving. Many
were soon in touch with the house again asking for further help, and
more were known to have had at least one further period of residence
in another small alcoholism hostel. It seems likely that the future
pattern of multiple-agency contacts was, for many ex-residents, the
same as it was prior to their admissions to Houses A and B.

Hostels for alcoholics frequently seem to be serving, not as
transitional or intermediate institutions, contributing to a rapid,
smooth, upward path from handicap to autonomy, but rather as 'stations'
on circuits or 'loop lines' (to use Wiseman's, 1970 terminology) consisting of a variety of therapeutic, penal, supportive and other
statutory and non-statutory agencies. To the sceptical it may appear
to be merely the accident of a particular agency's origins that
results in one rather than another being termed 'therapeutic' or 'rehab
ilitative'. The distinctions between different agencies become blur-
red and their common identity as stations on the 'rehab-route' becomes
more salient than their individual designations. Besides the lodging
houses, hotels, courts, police stations, reception centres, hospitals,
church missions and soup kitchens, the few small hostels for alcoholics
may sometimes appear, in quantity at least, to make a relatively small
contribution.

In a number of ways alcoholism hostels may actually help to perpetuate impermanence. Almost all the houses in our survey of London
hostels, including Houses A and B, assumed that residency there was
temporary: it was made clear from the beginning that a resident was
expected, sooner or later, to 'move on'. The houses were conceived as
being 'half way' from one place to another. As one staff member
emphatically put it, "This is not a home". Only two houses seemed not
to share this assumption. One was House G which was exceptional in
other ways, and was in many respects a communal 'three-quarter-way
house' or 'group home'. The 'halfway house' concept was also inappropriate to House H, a small house for female drunkenness offenders,
which was set up initially as a long-term 'resting place' for older
women alcoholics. Unlike most of the small hostels, House H was from
the outset conceived of as a 'home'. At the larger women's hostel
(House I) the staff were clear that they were doing a variety of jobs
in parallel, and that they were combining a halfway house and a home
under the same roof. However, the staff member in charge was equally
clear that, "We are attempting too much"! Many other members of staff
felt that these two jobs were difficult to combine in the same place.
Hence the same confusions arise about the purpose of, and ideal length
of stay at, alcoholism hostels as arise in other types of hostel such
as those for the psychiatrically ill and those for youthful and adult
offenders.

Drinking Assumptions

A special feature of alcoholism hostels, as distinct from hostels
of other types, concerns assumptions about alcoholism and drinking.
In many ways these assumptions seem to us to help perpetuate the
alcoholic resident's inpermanence. Virtually universally shared, for
example, are the assumptions that all residents are in the category

'alcoholic', and that all instances of drinking by people in that category are 'uncontrolled' or lead very rapidly to further drinking which is uncontrolled. Whatever its advantages, the 'no drinking' rule, which operates in some form in all hostels, has the effect of limiting to very special circumstances opportunities for staff observation of drinking. Very often, perhaps usually, staff have no first-hand evidence of the drinking behaviour of a resident, and rely purely on self-report and hearsay. Concepts of the drinking of 'alcoholic' residents are usually quite undifferentiated; it is supposed that the individual has one or other extreme status at any moment in time. He is either abstinent or 'drinking'. The status 'drinking' implies far more than it would if used to describe a non-alcoholic. It implies relapse, a 'slip', failure, return to an uncontrolled and unsettled way of life, an excluding of the self from the sober world of 'therapeutic' establishments. Many, perhaps most, residents share these assumptions. He is either doing well or badly, is sober or drunk, is settled or moving on. In everyone's minds, settling at one particular 'station on the loop' is associated with sobriety, meaning abstinence, and moving on is associated with 'slipping' back into uncontrolled drinking.

Such thinking is particularly inappropriate when it is borne in mind that all but a small minority of alcoholics in hostels will drink alcohol again within a few weeks or months of leaving, as is indeed the case for groups of excessive drinkers who have received treatment or advice in any setting (Orford et al, 1976). Relapse, mostly occurring soon after treatment, is the rule rather than the exception for people with appetite or habit disorders such as excessive drinking, smoking or drug addiction (Hunt and Matarazzo, 1970). The same may be true when the problem is the committing of delinquent acts. This fundamental feature of behaviour disorders may account for the fact that early and irregular leaving is so much more of a problem in small hostels for alcoholics, drug addicts and offenders than it is in hostels for people with psychological problems that principally involve abnormalities of feeling and thinking.

Hence the belief in the division between the two worlds of the sober hostel and the intemperate world outside, which is fostered by prevailing beliefs about alcoholism and abstinence, is an exaggerated and unrealistic one. Insofar as the drinking world is scarcely ever totally left behind, it could be argued that an attempt at integration, rather than division, would best serve the long-term interests of alcoholism hostel residents. Otherwise there are likely to be repeated, and painful, moments of dislocation or discontinuity.

Prevailing belief results in an amplification of drinking instances, both in fact and in fantasy. Probably most residents, whilst publicly subscribing to the idealized version, reside in fear and anticipation of the time when they may drink and leave, or leave and drink. Leaving and drinking are inseparable by virtue of the assumptions, and the rules of the establishment which confirm these assumptions. Such a strong set of beliefs seems bound to assist in creating its own supportive evidence. Any instance of drinking is very likely to be construed as failure, is more likely to lead to further drinking, leaving, and removal to a way of life which provides fewer constraints and makes uncontrolled drinking more likely. Not that evidence is altogether necessary. Once any resident leaves a house in other than a completely planned and orderly way, he is likely to be assumed drinking, whether evidence for this exists or not. The assumption of resumed drinking by disappearing ex-residents has the function of help-ing to maintain the system of beliefs on which the house is based.

The possibility that the occasional ex-resident may drink in a 'controlled' or 'mild' fashion is recognized by some, and some resid-ents from time to time give partial support to this notion. Usually this knowledge is 'underground' and not for the ears of staff, or for public announcement. As one ex-resident told the research worker, it is not wise for residents to report all instances of drinking to staff because untoward consequences need not follow and staff tend to get over-concerned. Abstinence, according to most staff, is merely a means to an end. Whether it should be the universally chosen means is not certain. In any event the means, almost always abstinence, can easily come to assume greater apparent importance than the ends them-selves, and this has not escaped the notice of alcoholism hostel planners. For example, in the Scottish hostel report it is stated:

> ...despite this lack of emphasis upon sobriety and relapse
> as concomitants of success and failure, the goal of
> abstinence assumes a higher importance...than is theor-
> etically intended. ...there is a very real focus upon
> abstinence as part of rehabilitation. It may be also
> that the no drinking rule imposed externally in the sett-
> ing up of the hostel, although it received the sanction
> of the resident group almost immediately, served to lay the
> initial foundations for a heightened awareness of sobriety...
> (Edinburgh Corporation, 1974, pp.22-3).

Similarly, Cook, having argued for the benefits of a fairly strict no drinking rule, nonetheless goes on to state that, "one difficulty of a strict no drinking rule is that the community can too easily lapse into having abstinence as the only criterion of success" (1975, p.20).

Long-Term Needs

Even when early and irregular leaving is avoided, concepts of 'rehabilitation' and the 'halfway house' often seem inappropriate. For one thing there is what might be called a 'honeymoon effect' which we observed at Houses A and B (Chapter 10). The data suggested that many men who stayed for at least a few weeks were likely to ex-perience a welcome sense of achievement, security and comradeship early on, but that in many respects the honeymoon feeling rapidly wore off for many. This is, of course, by no means an inevitable process. However it represented the overall direction of several trends which were opposite to what an idealized account of the hostel might suppose.

The same problems of long-term need for support, that arise for so many residents of hostels for the ex-mentally ill, then arise for a substantial proportion of that minority of alcoholism hostel residents who remain in the hostel for more than a few weeks. Although staff of just over half of the houses in our survey of London hostels stated an ideal length of stay of one year or less, all of the 11 houses had had at least one resident staying for one year or more, and in 6 instances at least one resident had stayed for more than 2 years, and in 2 cases at least one resident had stayed for more than 4 years.

On the basis of the pilot study carried out at House C it was concluded that:

> ...the length of time required in a halfway house facility will depend on the social resources available to the individual...a halfway house which admits clients unselected in terms of these resources must remain flexible about length of stay, it being likely that a proportion of clients admitted will require to stay up to one year or more (Orford et al, 1974, p.223).

Furthermore, at Houses A and B the small minority of residents whose manner of leaving corresponded to the ideal were not necessarily trouble-free after they left, and half of this very small number used further special residential or occupational support. Four of 6 men who left in an orderly and planned fashion after several months, went on to live in flats managed by one of the organizations which also ran alcoholism hostels, or else moved to House G (which some would consider more of a 'three-quarter-way' than a 'halfway' house). Two men who settled subsequently took on the special role of 'recovered alcoholic' working in the alcoholism field, and were paid by one of the same organizations.

Almost all staff of alcoholism hostels seem to find a problem in placing a proportion of residents even after a successful period of residence. The problem is the same one, although perhaps in less acute form here, as is faced in most after-care hostels for ex-psychiatric patients, where many people who might at one time have become long-stay hospital patients are now becoming long-stay hostel residents. The idea of 'three-quarter-way houses' (an ugly term implying merely a lesser degree of impermanence) containing semi-independent flatlets, as well as the idea of 'group homes' are ones that are gaining ground. Houses A and C had these facilities at the time of the study, House B has set up such a facility since, and others were planning them or expressing the need for them.

### Prospects for Small Alcoholism Hostels

As is the case with other types of small hostel, the problems of alcoholism hostels seem to derive from an attempt to force people into an over-simple concept of what residential community care for alcoholics is for. This concept had no place for the majority of actual hostel users who either relapsed quickly, or who stayed and then had nowhere very satisfactory to go. The growth of alcoholism hostels has demonstrated that the need for community care for alcoholics exists on a large scale, and available figures on hospital admissions, drunkenness offences, and alcohol consumption itself, suggest that the need will rise in future rather than decline. Future prospects should therefore rest, not upon abandoning the small hostel idea on the grounds that it involves too many problems, but rather upon a recognition that these problems call for clearer thinking and planning (1) for varieties of alcoholism hostel, (2) for adjunctive facilities as part of a more comprehensive system, and (3) for genuine alternatives against which hostels themselves might be judged.

### Adjuncts

With the development of alcoholism hostels has come a growing recognition that hostels or halfway houses are insufficient on their own to meet the needs to which they were a response. After only a few years of operation at House C, for example, one of the first alcoholism hostels in London, it was already apparent that a variety of adjunctive facilities were necessary. There was discussion of the need for 'a maintenance unit' to provide non-residential help for ex-residents and others, the need for a restaurant service, for a 'three-quarter-way house' and for an 'admission unit'. There was clearly a recognition even then that, "...the process of dealing with alcoholics is a long-term continuing one" (Ingram-Smith, 1967, p.304). Around the same time, the experience of setting up House A led to the following comment:

> There are many problems still outstanding. Most pressing perhaps is that of what is to happen to men when they eventually leave the house: we suspect some alcoholics may be able to maintain sobriety indefinitely in an atmosphere such as the house provides, but that they would not survive the shock of returning to solitary lodgings. We may set up a series of small local lodging houses for ex-residents with no wardens or staff of any description... (Edwards et al, 1966, p.1408).

Cook has recently described in his book, Vagrant Alcoholics, how early experience at House B led to the setting up of the larger project whose aim was to provide an integrated service linking a variety of different types of facility for vagrant alcoholics. He goes so far as to say:

> Certainly the houses should never again be the fortresses and isolated units that they once were. We would ourselves feel it difficult to advocate the setting up of a house for alcoholics unless it was to be accompanied by other facilities supporting and feeding it, these in turn supported by the house itself (1975, p.94).

Making a similar point, Shandler (1972) advocates a total, "System of services that are needed to provide housing and treatment for the public inebriate". His system would include no less than 10 elements ranging from 'emergency screening and referral centres' through detoxification units and transitional or temporary housing accommodation to 'domiciliary housing' and supervized boarding homes and hostels.

Housing and work opportunities are two crucial resources in the long-term process of gaining independence and overcoming handicap, for people who lack the personal and social resources necessary for rapid 'rehabilitation'. Under prevailing conceptions of the role of alcoholism hostels, each is accorded a position of relatively low priority. Some however, such as Shandler, are aware that the first of these cannot be ignored. Reporting on the skid row programs in Philadelphia, he writes:

> Like many professionals from the social sciences, public and mental health fields, we were enamoured by the mystique of therapy and its ability to equip any person to handle everyday problems...it did not take too long or too many follow-up reports to realize that the program's lack of emphasis on housing was creating a revolving door...

Formal treatment can only go on for a limited amount
of time. At some point, if successful, he must make
it by utilizing his daily resources. Housing is the
most critical of the resources and if he gains support -
physically and emotionally - from his living arrangement,
he is well on the way. Housing is then the longest-
acting component of this rehabilitation plan (1972,
pp.49, 63).

It is also quite noticeable that alcoholism hostels in London,
despite their emphasis upon the obtaining of outside employment, provide next to no direct vocational or occupational help. However,
it has been noted in a variety of different contexts, including that
of homelessness and alcoholism, that successful 'graduation' is often
associated with obtaining employment with, and sometimes accommodation from, a rehabilitation organization. Just as the status of
some long-term residents in hostels for the mentally ill becomes uncertain, partly that of a patient and partly that of an employee
(Apte, 1968, pp.56-7), so it has also been noted that a high percentage of successful graduates from drug rehabilitation programs
continue to work in the drug field or in some other social service
occupation (e.g. Smart, 1974).

The limited role of the halfway house or transitional hostel in
the long-term process of acquiring or reacquiring social status, is
reflected in the development of total plans or projects involving far
more than just a halfway house. For example, in the wider project
described by Cook much mention is made of various forms of longer-
term, independent housing, and of the development of a New Careers
Scheme whereby selected hostel graduates are employed as project
staff (1975, pp.101-6).

Varieties

There is also greater awareness now that needs vary and that no
single type of hostel can be totally adequate to meet all requirements. For example, the study at Houses A and B found wide variation
in the degree to which men had, at any time in their adult lives, led
a socially stable way of life (Chapter 6). Rehabilitation, implying
a return to social stability and autonomy, is only strictly applicable
when a person has the past experience and present social resources
that will equip him in a short space of time to lead a fully independent existence in a competitive society. Quite apart from differences
in personal and social resources, different regimes are likely to
appeal to people with different preferences. The 'paternalistic'
hostel may appeal more to the sort of person who fits relatively
easily into a role complementary to that of the fairly controlling
staff member. The more assertive person, with leadership qualities
of his own, would probably find it difficult to settle happily in
such an environment.

One of the best demonstrations of interaction effects in research
on social treatments is that reported by Wilbur et al (1966). They
assigned a sample of tuberculous alcoholics to one of 2 in-patient
treatments, one run on 'therapeutic community' lines, the other a
very much more traditional and authoritarian regime. Before treatment they assessed the personality of each patient, making use of the
concept of 'interpersonal maturity' (Sullivan et al, 1957). The

results showed that amongst patients of high interpersonal maturity
those assigned to a therapeutic community regime responded better than
those assigned to the authoritarian regime. On the other hand,
amongst patients of 'low maturity level' those assigned to the more
traditional regime responded better than those assigned to the therapeutic community regime. These results suggest that there is probably
a need for a variety of hostels, different in their internal organization, rather than the creation of new hostels all of which attempt a
middle-of-the-road position in an attempt to satisfy everyone. The
latter course probably leads to lack of clarity about methods, and
may in the end satisfy relatively few. The need for variety to meet
variation in need is stated, for example, in the Scottish hostel
report:

> Ideally, of course, there should be a wide spectrum of
> hostels ranging from the very supportive, rather instit-
> utional place to one where the men are totally indepen-
> dent, and with lengths of stay ranging from a couple of
> months to an indefinitely long-term living situation for
> men who are too inadequate or too damaged ever to be self-
> sufficient. Obviously a single small hostel...can never
> expect to cater for the needs of all the men who require
> hostel accommodation (Edinburgh Corporation, 1974, p.40).

Alternatives

Continued thought should also be given to planning innovative
alternatives to small hostels as presently conceived. For instance,
one project which exists in the London area (The Peter Bedford
Project) makes non-specialist provision for a proportion of single
homeless people who would fall in the category 'alcoholic' and provides a contrast with small alcoholism hostels in other ways. The
project, incorporating a housing association, runs a number of small
houses. Staff are nearly all non-residential and the relationship
with residents is that of landlord and 'tenant'. The project also
incorporates a trading company which employs over half the working
tenants. A further aspect which sets this project somewhat apart
from most is that a sizable proportion of the project's tenants
(roughly $\frac{1}{3}$) are people who have approached the project with housing
needs, rather than with any 'problem' or form of deviance which would
enable them to be categorized, for example, as 'alcoholic', 'compulsive gambler' or 'ex-prisoner'.

In conclusion of this chapter, and Part I of the book, two things
may be stated with some confidence. The first is that small alcoholism hostels, sharing as they do in the general move away from institutional care and towards community care, have established themselves
as essential components of modern alcoholism services. The second is
that there exists a number of key problems in their operation and
these have as yet not been satisfactorily overcome. Hence the vital
need for continued thinking and innovation.

Part II now presents the detailed research findings at Houses A
and B. At the end, in Chapter 11, we return to the concerns of this
chapter and briefly make some general recommendations for the future.

# Part II

# Report of Research at Two
# Small Alcoholism Hostels

# Chapter 5

# Research Method at Houses A and B

The remainder of this book is devoted to a detailed report of the research at two specialized alcoholism hostels - Houses A and B. Chapters 6-10 present the research findings and each concludes with a summary. The final chapter consists of recommendations to the many individuals and bodies involved in some way with alcoholism hostels - central and local Government, non-statutory planning and managing bodies, staff and residents.

The present introductory chapter begins with brief background notes on the two houses themselves and proceeds to an outline description of the research and the way it was mounted.

The Houses

House A

There is relatively little written material on House A. There is, however, a published paper by Edwards et al (1966) describing the setting up of the house and the experience of the very early days there. We have also drawn on an annual report which was written some years later during the time that the research was carried out (Helping Hand, 1972). The report by Edwards et al describes a fortuitous meeting between the Camberwell Council on Alcoholism, which had designed "a very rough blueprint for a hostel", and the founder of a charitable body concerned with alcoholism. A house was bought and the first residents installed "within six months" of this meeting. The report goes on to describe the house itself as:

> ...situated in a predominantly Victorian suburb of South London. There is room for 12 men to sleep (in double bedrooms), a large sitting room with comfortable chairs and a television set, and downstairs there is a dining room adjacent to the kitchen (p.1407).

There was a call-box in the hallway for the use of residents and the staff member had his office next to the living room. With large pleasant gardens front and rear, House A could well pass as 'just another house in the road'. The tone of the house was set by its most important rule, banning the use of alcohol either in or away from the house, and by its expectation that residents would, at least after a while, look for outside employment. Both these matters will, however, be examined far more closely in Chapter 7.

The Edwards et al report was titled; Setting up a Therapeutic Community, and the annual report described the house as, "An experiment in alcoholic rehabilitation using some of the experiences of therapeutic communities pioneered by Maxwell Jones". The house was described as "group centered" and its effectiveness as arising out of the, "potential inherent therapeutic value of an homogenous group". The emphasis was on involvement and responsibility and partnership between staff and residents. Much stress was laid upon the weekly house meeting where attendance was compulsory. As Edwards et al put it, "Wednesday evenings are very important in fostering the idea of shared responsibility". Residents elected a group leader who had special responsibility for domestic arrangements and liaison with house and domestic staff (during the time of this research the domestic role of the group leader was reduced and the elected resident became known as the 'group spokesman'). The annual report described a number of working sub-groups of residents responsible for 'house and garden', 'encounter' (visiting hospitals, the reception centre and Alcoholics Anonymous meetings with a view to recruiting new members) and 'publicity'. This last sub-group had the responsibility of inviting interested outsiders to a weekly evening 'visitor's meeting' at which attendance for residents was voluntary. It also had the task of producing the house magazine, Achievement, which was devoted to articles by residents, ex-residents and visitors and which played a quite significant role in the life of the house.

Residents were expected to care for their own room and to cook their own meals at weekends. Two women were employed part-time, one to clean living rooms and kitchen, the other to prepare weekday evening meals. Except where extensive work was necessary, repairs and redecoration of the house was often done by residents themselves.

Since House A was set up, the same charitable organization had obtained two adjacent properties on the other side of the same road and the three houses together formed a complex of related facilities. One had been used as a short-stay assessment or 'induction' unit from which it was intended that men should be referred to House A or to other alcoholism hostels or other services. The second house was divided into a small number of independent flatlets which were often occupied by ex-residents of House A.

The organization had expanded in other directions also and by then managed a range of additional projects for both alcoholics and drug addicts. This required a complex organization consisting of head office staff, a council of management and 3 sub-committees concerned with finance, house and development, and publicity. Members of this organization rarely controlled or supported the work of the house closely, although they may occasionally have made decisions which affected its everyday life. At the time of the research there was a full-time Social Worker Director with special responsibility for liaison between the organization's head-quarters and its various projects, including House A. The annual report also refers to the vital role played by a 'support group' consisting of a general practitioner, a psychiatric social worker and a liaison probation officer. Reference is also made to a 'joint house advisory committee' set up with resident participation from both Houses A and B. The function of this committee was to "provide the residents, staff, management and occasionally interested outsiders with the opportunity to exchange ideas and advise on the running of the houses".

House B

House B has been rather better documented. A published paper by Cook et al (1968) described the first year at the house, a subsequent paper described the first three years (Cook and Pollak, 1970), and a recent extended account of House B and the project of which it is now a part has recently been written by Cook (1975). Unlike House A, which was designed to cater for 'alcoholics', with no further specification, House B was from the outset intended to specialize in the problems of the 'chronic drunkenness offender', the 'vagrant alcoholic' or the 'skid row alcoholic'. The purpose of the house, as described in a number of published and unpublished documents, was to demonstrate a "constructive, humane and economical alternative to the repeated imprisonment of the skid row alcoholic".

As at House A, the intention was that House B should have the external appearance of an ordinary dwelling. This intention was perhaps not quite so well achieved as at House A. House B was a relatively large, detached house standing on the corner of two roads, one of which carried a considerable volume of traffic, and the surroundings were more urban than suburban. The house had a capacity of 10 men in single, double, and in one case treble, bedrooms. There was a large lounge with a television, a dining room and a large kitchen. A billiard room doubled as a staff office. A single phone was available to both staff and residents. There was a small garden.

Unlike House A, House B did not originate as part of an already existing social work organization. Indeed it was itself the beginning of the establishment of a larger voluntary organization specializing in the care of vagrant alcoholics in South London. The development of this wider project is described in detail elsewhere (Cook, 1975). By the time the research started, the project had acquired a second house (House G) which admitted men with longer previous periods of sobriety, as well as a small short-stay house for men who were awaiting admission to House B and other houses. A non-residential side to the project's work had also begun with the setting up of a small number of 'shop front' day centres where help was available for homeless alcoholics, some of whom would subsequently be admitted to House B. The project also employed a research sociologist who was conducting a participant observation study of skid row in London (Archard, 1975), and later developments included the acquisition of further houses and the setting up of a New Careers scheme which enabled the project to employ a small number of recovered alcoholics. In comparison with the organization that managed House A, the House B project organization was local, managerially relatively simple, and much involved in the control and support of the house itself.

Many important features of House B were similar to those already described for House A. Drinking was banned, residents were able to hold full-time jobs, and weekly group discussions were seen as an essential element of the 'therapeutic community'. Domestic arrangements were similar to those at House A, with residents responsible for their own room, for cooking at weekends, and for decorations and minor repairs. Residents were involved in selecting new members and were supposed to have the responsibility of discharging fellow residents if the need arose. The same could be said of House A. During the time of the research, residents at House B were involved in the selection of a new staff member, and for the first time were invited to elect a representative to the project's management committee.

## The Research

### Setting up the Research

The 'study proper' was preceded by a period of several months of deciding upon, developing and piloting techniques. This time also served the invaluable purpose of enabling the research worker to become thoroughly acquainted with the houses and making her a figure quite familiar to residents and staff. This not only gave the research team greater confidence that they had a true 'feel' of the houses, but also gave us the impression that the research came as very much less of an intrusion than it might otherwise have done. Pilot work was gradually introduced over this period so that residents and staff must have been well used to the presence of a research worker and her use of certain techniques by the time the study proper began.

An earlier task had been that of acquainting both staff and residents with the research worker's intentions and the obtaining of their permission to carry out the study. Not only was the capturing of the interest and involvement of residents and staff a necessity, but it was also in keeping with the spirit of both houses that the decision to agree to research being carried out be a joint group decision. No doubt the exact manner in which these decisions were made would have provided excellent case demonstrations of decision-making in these two small hostels, but the opportunity to document those decisions was missed perhaps on account of the great investment which the research team had in the outcome! At this early stage a commitment was entered into regarding confidentiality. It was understood that any information provided to the research worker in private would not be passed on to anyone connected in any way with the house. Staff had to accept that the research worker might receive information or opinions which could have been valuable to the staff but that these would not be passed on.

Fairly early on in the planning period it was decided to set up a two-weekly staff seminar at the research unit. This was partly at the instigation of the research team who wished to maintain regular informal contact with hostel staff so as to allay any fears and misunderstandings about research which might arise as well as to stimulate their own thinking about small hostels, and partly at the instigation of staff who seemed to value a regular opportunity to get together with research workers and other hostel staff to discuss matters of mutual interest. Staff from Houses A, B and C attended this seminar when they could, and so occasionally did staff from other hostels. With very occasional breaks these seminars continued for more than two years.

In choosing research techniques an attempt was made to strike a balance between those of different styles - tightly structured interview questions, relatively open-ended questioning, formal and informal observation. Certain techniques, such as the resident intake interview, were adapted with some modification from the pilot study at House C, whilst others, such as the group recording technique and the monthly resident interview, represented more drastic modifications. Still others, most of the staff interview for example, were new to this study. In one way or another most of the techniques used were designed by the research team or, like the group recording technique and the sociometric measures, were loosely based on others' research. The scale of residents' attitudes towards staff, adapted from Ellsworth (1965), was an exception. Needless to say some techniques, notably the group interaction recording, required more piloting than others. Quite a lot of time was wasted at the planning stage on account of our ambition to measure more than we had the resources to cope with. Some techniques were embarked upon which were never finally employed. For example, time was spent attempting to develop a reliable method of recording the rehabilitation 'aspirations' of each resident, against which subsequent progress might have been assessed. This particular technique went through a number of versions, but at the point at which the effort was abandoned it took three or more hours to administer to one resident and was still in a far from satisfactory form.

Techniques and Sample

The study proper lasted for 16 to 17 months (72 weeks to be exact) running from mid-February of one year to the end of June of the following year. The formal research techniques which were used can be conveniently grouped in the following way:

1. An intake interview conducted with each new resident within 3 days of his entry (Appendix B).

2. A subsequent, recurring, interview with each resident. The first such interview with each resident was held approximately 2 weeks after his entry (time after entry in fact varied between 10 and 18 days on account of the weekly system of interviewing at the 2 houses which will be described below) and thereafter interviews were held with each resident at 4-weekly intervals (Appendix C).

3. A 2-weekly interview with each full-time member of staff (less frequent interviews were held with part-time staff, senior staff and visitors) (Appendix A).

4. Interaction recordings of every alternate weekly house group meeting (Appendix D).

To simplify the research worker's life, which was divided during this period between the 2 houses and the research unit, the formal research program was organized so that alternate weeks were spent at each house. Thus group recordings, staff interviews and all resident interviews other than intake interviews (i.e. items 2, 3 and 4 listed above) were conducted at House A during one week, at House B during the following week, again at House A the next week and so on. In

order to carry out intake interviews within 3 days of a new resident's
arrival it was necessary to make 'intakes' an exception to this
program (i.e. item 1 above). For purposes of analysis the 72 weeks
of the study proper have been divided into 18 4-week 'months'. Whenever the focus of the analysis of the results is upon the houses
themselves rather than upon individuals (as is particularly the case
in Chapter 8) reference will be made to these 18 'months' of the
study proper.

It was naturally the case, however, that not all residents who
were in one or other of the 2 houses during the time of the study
proper had their 'intakes' during those 16 to 17 months. The study
proper was preceded by a run-in of approximately 4 months during which
time the resident intake interview was administered in its final form
to all newly arriving residents (see Table 3). The Intake Sample
(principally referred to in Chapter 6) therefore consisted of all new
entrants to the houses from the October preceding the start of the
study proper until the end of the study proper approximately 21 months
later. During this time 37 men entered House A and 28 men entered
House B. Of this number 2 entered House A twice (arbitrarily we
counted it as a new entry if a man left and stayed away for more than
4 weeks before returning) but one other new resident left too quickly
to be interviewed. At House B one man entered the house twice and one
other left too quickly to be interviewed. The Intake Sample therefore
consists of 38 separate admissions to House A and 28 to House B (representing 36 and 27 men respectively). When a description is provided
of the way residents left the houses (in Chapter 10) it is possible to
include the 2 men who left before intake interviews could be administered, and the numbers are therefore 39 at House A and 29 at House
B. In addition to the men who figure in these samples there were 7
men (5 at House A and 2 at House B) who were in the houses at the
beginning of the study proper, and who had already been in residence
for 4 months or more, but who were nonetheless interviewed at 4-weekly
intervals for as long as they stayed thereafter although they never
completed an intake interview.

From place to place in the following chapters (especially in
Chapters 8 and 9) mention is made of specific individuals. To preserve anonymity whilst attempting to recreate individual identities
which will have meaning for the reader, all individuals have been
provided with pseudonyms consisting of a first name followed by an
initial (e.g. Fred M). The initials have no special meaning but have
simply been assigned alphabetically as individuals are introduced in
the narratives in Chapter 9. The only exceptions are staff members
(including domestic staff) who have been given the initial 'S' (e.g.
Colin S, Joan S).

Impact on the Houses

There is a whole host of issues to do with the conduct of this
research itself which cannot be discussed here because of limitations
of space. One issue which must be touched on, however, concerns the
impact on the houses of such a major research intrusion, and also
the possible effects which this might have had upon the findings.
Certainly we have anecdotal evidence that the presence of a research
worker makes a difference. The first indication of this came at the
completion of the pilot study at House C at the point when the regular

Table 3: Phases of research activity at Houses A and B.

| | From | To | Activity |
|---|---|---|---|
| Phase I (pilot) | | mid. October of year prior to study proper | Pilot work only. Residents admitted in Phase I and still resident at start of Phase III received the recurring 4-weekly interview from start of Phase III until they left, but did not receive an intake interview |
| Phase II (run-in 4 months) | mid. October | mid. February | Residents admitted in Phase II received an intake interview and a recurring 4-weekly interview from the staff of Phase III until they left. |
| Phase III (study proper, divided into 18 4-week 'months') | mid. February | end of June of the following year | Full data collection program. |
| Phase IV (run-down) | end June | | No new residents interviewed. Remaining residents admitted before end of Phase III continued to receive 4-weekly interview until departure. |

program of research interviews was about to be curtailed. At that point the staff sought the advice of the research workers. It turned out that residents had found regular interviews with research staff so valuable that the staff were wanting advice on the setting up of a program of individual interviews with residents that would substitute for the research interviews! During the course of the study at Houses A and B the research worker continually had to resist the role of counsellor both to residents and occasionally to staff. On one occasion when a resident was asked whether he had had a recent opportunity for a personal discussion with the staff member at the house, he replied that his monthly interview with the research worker was 'enough'. The impression was formed that some members of staff found their 2-weekly research interviews of considerable value and most staff members consulted the research worker on various issues from time to time. The temptation to give definite advice was of course resisted during the study itself.

It is quite impossible to say, given the limitations in the design of the present study, in what way the findings were affected by the impact of the research. We can only state our impression that the conclusions of the present research were not affected, but the readers of this report will have to form their own conclusions.

# Chapter 6
# Referral and Selection, Residents and Staff

> Only a small number are able to conform to live in this environment. Only a small number are ready for it. Those who are not ready for it would destroy the house in no time at all (Staff member at House H).

> These are the 'low bottom' alcoholics... Alcoholism in this population is not an isolated affliction, but a major disruption of their entire life (Pattison et al, 1973, p.223, writing of an alcoholism halfway house population in the U.S.).

Whether their role is that of therapist, educator, or custodian, staff of facilities that deal in human beings display a high level of concern over the matter of who come to be their clients. This is certainly true of the staff of small alcoholism hostels. Much of their time is spent negotiating over the entry of prospective residents, and an observer cannot fail to notice how frequently conversations amongst hostel staff return to the question of referral and selection. These are undoubtedly major policy matters for hostels, and committees are also constantly debating the issues concerned.

Later chapters should make clear the very real basis which exists for staff preoccupation with referral and selection. Parts of Chapters 7, 8 and 9, in particular, will attempt to show how the changing character of a small residential community of this type is determined, amongst other things, by the current composition of the resident group. In this light, the processes of referral and selection of new residents can be seen as integral, indeed central, parts of the operation of the hostel community. The first part of the present chapter gives an account of research material focusing specifically upon these processes. Much of this material comes from an analysis of forms, which the staff member in charge at each of the 2 houses was asked to complete, detailing each referral (See Appendix A). The member of staff kept a supply of these forms for ready use between research interviews, and the information recorded was then elaborated at the next research interview with that staff member.

Once admitted it is the resident group, together with staff, who together form the body of people out of which the everyday life of the small hostel community is fashioned. The second part of this chapter turns to consider the men who succeeded in overcoming the admission barriers to Houses A and B. It also considers how, and by whom, the houses were staffed. It is against this necessary background that subsequent chapters describe events of significance in the lives of the houses themselves. Data on characteristics of residents were obtained by administering the standard intake interview (Appendix B) to each member of the Intake Sample within 3 days of his entry.

A variety of questions can be asked of these personal data. Just how unattached, or marginal in society, were residents at the time of the study? Does the appellation 'skid row alcoholic' apply to all residents, to most, or only to a few? And what of residents' past histories? Ogborne and Smart (1974, pp.6-8,18) have recently suggested that alcoholism halfway house residents are likely to display a number of previous social advantages in comparison with chronic drunkenness offenders in prison. The former, in comparison with latter, have been shown, in a number of North American reports at least, to have been better educated, to have had higher status jobs and to have more frequently been married at some time. Were residents of Houses A and B predominantly men whose social position had declined from one of relative social advantage, or had they occupied a very low status position in the social hierarchy from early adult life?

Did the differing sources of referral to Houses A and B, and the different referral and selection procedures in operation, produce different resident group compositions at the 2 houses? By reputation the 2 houses were very different. House B had the reputation of catering for skid row chronic drunkenness offenders. House A, on the other hand, was thought by some to have a much more 'middle-class' bias. Others had argued that the degree of this bias was exaggerated and that the 2 houses were not dissimilar in terms of the social histories of their residents.

## REFERRAL AND SELECTION

### Sources of Potential Residents

A count of the number of referrals made to Houses A and B from different sources during an 18-month interval (shown in Figure 7) bears out the survey finding that the bulk of referrals came from a small number of types of source. Of a total of 216 referrals to these 2 houses during this time (124 to A and 92 to B), only 12 were direct self-referrals (7 to A, 5 to B) and the remainder were referrals from one agency or another. Doctors and social workers at psychiatric hospitals and units, probation officers, and welfare officers in the prison service and at the large South London DHSS reception centre for the 'destitute' were the major outside agents of referral. Additional referrals came from staff working in other parts of the same organization that managed Houses A and B. In particular, the largest single category of referrals to House B (33 referrals, also referring 12 to A) consisted of referrals from social workers at one or other of the small number of walk-in 'shop-front' offices, situated in South East London and run by the same organization that managed House B. The short term assessment centre, situated across the road from House A and run by the same management, was also a regular source of referral to both houses (10 to A, 8 to B).

These few sources virtually exhausted the referrals made to the 2 houses during the period of the study. Medical social workers working in non-psychiatric settings provided only 4 referrals to House A and none to House B; social workers working as part of the statutory

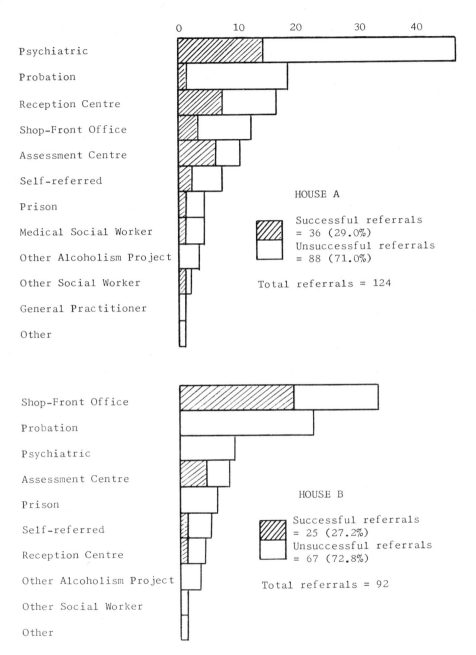

Figure 7: Sources of successful and unsuccessful referrals to Houses A and B.

local authority services provided merely 3 referrals (2 to A, 1 to B), and there was just one referral to House A from a general practitioner. Health visitors, community nurses, doctors in industrial and occupational schemes, and family counsellors provided no referrals. More surprisingly, no single referral came from Alcoholics Anonymous. Nonetheless referrals may have been influenced by recent or past attendance at Alcoholics Anonymous in some cases even if there was no formal referral. Formal referrals are obviously less likely from that source than from agencies with paid professional employees.

## Admission and Non-Admission Rates

There was no way of ascertaining the true ratio of admissions to total referrals for most of the houses in the survey, but Figure 7 shows the details for Houses A and B. During the 72 weeks of the study of the 2 houses, 29.0% of referrals resulted in admission at House A, and 27.2% resulted in admission at House B. These figures are remarkably similar and possibly fairly typical.

Before considering how and why such a large number of referrals never result in admission, the differing non-admission rates of referrals from different sources should be considered. Figure 7 shows quite clearly how uneven was the spread of non-admissions. Some referral agents fare much better than others in getting prospective residents admitted. Noticeably, it is the agents operating under the same organizational umbrellas as the houses themselves which had the greatest success. Indeed they were the only agents whose referrals had a success rate higher than 50% (assessment centre to House A 60%, shop fronts to House B 58%). Both these sets of referral agents were in fact less successful in referring to the other house, outside their own organization (shop fronts to House A 25%, assessment centre to House B 50%).

Amongst other agents referring to House A there appears to have been a fairly sharp division between 2 fairly successful categories (doctors and social workers in a psychiatric setting 30%, reception centre welfare workers 44%) and the rest. Amongst the rest, probation officers referred the second highest number of potential residents but were conspicuously unsuccesful. Only one probation referral out of 18 which was made during this period resulted in admission.

At House B the division was sharper still. Indeed, referral agents operating outside the organizations that ran Houses A and B were virtually totally unsuccessful in referring residents to House B during the study period. Probation officers tried 22 times, doctors and social workers in a psychiatric setting tried 9 times, and prison welfare officers tried 6 times, but in no single instance was any one of these agents successful. It seems that this cannot be explained as a simple re-routing of external referrals through the organization's own channels, as only one successful external referral was known to have been successfully admitted later via the approved intra-organization route.

## Stages in the Referral-Selection Process

The data from the survey gave the impression that entry to a small hostel community for alcoholics was guarded very carefully.

At Houses A and B the process typically involved the following 6 stages:

> Stage 1 - Referral agent approach.  A phone call or letter from the referral agent to the staff member in charge of the house.
>
> Stage 2 - Staff interview.  An interview between the staff member and the prospective resident took place· at the house it-self or, if impossible or inconvenient, elsewhere - for example in prison if the prospective resident was yet to be released.  At this stage the staff member might send for social or medical reports from the referral agent or from an agent with whom the prospective resident had been in contact previously.
>
> Stage 3 - Meal at the house.  The prospective resident was usually invited to attend an evening meal, or occasionally at House A an open visitors' meeting.  At House B a prospective res-ident might be accommodated temporarily in a nearby small 'first-stage house'.  While staying there the prospective resident might continue to visit the house informally a number of times.
>
> Stage 4 - Group interview.  Either on the same night as the meal at the house, or some days later, the prospective resident met the existing resident group formally, and was interviewed and later discussed by them.
>
> Stage 5 - Acceptance.  If the prospective resident was accepted by the group, a mutually convenient date for moving into the house would be arranged.  This date was usually within a week, and often within a day or 2, of the group interview.
>
> Stage 6 - Arrival.  The process was finally completed when an accepted candidate arrived to take up residence.

During the course of the study, shortly after a new staff member had taken over responsibility at House A, the referral-selection pro-cess at House A was changed with the introduction of a 3-week pro-bationary period (similar to that operating at House F run by the same organization) which effectively replaced stage 4.  Formal con-sideration by the resident group took place 3 weeks after admission rather than prior to admission.

Naturally enough the whole referral-selection process took a variable length of time depending on a whole variety of factors, and occasionally parts of the process might be modified or even by-passed, especially if a prospective resident was already well known to staff or existing residents.

Figure 8 shows the stages at which most unsuccessful referrals stopped proceeding.  At both houses the largest number (36 at A, 38 at B) failed at the very first stage and never proceeded to the staff interview stage.  A further sizeable number (28 at A, 28 at B) failed at the second stage, after the staff interview, and did not proceed to the next stage involving a meal at the house.  By that stage the pro-cess of filtering out the majority of referrals was virtually complete at House B.  With the exception of one man who was turned down after the group interview, every prospective resident who got as far as having a meal at the house was subsequently admitted.  The same was not true of House A where 24 referrals failed despite getting as far as having a meal at the house.  Three of these did not get as far as a group interview, 18 had a group interview but a mutually agreeable

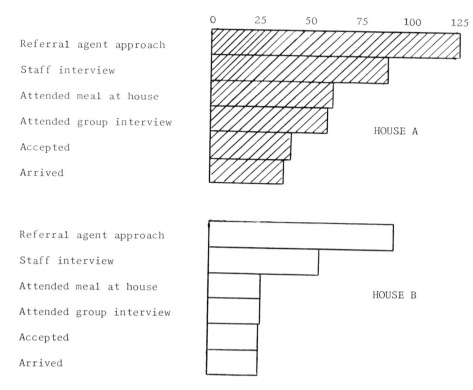

Figure 8: Numbers of potential residents entering each of 6 successive stages in the referral-selection process at Houses A and B.

arrangement for admission was not made as a result, and in 3 cases such an arrangement was made but the prospective resident did not arrive for admission.

Reasons for Non-Admission

It would be wrong to assume that all instances of non-admissions are attributable to deliberate selection by staff or existing residents. In many cases, especially at House B, there was deliberate selection, but in other instances, especially at House A, neither existing residents nor staff were active agents in turning away a prospective resident. In some cases the prospective resident or referring agent withdrew the application, in some cases the prospective resident was known to have 'drunk' or relapsed and had therefore effectively excluded himself from consideration, and in other instances the prospective resident simply did not turn up for the next stage of the selection process. Table 4 shows the breakdown of non-

Table 4:  The proportions of non-admissions at Houses A and
B which were due to active rejection.

| | HOUSE A | | | |
|---|---|---|---|---|
| | Actively Rejected | Not Actively Rejected | Others | No. admitted in same period |
| Months 1-6 | 12 (35%) | 17 (50%) | 5 (15%) | 9 |
| Months 7-12 | 5 (13%) | 30 (81%) | 2 ( 6%) | 11 |
| Months 13-18 | 8 (47%) | 6 (35%) | 3 (18%) | 16 |
| TOTAL | 25 (29%) | 53 (60%) | 10 (11%) | 36 |
| | HOUSE B | | | |
| | Actively Rejected | Not Actively Rejected | Others | No. admitted in same period |
| Months 1-6 | 26 (74%) | 7 (20%) | 2 ( 6%) | 7 |
| Months 7-12 | 12 (63%) | 2 (11%) | 5 (26%) | 10 |
| Months 13-18 | 10 (77%) | 3 (23%) | - | 8 |
| TOTAL | 48 (72%) | 12 (18%) | 7 (10%) | 25 |

admissions into those Actively Rejected by the house and those Not
Actively Rejected for each of 3 successive 24-week intervals. (Non-
admissions were coded as Actively Rejected, or Not, by one research
worker and checked by another. Mixed or unclassifiable non-admissions
appear as Others).

Table 4 shows the variation between the 2 houses, and also illustrates an important principle, to which we shall return at length in
Chapter 8, namely the principle of variation in the operation of a
hostel over time. Nothing stands still for long in small hostels, and
like all other aspects of community life the details of admission and
non-admission can change dramatically from one time period to another.
House A had relatively few Actively Rejected non-admissions in each of
the 24-week periods in comparison with House B, and had relatively
many Not Actively Rejected non-admissions. The contrast is apparent
in the first 24 weeks, but is most marked in the middle third of the
study. This can only be understood in the knowledge of the state of
House A at that time, which will be described in more detail in Chapter 9. Briefly, it may be said here that House A was relatively
empty of residents during this period and for a variety of reasons
may not have been as attractive to potential residents as it was at
other times. New referrals were therefore encouraged, indeed sought
after, and the number of Actively Rejected was low. Indeed, prospective new residents were more likely to reject the hostel than the
other way about.

During the last 24 weeks the position at House A had completely changed, with a relatively high ratio of admissions to non-admissions and, for the first time, more Actively Rejected than Not Actively Rejected non-admissions. A new member of staff had introduced the new probationary period policy and was in the process of building up an attractive, new resident group.

Over the 72 weeks as a whole Not Actively Rejected non-admissions outnumbered others at House A at each stage of the referral-selection process (with the exception of Stage 3 - 2 out of 3 failures after the meal and before the group interview being active rejections by residents or staff). In contrast, Actively Rejected non-admissions outnumbered others at House B at each of the 2 stages where failures occurred, namely Stages 1 and 2.

Selection Criteria

Aside from the requirement that all residents be suffering from alcoholism and, at House B, that residents be offenders qualifying the hostel which accommodated them for Home Office financial support, neither House A or B appear to have had any very explicit selection criteria. In fact the alcoholism criterion was never cited as grounds for rejection during the study period. The assumption seemed to be that negative diagnostic errors (failing to call someone an 'alcoholic' when he is) are much more numerous than positive diagnostic errors (calling someone an 'alcoholic' when he isn't) and that anyone referred to a hostel for alcoholics is therefore almost certain to come within a broad working definition of the term 'alcoholism'. These working assumptions do not, however, prevent some later speculation on the part of residents, and sometimes on the part of staff too, about whether particular individuals are exemplars of the species 'true alcoholic'.

The offender criterion, in the case of House B, was relaxed towards the end of the study when the DHSS took over responsibility from the Home Office for the rehabilitation of chronic drunkenness offenders. Per capita (or more accurately 'per bed') Government grants were then no longer contingent upon offender status.

In practice, however, it would appear that there is a whole range of fairly practical reasons for turning down individual people, but they are grounds that can only be individually applied and occur too infrequently to be stated as definite selection criteria. For example, amongst the reasons given for active rejections were the following:

| House A | House B |
|---|---|
| Old Age | Too young |
| Bad health, physically unfit | Not a Londoner |
| Drug taker | No criminal record |
| Required short stay only | Not a skid row man |
| Unwilling to pay rent | Drug taker |
| Too close contact with family | Possibly homosexual |
| Job too far away | |
| Needing more hospital treatment | |

However, beyond these fairly objective but individual criteria, are the 2 more subjective criteria mentioned in one form or another at nearly every house in the survey and already discussed at some length in Chapter 2. These were firstly, desire or motivation for 'sobriety', and secondly, ability to mix amicably with other residents. Staff at

Houses A and B shared this widespread concern with these 2 difficult-to-make-explicit criteria. Amongst exact wordings offered in explanation for Actively Rejected non-admissions during the study period were the following:

| House A | House B |
|---|---|
| Too many problems | Not ready for House |
| No real interest | Bad record for violence |
| Too little faith in group | Expressed a distaste for group |
| meetings | living |
| Psychologically unsuitable | Insincere |
| Lacks sincerity, poorly | Lack of motivation and insight |
| motivated | He couldn't tell the House from |
| Not open enough about past | the Salvation Army |
| | Residents considered him a |
| | 'nutter' |

## CHARACTERISTICS OF RESIDENTS

### Sex, Age and Country of Birth

Like the majority of small alcoholism hostels in the London area, Houses A and B had exclusively male resident groups throughout the study period and all 4 members of staff who were in charge during some part of this period were male. Hence the communities were virtually all-male ones. Only the part-time domestic staff, and at House A the occasional attached student, were female. Although it rarely seemed to be a major issue, concern was expressed from time to time about this all-maleness. Indeed, shortly after the conclusion of the study a new policy was introduced at House A allowing the admission of female residents. The all-male policy remains at House B. One of the effects of this male exclusiveness seems to be the enhancement of the importance of female ancillary staff.

Of 66 intakes during the study (the Intake Sample; 38 at A, 28 at B) only 2 were men in their 20's (1 at each House). Twenty were in their 30's (8 at A and 12 at B), the largest number were in their 40's (17 at A, 14 at B), and the remainder were in their 50's (12 at A and only 1 at B). Although the age distributions at the 2 houses were therefore somewhat similar, the distribution was displaced towards the higher ages for House A (range 29 to 58 years, mean 44.8) in comparison with House B (range 27 to 52 years, mean 41.1). Pilot data from an earlier period at House C were of the same order (range 27 to 62 years, mean 43.4).

All but 1 member of the Intake Sample (at House B, from St. Helena) stated their country of birth to be within the British Isles. However the English were outnumbered by the Scots and Irish, particularly at House B. The Intake Sample at House A was 16 English (42%), 15 Scots (40%), 4 Southern Irish (11%), 2 Northern Irish (5%), and 1 Welshman. At House B the numbers were, 5 English (18%) 10 Scots (36%), 8 Southern Irish (29%) and 4 Northern Irish (14%).

### Education, Occupation and Adult Social Stability

These 3 social history variables illustrate 2 important facts about resident characteristics at small alcoholism hostels. The first con-

cerns the wide variation to be found amongst house residents. The
second concerns the concentration of particular types in different
houses, with the obvious implications this has for the nature of the
houses themselves.

The first variable is simply the age at which a resident stated
that he completed full-time education. The second is the status
rating of the highest status occupation a resident reported ever
having held (Figure 9). Occupational status ratings were based upon
the Hall-Jones scale of the prestige of different occupations as
judged by a British population (Hall and Jones, 1950). The scale
classifies occupations into 7 groups ranging from those of highest
prestige (professional, higher administrative, and managerial occupations) to those of lowest prestige (non-skilled manual occupations).

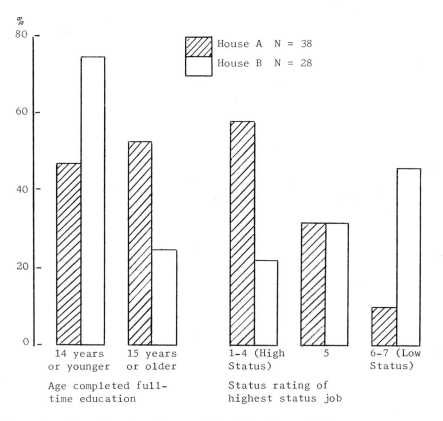

Figure 9: Educational and occupational background of Intake Sample at
Houses A and B.

The third variable is more complex, and consists of the sum total
of the 5 items shown in Table 5. This scale is designed to measure
the level of 'previous adult social stability' and is based on an item
analysis of House C pilot data (Orford et al, 1974). The scores obtained by new residents at Houses A and B are shown in Figure 10.

Individual variation is abundantly evident in Figures 9 and 10.
The social histories of individual residents vary from those indicating
education to a relatively advanced age, prestigeful occupations, and
a high level of adult social stability, to those displaying the
opposite characteristics. What is equally apparent, however, is the
concentration of social histories of particular types in one or other
of the 2 houses. House A had the higher proportions of residents who
stayed in full-time education beyond the age of 14, of residents who
had at one time or another held occupations of relatively high prestige (categories 1 to 4), and of residents with scores above the mid
point on the scale of previous adult social stability (scores of 13
or higher).

Recent Social Stability

Almost all the new residents at Houses A and B had spent some time
in prison or in hospital, or living in a small hostel making special
provision for alcoholism, within the 12 months prior to their arrival.
Only 6 men provided exceptions to this statement (3 at A, 3 at B).
Most obvious however was the contrast between the recent experience
of the new residents of the 2 houses. At House A, the majority (68%)
had been in hospital during the 12 months prior to their arrival at
the house, but only a minority had been in prison (42%), and a still
smaller minority (29%) had lived in an alcoholism hostel. In contrast,
at House B, the majority of new residents had spent some time in prison
(68%), the majority had spent some time living in an alcoholism hostel
(61%), whereas only a minority (28%) had spent any time in hospital.

There was wide variation also in the way of life residents had led
when not in prison, hospital or hostel (Figure 11). When new residents
were asked to roughly apportion the last 12 months spent outside
prison, hospital or hostel into periods spent living with family or
relative(s), friend(s), living alone in rented accommodation, staying
at a reception centre, in common lodging house(s), or 'sleeping rough',
major differences emerged. At one extreme were men (10 at A, 15 at
B) who had not lived with family or friends within that period of
time, but who had spent over half of the time (an estimated 30 weeks
or more) living in a reception centre or in common lodging house(s)
or 'sleeping rough'. At the other extreme were 6 men at House A who
had no experience of reception centre or lodging house living, or of
'sleeping rough' during that time, but who had spent 3 months or more
living with family or friend(s). As was the case with so many resident variables, there were large differences between the houses as
Figure 11 shows. At House A residents had had much more recent experience of living with family or friends, whilst House B residents
had often spent much of the previous year leading a way of life involving reception centres, common lodging houses and 'sleeping rough'.

There were parallel differences, again both between and within
houses, in terms of recent contacts with family members. At House A
the majority (68%) had had more than a single, isolated contact with
a family member within the 12 months prior to coming to the house,

Table 5:   Scale of previous adult social stability.

| | SCORE | | | |
| | 1 | 2 | 3 | 4 |
| --- | --- | --- | --- | --- |
| Age left childhood home (yrs) | 16 or younger | 17 | 18-21 | 22 or older |
| Longest at 1 address (mths) | 15 or fewer | 16-36 | 37-84 | 85 or more |
| Longest contin. period with 1 employer (mths) | 18 or fewer | 19-36 | 37-60 | 61 or more |
| Age 1st convicted (yrs) | 25 or younger | 26-35 | 36 or older | Never |
| Age 1st slept rough, or used rec. centre or cheap lodging hse. (yrs) | 28 or younger | 29-40 | 41 or older | Never |

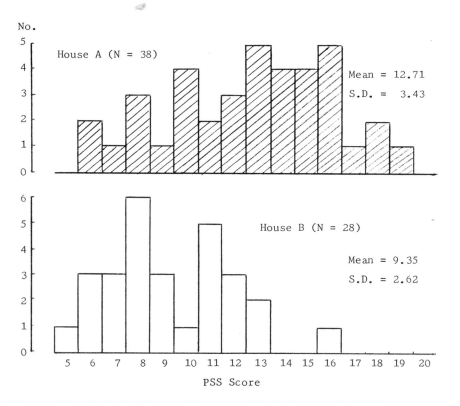

Figure 10:   Distributions of Previous Adult Social Stability scores for Intake Sample at Houses A and B.

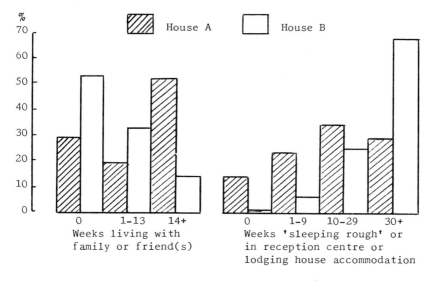

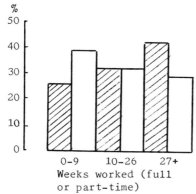

Figure 11: Life style in the most recent 12 months spent outside institutions (Intake Sample at Houses A and B).

and 29% had had more than 1 contact within the month prior to their arrival. At House B only a minority (32%) had had more than a single contact within the previous 12 months, and 18% had had more than 1 contact in the preceding month. Roughly ½ these contacts were with wives or children and roughly ½ were with parents, brothers or sisters.

In terms of weeks in and out of work (again roughly apportioning the most recent 12 months spent outside prison, hospital or hostel, and counting part-time work as being 'in' work), Figure 11 shows variation amongst residents at both houses, but in this instance an absence of any obvious difference between the 2 houses. At both houses there were new residents who had scarcely worked at all and others who had scarcely been out of work.

Drinking Troubles

Residents were asked about their experiences of a number of possible troubles which could be attributed to their drinking (the exact wording of these questions is shown in Appendix B). The details are shown in Table 6. Multiple experiences (6 or more times) of amnesia and tremor were almost invariable, whilst roughly $\frac{2}{3}$ reported multiple drunkenness offences, and sizeable minorities reported multiple experiences of hallucinations, reported drinking 'crude spirits' (methylated or surgical spirits) 6 or more times, and admitted 'trying to take thei own life' on at least 1 occasion.

Once again, however, there were substantial differences between Houses A and B. Nearly all new residents at House B, as opposed to less than $\frac{1}{2}$ at House A, had multiple convictions for drunkenness offences. The same was true for multiple occasion crude spirit drinking (71% at B, 24% at A). Again rather more than $\frac{1}{2}$ at House B, as opposed to approximately $\frac{1}{4}$ at House A reported multiple convictions for offences other than drunkenness. For suicide attempts the difference was in the opposite direction with the majority at House A reporting at least one such incident, in comparison with a minority at House B.

Table 6:  Drink-related and other troubles reported by members of Intake Sample at Houses A and B.

| | HOUSE A (N=38) | | HOUSE B (N=28) | |
|---|---|---|---|---|
| | Ever | 6+ Times | Ever | 6+ Times |
| Amnesia | 38 (100%) | 37 (98%) | 26 (93%) | 23 (82%) |
| Tremor | 37 (98%) | 36 (95%) | 23 (82%) | 20 (71%) |
| Hallucinations | 22 (58%) | 14 (37%) | 17 (60%) | 13 (46%) |
| Suicide attempt | 20 (53%) | 3 ( 8%) | 8 (28%) | 2 ( 7%) |
| Drunkenness offence | 35 (92%) | 18 (47%) | 28 (100%) | 23 (82%) |
| Other offence | 25 (66%) | 10 (26%) | 24 (86%) | 16 (57%) |
| Crude spirit drinking | 17 (45%) | 9 (24%) | 23 (82%) | 20 (71%) |

Previous Treatment for Drinking

The majority at both houses had attended meetings of Alcoholics Anonymous on at least 1 occasion in the past, most had had some hospital treatment specifically for alcoholism, whether as an in-patient or out-patient, and most had had a period of residence in a small hostel of some kind. However, much of this experience was brief. This was particularly the case for contact with Alcoholics Anonymous, and was more often the case for new residents at House B than at House A. Almost 2 out of every 3 A.A. attenders amongst new residents at House B had never been as many as 6 times, and the same was true of almost 1 in every 3 A.A. attenders at House A. Many House B residents who had received hospital treatment for alcoholism had never made as many as 4 attendances at out-patients or stayed for as long as 4 weeks as in-patients. In contrast, hospital treatment had almost always been more intensive than this for House A residents. Similarly, many residents at House B who had previously been in a hostel had stayed for less than 4 weeks whilst nearly all House A residents who had previously been in hostels had stayed longer.

By combining data on the 3 types of previous treatment or rehabilitation experience the contrast between residents of the two houses is shown up more clearly. New residents at House A were particularly likely to have had multiple or prolonged experience of all 3 types (12 at A, 3 at B), or to have had multiple or prolonged A.A. and hospital experience without previous prolonged hostel experience (9 at A, 2 at B), or to have had prolonged hospital treatment experience without multiple or prolonged experience of the other two types (7 at A, 2 at B). On the other hand, new residents at House B were more likely to be without multiple or prolonged experience of any type (3 at A, 7 at B), or to have had prolonged hostel experience without multiple or prolonged A.A. and hospital experience (3 at A, 6 at B), or to have had prolonged hostel and hospital experience without multiple A.A. attendancies (2 at A, 5 at B).

Recent Drinking

Data based upon each resident's report of the recency of his last alcoholic drink before arrival at the house are remarkably similar for the two houses, and are at first glance somewhat surprising. No single new resident at either house reported drinking at any time within the 7 days prior to arrival and only 4 new residents (3 at A, 1 at B) reported drinking at all within the 14 days preceding arrival. In fact a clear majority denied drinking at all within the 4 weeks before coming to the house (29 or 76% at A, 22 or 79% at B). Of both these totals, the majority reported their most recent alcoholic drink to be more than 6 weeks distant by the time of their arrival.

Nor are recent periods of abstinence necessarily 'forced' according to residents' accounts. A substantial number (39% at A, 29% at B) claimed 3 months or more continuous abstinence in the recent past whilst living outside an institution or hostel and a further substantial proportion (32% A, 36% B) claimed at least 2 to 3 weeks.

STAFF AND STAFF NUMBERS

Chapter 1 documented the variation which exists amongst hostels for alcoholics, in terms of staff numbers and staff-to-resident ratios.

Houses A and B are both examples of the smaller hostel (capacity of 12 or fewer residents), manned by a single non-resident member of staff. It is important to realize that this is not the only type of hostel for alcoholics in existence. Amongst the houses in the survey the larger hostels tended to have several members of staff and, even allowing for their larger numbers of residents, more favourable staff-to-resident ratios. Houses A and B, with effective staff-to-resident ratios of 1 to 12 and 1 to 15 respectively (the staff member at House B spent roughly $\frac{1}{3}$ of his time being responsible for House G), were 2 of the least staff-intensive houses in the survey sample.

## Ancillary Staff

As small houses they also had relatively little ancillary or domestic help. During the period of the study House A had a part-time cook, who cooked an evening meal only 5 days a week (excluding Saturdays and Sundays), and a part-time cleaner who worked approximately 20 hours every week. The house also shared a part-time secretary with the short-term assessment centre which was situated in the same road, opposite the house. She worked 20 hours a week, her office was situated in the assessment centre and not in House A, and the bulk of her work concerned the assessment centre. In addition, during the time of the study the position of bursar (20 hours a week) was filled for varying lengths of time by 4 different people, one of whom was the wife of the staff member. House B had only a part-time cook who prepared evening meals 5 days a week. The staff member in charge at House B also had access to the services of a secretary but she provided services for the very much larger project of which House B was a part, and was situated in the project offices some miles from House B.

## Visiting Professional Staff

Houses A and B had both had the services of visiting psychiatrists some time in their history, but neither had this type of support during the period of the study. The only regular visitor to House A during this period was a woman who had wide professional experience in the alcoholism rehabilitation field, as a research worker, a staff member at the assessment centre and later as organizer of a local alcoholism council. For 10 months in the first year she visited House A informally one evening a week and provided support in other ways, for example in the production of the house magazine. House B was supported more directly throughout the study period by staff of the wider project of which it was a part. The project director, himself the first ever staff member in charge at House B, usually attended every other weekly house meeting and had regular weekly meetings with the staff member in charge. In addition the project attempted a policy of continuity of responsibility for individual clients, and project social workers who had managed a client's passage through the project's own referral and selection channels retained some responsibility during his residency at House B. Regular visitors to House B throughout the study period therefore included 2 or 3 individual social workers although the main purpose of their visits was to see a small minority of the existing residents.

Support Groups

Because both Houses A and B were part of larger organizations, there were no committees for the houses themselves (although the larger organization had committees dealing with matters such as staffing and finance that affected the house), but the staff member in charge had available to him the advice of a relatively small (3 to 5 people) 'support group'. At House A this group consisted of a psychiatric social worker, a probation officer, a general practitioner, and the senior social worker of the parent organization of which House A was a part. The latter was a former staff member in charge at House A. It was the intention that the group should meet approximately monthly to advise and support the staff member in charge. However in practice its meetings were irregular and its status was in some doubt in the Summer and early Autumn of the first year of the study when its support was most needed (see Chapter 9). The support group at House B (shared with House G) consisted of 2 senior social workers, 1 of whom was the project director, a psychiatrist, a probation officer and a community worker who was also a clergyman. This body met, with the staff member in charge, approximately monthly throughout the period of the study.

Staff Training

The first staff member in charge at House A during the study period (staff A1) was in his early 40's and, despite his training and experience as a probation officer, had had no previous experience in residential work nor in specialized work in alcoholism. Staff A2 took over $\frac{2}{3}$ the way through the study period (see Figure 12). He was a young man, in his 20's, and had previously worked as a qualified psychiatric nurse. In that capacity he had worked with alcoholics in a hospital setting but had not specialized in the problem. However, before taking up the appointment as staff member at House A he had worked for 6 months as social worker in charge at the neighbouring assessment centre.

Staff B1 was a young man, in his 20's, who had had no previous experience or training in residential work. He had a university degree in philosophy and had done a post-graduate course in computer programming. However he was by no means unfamiliar with the problems of alcoholism rehabilitation as his father had been in charge of an alcoholism hostel for a number of years. Staff B2 also took over about $\frac{2}{3}$ the way through the study period. He also had no previous experience or training in residential work, and other than brief experience as a voluntary worker with homeless alcoholics had no specialist experience of the problem. His own recovery from a 'compulsive gambling' problem was a motivating force and he was widely involved in local community action groups.

SUMMARY

Similarities Between Houses A and B

Referral and Selection

1. The bulk of referrals came from 3 types of source: the hostel's own assessment and induction system; psychiatric hospitals; and

116

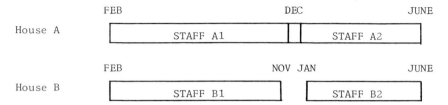

The 2 staff at House A overlapped for approximately 2 weeks whilst House B was without a member of staff in charge for approximately 4 weeks.

Figure 12: Staff members in charge at Houses A and B during the study period.

probation officers, prisons and the local reception centre. Comparatively very few came from other sources.

2. Only 25 to 30% of referrals resulted in admission. Referrals from the hostel's own assessment and induction system were most successful (60%), whilst probation officer referrals were least successful (1 out of 40 referrals successful).

3. The process of referral, selection and admission was a lengthy one involving 6 successive stages. Most unsuccessful referrals failed at 1 of the first 2 stages.

4. Selection criteria were mostly not objective or explicit, and varied from time to time depending upon staff and the current composition of the resident group. Some applicants were rejected for one of a number of practical reasons. Otherwise, potential residents were rejected for one or other of 2 major reasons; lack of motivation, and expectations of difficulties in mixing amicably with existing residents.

5. Not all failures of admission were due to deliberate selection. Roughly ½ were due to applications being withdrawn, or prospective residents relapsing or not showing up for the next stage.

Characteristics of Residents

6. Both houses admitted only men. Ages ranged from early 20's to late 50's (average 40-45 years).

7. Residents displayed considerable heterogeneity for recent social history. Many had been unemployed for a long time, others had mostly been in work. Many had had no contact with their families for many years, others had been living with their families fairly recently or had had contact with them. Many had 'slept rough' or lived in reception centres or lodging houses most of the previous year, others had lived that way relatively infrequently or not at all. It would have

been very difficult to draw a line between 'vagrant' or 'skid row' men and others.

8. There was even greater variation in previous social history. Some men had been relatively educationally advantaged, had obtained jobs of relatively high status in the past, had been residentially and occupationally stable for a number of years, and had appeared in court for the first time in middle-age, if at all. Other residents were much more lacking in previous adult social stability. They were educationally and occupationally disadvantaged, had never achieved residential or occupational stability, and had made court appearances as juveniles or in early adult life.

9. Almost all reported multiple experiences of alcoholic amnesia and tremor. Most admitted multiple drunkenness offence convictions and at least some crude spirit drinking. Substantial minorities admitted regular crude spirit drinking and at least one suicide attempt. Most had attended Alcoholics Anonymous, most had received hospital treatment for alcoholism, and most had lived in a small hostel previously.

10. No resident admitted to drinking within the 7 days before admission, and 75 to 80% claimed not to have had a drink in the previous 4 weeks. Approximately 1 in 3 stated that they had abstained for 3 months or longer in the previous 12 months whilst living outside prison, hospital or hostel.

Staff

11. House A had a single member of staff for up to 12 residents; House B had $\frac{2}{3}$ equivalent of a staff member for up to 10 residents. Both were non-residential. There was a single change of staff at each house during the study. Of the 4 staff members involved in the study all were men, 3 were in their 20's, and only 1 had any previous experience of residential hostel work specializing in alcoholism. Another had previously worked as a probation officer. Staff at each house had a professional 'support group', and part-time domestic help.

## Differences Between Houses A and B

Referral and Selection

1. A much higher percentage of referrals to House A came from psychiatric hospitals; a higher percentage to House B came via the hostel's own assessment and induction units.

2. House B referrals scarcely ever resulted in admission unless they came by this channel; House A referrals were sometimes successful from sources other than the hostel's own assessment centre.

3. Once a referral had proceeded to the stage of meeting residents at a meal it was almost certain to result in admission at House B. At House A 1 in 3 of referrals reaching this stage were unsuccessful.

4. House B staff were more actively selective than staff at House A at each of the first 2 stages. Failures of referral at House A were more often due to withdrawal of application or failure of the prospective resident to show at the next stage. There was however marked

variation over time in this respect at House A.

Resident Characteristics

5.  The average age of residents at House B was slightly lower with relatively few men in their 50's, and the English were outnumbered by Irish and Scots by 4 to 1 at House B.

6.  The majority at House A had been in hospital in the previous 12 months, and only a minority had been in prison, and a minority in a hostel; the reverse was the case at House B.

7.  The 2 resident groups were distinctly different in terms of social history.  Many more House B residents reported multiple drunkenness offence convictions, admitted regular consumption of crude spirits, had had no recent contact with family, had much recent experience of 'sleeping rough' or in lodging houses or reception centres, had relatively low educational and occupational attainments, and had never been particularly socially stable at any time in their adult lives.

8.  Experience of Alcoholics Anonymous, hospital treatment for alcoholism, and small hostel residence was in each case more likely to have been brief for House B residents.  If the latter had experienced multiple or prolonged contact with any of these 3 sources of help, it was most likely to have been in a hostel.

# Chapter 7
# Everyday House Routines

In trying to adopt more active therapeutic measures many
difficulties were encountered. ...without adopting a
more directive approach it was impossible to initiate a
regular group discussion. They were unwilling to make
majority decisions on hostel policy, and tended to present
a facade of behaviour in a group, saying only what they
thought would be acceptable to the other men (Cook et al,
1968, p.241, writing of the first year's operation at
House B).

What goes on in these small hostels once the residents, described
in the previous chapter, have successfully gained admission? What
events take place, and what is their significance? What rules and
expectations govern the behaviour of the members of these communities?
What day-to-day decisions have to be made, and issues settled? Where
does the responsibility for enforcing rules and making decisions lie?
The questions that could be asked about the everyday life of a small
hostel are unlimited in number and only a few have been raised here.

For example, the researchers were made aware early on that almost
all personnel connected with small hostels held strong views on issues
to do with 'where power lies' in the day-to-day running of a hostel.
In particular, those who had planned Houses A and B and those who
staffed them held tenaciously to the view that their houses differed
markedly from many other hostels, that their own houses were 'therapeutic communities', and that this way of going about things was in-
herently superior. Central questions to which this chapter is therefore addressed are, To what extent were Houses A and B 'democratic'?,
and, To what extent did they in fact embody the ideas of a 'therapeutic community'? Was there evidence, for example, of the 'freedom
of emotional expression' in group meetings, or of the shared distribution of decision-making authority throughout the membership of the
house, which are supposedly amongst the most important ingredients of
the therapeutic community? (Jones, 1952, 1968; Rapoport, 1960).

Other key questions concern the amount of staff-resident contact,
and the operation of a no drinking rule. Does the 'group work' emphasis, and the opportunity which the small hostel provides for a variety
of informal contacts, replace the traditional casework relationship
between staff and residents? Are hostel staff managers and facilit-
ators, or do they retain a more traditional 'therapeutic' role? Much
emphasis is placed upon the no drinking rule in therapeutic alcoholism

hostels. How absolute was this rule in practice and how total was the concensus of opinion about it?

## Work and Finance

At neither house was work said to be compulsory, nor was it necessarily always encouraged. New residents were not expected to start work immediately, or within any stated period of time, and might in fact be discouraged if it was felt that they were 'rushing' into work before they were 'ready' for it. Nonetheless outside employment was undoubtedly a major part of routine. The generally shared expectation was that a resident would try his best to obtain outside employment once he had settled down at the house, and for this reason there was no organized routine or daily program at either house for those not working. The view was undoubtedly shared by residents and staff alike that gainful employment constituted an integral part of the 'total rehabilitation', 'change in life style', 'leading a fuller life', or the 'becoming a useful member of society' which are amongst the stated purposes of small alcoholism hostels (see Chapter 2). Of course working also released a resident from reliance upon limited social security payments most of which would go towards paying rent. Once a resident was considered to be sufficiently settled, there might be a considerable amount of informal pressure on him to try to obtain work.

In practice the proportion of current residents in work varied considerably from time to time. During the period of the study there were times when nearly everyone was in work. For example, at House A nearly all residents were in work at the beginning of March of the first year, and all residents were in work during the early part of October at House B. At other times the position was reversed and only a minority were in work leaving the majority at somewhat of a loose end for much of the daytime. For example, only 2 of the 6 residents at House A were in work at the end of the following January, while at House B only a few residents were in work during August of the first year. Given the lack of job skills of many residents often combined with an irregular recent work record, scope was often limited, particularly for residents at House B. Many of the jobs obtained by residents were not considered totally satisfactory by them; for example minor factory work, street cleaning and warehousing. Others, such as building site labouring, whilst possibly being fairly well paid, provided little permanency and no further training. Some residents at House A plus the very occasional resident at House B were able to obtain skilled work, such as painting and decorating, and a few at House A were able to take advantage of their training and previous experience of non-manual jobs, and obtain jobs such as building foreman, clerical worker and journalist.

As at other houses in the survey, residents were required to pay a weekly rent of £6-7 (the average weekly earnings in Britain then stood at £36). Arrangements were made with the local Social Security office so that unemployed residents received money to pay this rent plus £1.85 pocket money. It was a rare event for a resident to be unable to pay his rent for the week and there were no instances during the study period, at either house, of residents being asked to leave or otherwise being penalized for non-payment. At House A the matter was occasionally discussed at the staff's discretion at the weekly group meeting. Staff assisted in making initial arrangements for the collection of clothing grants etc. They also occasionally held money for individual residents to assist in saving and as an insurance against spending on drink, and they also assisted individuals in making the necessary arrangements to make payment to a court, or to their families.

## House Group Meetings

The 'group therapy and business meeting' at House A and the 'house meeting' at House B were each held on a single regular weekday evening and lasted for up to 2 hours. Attendance was compulsory at House A but there was a degree of flexibility in the attendance rule and it was agreed that a resident might be excused up to 1 in 3 weekly meetings on the grounds of evening shift work. Attendance was not compulsory at House B, but all residents were strongly encouraged to attend regularly and if a resident failed to attend without good reason the matter was likely to be raised in the group. At each house, therefore, the group meeting was an important event in the weekly diary and normally all were expected to attend. This expectation included the staff member in charge, and at House B the director of the overall project of which House B was a part also attended, usually on alternate weeks.

At House A part of the meeting time was spent on 'house business', but most of the time (approximately $1\frac{1}{2}$ hours) was devoted to 'group therapy'. In accordance with this designation of the group meeting, and in accordance with the 'therapeutic community' pretentions of the house, residents were expected to participate by allowing some degree of self-disclosure.

The expression 'group therapy' was not used at House B in speaking of their weekly meetings. An annual report described the meetings in the following terms:

The meeting acts as a forum for the exchange of views and ideas as well as for discussion on the wider problems of coping with sobriety. For the staff, the primary function of these meetings is to focus attention on the implications of decisions taken. The decisions and the consequences are then the responsibility of the residents (Alcoholics Recovery Project, Report, 1973, p.8).

The resident group at House A elected a 'group leader' who served for an unlimited term, and who had particular responsibility for domestic arrangements and for liaison with the staff member in charge and with domestic staff. For example, his responsibilities included ordering milk and bread etc., paying tradesmen and overseeing other residents' domestic duties. He was also the one called upon to take charge when a man returned drinking or was difficult when staff were away. Towards the end of the study, following the events of previous months (see Chapter 9), residents and staff reduced the domestic role of the group leader and the elected individual became known as the 'group spokesman'. At House B the meeting elected a 'group chairman' monthly. The function of the elected resident was simply to chair the meeting and he had no further responsibilities beyond that.

Measuring Groups

Existing methods for quantifying what takes place in a group meeting were found to be inapplicable to this type of free-flowing non-task group. The method finally used at Houses A and B during the study period was evolved and piloted at earlier meetings at both houses. The technique was then used at the 2 houses on alternate weeks throughout the study period.

The research worker sat in the group, as a non-participating observer, and made a continuous recording of the following information:

1.  Who speaks? Each participant was assigned a row on the recording form and an entry was made in the appropriate row whenever he spoke.

2.  To whom? A record was made of the individual participant (or whole group) to whom the utterance was directed.

3.  With what amount of emotional expression? Each utterance was judged to be at 1 of 3 levels of emotionality: little or no emotion (alpha); emotion shown by content only (beta); emotion shown both verbally and by gesture or tone (gamma). Emotion could be either 'positive' (e.g. humour, joy, relief) or 'negative' (e.g. anxiety, irritation, anger).

Further details of this recording technique, along with example ratings are provided in Appendix D. Some estimate of the reliability of the technique was obtained by having a second non-participant observer sit in on 2 meetings (1 at each house) and make independent recordings. Details of one of these reliability checks are also provided in Appendix D. In summary, these checks suggested that the technique was sufficiently reliable to provide a measure of the relative total volume of speech made and received by the different participants in a group, and of the relative overall levels of emotionality of different groups. However, the technique is probably not sufficiently reliable in the form used, to provide more detailed measures, for example of the relative amount spoken by individual participants to individual other participants, or of the relative levels of emotionality of different participants when speaking to different others.

One of the most evident features of these data was a contrast in the level of emotionality shown at the 2 houses. Unemotional utterances predominated at House B whilst there was a more equal balance of emotional and unemotional utterances at House A. That this contrast was a regular feature of meetings at the 2 houses is shown by the figures in Table 7 which shows data from 12 meetings covering the first 24 weeks of the study and 12 meetings covering the last 24 weeks at each house. On average 52% of resident utterances in the first 24 weeks at House A were emotional (beta or gamma) and the same was true for 57% of utterances in the last 24 weeks. Comparable percentages for House B were 16% and 23%. At House A emotional remarks constituted 50% or more of the total in all but 3 meetings in the first 24 weeks and in all but 2 meetings in the last 24, whilst emotional remarks never constituted as much as 50% of the total at House B.

Table 7 also shows staff at House B to have been less emotional in remarks they made at group meetings than staff at House A. However, the contrast here is much less strong, as staff were consistently much

Table 7: Emotionality and staff dominance of group meetings at Houses A and B.

**12 Meetings from 1st 24 WEEKS**

| HOUSE A | | | | | HOUSE B | | | | |
|---|---|---|---|---|---|---|---|---|---|
| No. present+ | Emotion* Res. | Staff | Staff rank Speak | Rec. | No. present+ | Emotion* Res. | Staff | Staff rank Speak | Rec. |
| 11+1 | 54 | 13 | 4 | 5 | 9+2 | 15 | 7 | 1,2 | 1,2 |
| 10+1 | 34 | 2 | 3 | 5 | 8+1 | 4 | 3 | 1 | 1 |
| 10+1 | 53 | 0 | 8 | 8 | 8+1 | 6 | 1 | 1 | 1 |
| 8+1 | 50 | 11 | 5 | 3 | 7+1 | 12 | 0 | 3 | 1 |
| 8+1 | 55 | 0 | 8 | 8 | 7+1 | 4 | 1 | 1 | 1 |
| 9+1 | 68 | 30 | 5 | 6 | 8+2 | 32 | 37 | 1,2 | 1,2 |
| 7+1 | 46 | 18 | 1 | 1 | 9+2 | 19 | 16 | 1,3 | 1,3 |
| 7+1 | 58 | 16 | 1 | 1 | 9+1 | 12 | 15 | 2 | 1 |
| 7+1 | 61 | 32 | 4 | 2 | 7+1 | 16 | 13 | 1 | 1 |
| 6+1 | 53 | 9 | 1 | 1 | 6 | 25 | - | - | - |
| 6+1 | 53 | 6 | 3 | 1 | 5+2 | 36 | 15 | 2,3 | 1,2½ |
| 6+1 | 42 | 16 | 1 | 1 | 5+1 | 9 | 7 | 2 | 1 |

**12 Meetings from last 24 WEEKS**

| HOUSE A | | | | | HOUSE B | | | | |
|---|---|---|---|---|---|---|---|---|---|
| No. present+ | Emotion* Res. | Staff | Staff rank Speak | Rec. | No. present+ | Emotion* Res. | Staff | Staff rank Speak | Rec. |
| 4+1 | 58 | 1 | 2 | 1 | 8+2 | 8 | 5 | 1,3 | 1,2 |
| 3+1 | 11 | 3 | 1 | 1 | 7+2 | 31 | 8 | 1,5 | 1,2 |
| 5+1 | 65 | 21 | 3 | 4 | 9+2 | 16 | 6 | 4,5 | 1,4 |
| 5+1 | 78 | 14 | 4 | 3 | 9+2 | 15 | 3 | 4,7 | 1,7½ |
| 5+1 | 71 | 3 | 4½ | 3 | 8+2 | 16 | 2 | 1,7 | 1,6 |
| 7+1 | 52 | 33 | 7 | 5 | 7+1 | 30 | 3 | 1 | 1 |
| 6+1 | 66 | 15 | 4 | 3 | 6+2 | 35 | 9 | 1,5 | 1,3 |
| 6+1 | 72 | 17 | 2 | 2 | 6+2 | 10 | 1 | 1,6 | 1,6 |
| 8+1 | 53 | 16 | 1 | 1 | 6+2 | 14 | 0 | 1,6 | 1,5 |
| 8+1 | 49 | 14 | 1 | 1 | 6+1 | 42 | 5 | 1 | 1 |
| 9+1 | 54 | 17 | 3 | 3 | 6+2 | 20 | 7 | 2,3 | 2,3 |
| 6+1 | 59 | 25 | 1 | 1 | 8+1 | 42 | 3 | 1 | 1 |

+ Residents plus staff. Students on placement were present occasionally but they rarely contributed and have been ignored in this Table.
* Percentage of utterances rated Beta or Gamma.

less emotional than residents at both houses, but particularly at House
A. Staff were less emotional than the average resident on every single
occasion at House A. The same was true during the last 24 weeks at
House B when staff were consistently almost totally unemotional. Only
during the first 24 weeks at House B were staff anywhere near as emotional as residents. On 2 occasions during this time staff even displayed a fequency of emotional remarks greater than that of the average resident.

Table 7 also shows the position of the staff member(s) in the rank
orders of all participants in terms of volume spoken, and volume received. Staff at House B were much more likely than staff at House A
to head the rank-order lists. In fact, with the exception of a single
meeting at which the 2 members of staff present were pushed into 2nd
and 3rd places for volume spoken, a member of staff was the most voluminous speaker at each meeting attended by a member of staff during
these 2 24-week blocks. Meetings at House A were much less frequently
staff-dominated (at least as judged by this one index) and occasionally staff took very much a back seat. This contrast between the two
houses can be shown by comparing actual and chance-expectancy staff
rank positions for volume of speech (Table 8). If the staff role conferred no special speaking rights or expectations, then staff would
have been expected to occupy the 1st rank, for volume spoken, no more
than about 3 times out of 24 meetings, and would have been expected to
occupy 2nd, 3rd or 4th ranks equally often. They would even have been
expected to occupy ranks as low as the 7th, 8th and 9th on some occasions when the group was of at least that size. In practice, however,
staff occupied the top rank much more frequently than would have
been expected, and occupied lower ranks less often than expected.
This was particularly the case at House B where the staff member in
charge occupied the 1st rank 5 times more frequently than expected.
The discrepancy between actual and expected staff ranks was less
marked at House A. The 1st rank was occupied roughly 3 times as often
as expected, the 5th rank was occupied as often as expected, and the
7th and 8th ranks were occupied on 3 occasions.

Table 8: Staff domination of meetings - a comparison of expected and
actual rank order positions for volume of speech of staff at Houses
A and B.

| Rank order position | HOUSE A Expected | Actual | HOUSE B Expected | Actual | | |
|---|---|---|---|---|---|---|
| 1 | 3.2 | 8 | 2.7 | 14 | a | Staff member tied for |
| 2 | 3.2 | 2 | 2.7 | 3 | | 4th place on one |
| 3 | 3.2 | 4 | 2.7 | 4 | | occasion |
| 4 | 3.2 | 3.5a | 2.7 | 2 | | |
| 5 | 3.0 | 3.5a | 2.7 | – | b | No staff were pres- |
| 6 | 2.8 | – | 2.7 | – | | ent at one of the 24 |
| 7 | 2.3 | 1 | 2.5 | – | | meetings |
| 8 | 1.4 | 2 | 2.2 | – | | |
| 9 | 0.9 | – | 1.2 | – | | See text, above, for |
| 10 | 0.5 | – | 0.6 | – | | examples of how this |
| 11 | 0.2 | – | 0.3 | – | | Table should be read. |
| 12 | 0.1 | – | – | – | | |
| | 24.0 | 24.0 | 23.0b | 23.0b | | |

### Staff-Resident Contact

In the course of the study period at Houses A and B, staff members in charge were asked to keep a log of the number of hours they spent at the house and available to residents. This was to exclude any time spent in the house but not available to residents, such as time spent in a committee or staff meeting. They were also asked to report the number of hours in the previous 2 weeks spent with each individual resident. This time was divided up into 3 categories of staff-resident contact as follows:

1. <u>House business.</u> This particularly concerned House A where the staff member in charge might have relatively formal, non-personal, contact with members of the resident group, such as the group leader or editor of the house magazine who had special responsibilities.

2. <u>Formal - personal.</u> To be included in this category it was necessary that a contact had involved sitting down alone with an individual resident, in circumstances allowing some privacy, for the purpose of discussing matters of personal relevance to that individual resident.

3. <u>Informal.</u> This included all contacts of an informal nature whether public or private.

Further details of the method are given in Appendix A, and some results of applying the technique at Houses A and B are shown in Table 9. First of all it can be seen that both staff members in charge at House A spent roughly 40 hours per week at the house, at least in theory available to residents during that time. Staff members in charge at House B spent correspondingly fewer hours a week at the house on account of their extra responsibilities for House G. Except for house meetings, staff time at the houses was on the whole confined to daytime hours during weekdays. With the exception of staff B2, who spent an average of 5 hours at the house each weekend over 1 particular 6-week period, staff rarely came to the house at weekends (staff B1 averaged less than ½ hour per weekend, A1 was available for 1 hour on only 1 weekend during the whole of the year, and A2 did not recall attending at the weekend at all during the 6 months).

Despite the apparent similarities between staff members in terms of total time available, there were major differences in reports of how that time was used. Staff A1 reported spending only an average of just over 3 hours per week in contact with residents, and of this time a fair proportion was spent conducting house business. This picture contrasts with that reported by staff A2. He reported spending almost 4 times as many hours in contact with residents, including over 3 times as much formal-personal contact and 5 times as much informal contact. Most residents at House A had 4 hours or more of staff A2's attention every week, whereas those in residence the previous year mostly had ½ hour of the staff member's attention or less. Staff A1 seemed to make it his business to maintain some contact, however brief, with all residents. Only 2 residents, throughout his year, went as long as 2 weeks without any contact with the staff member, and one of these was Dick D, an ex-group leader who was coming to the end of a fairly lengthy stay in the house and was rarely being seen by anyone. Staff A2, with his much higher rate of contact with residents, maintained regular contact with all.

Table 9:  Average hours per week spent at the house and in contact with residents, reported by staff at Houses A and B.

| STAFF MEMBER | A1 | A2 | B1 | B2 |
|---|---|---|---|---|
| Available in the house | 39.6 | 37.2 | 28.8 | 27.9 |
| Total contact with residents | 3.4 | 13.5 | 28.6 | 4.3 |
| House Business contact | 0.9 | 2.6 | 0.0 | 0.1 |
| Formal-Personal contact | 0.9 | 3.4 | 4.5 | 1.7 |
| Informal contact | 1.6 | 7.6 | 24.1 | 2.5 |

An even more dramatic contrast between the 2 staff members occurred at House B.  Whereas staff B1 reported spending virtually all his available hours in contact with residents, staff B2 like staff A1 reported spending relatively few of his available hours with residents.  In terms of individual contact categories, he spent fewer hours in formal-personal contact with residents, and many fewer hours in informal contact (2½ hours on average in comparison with B1's unusually large average of over 20 hours).

Staff B1 gave most of his residents 4 hours or more a week of his time, whereas most residents of the following year had less than ½ hour a week of their staff member's (B2's) time, and the latter did not always keep contact with every resident.  Over 6 months there were 16 separate instances (involving 10 separate individual residents) of a resident going for 2 weeks without individual contact with the staff member.

It is of course important to bear in mind that staff provided all the data on staff-resident contact and an unknown degree of bias may have been operating, although it seems unlikely that this could have accounted for the large differences between individual staff members.

House Conduct

The Control of Drinking

Each resident was asked what action he thought should be taken about drinking and about a series of other behaviours.  Eight standard statements briefly describing these behaviours (shown in Table 10) were evolved and piloted during the pre-study period.  The first concerns drinking itself ('drinks').  The wording of the statement is important. The hypothetical rule-breaking resident drinks <u>away</u> from the house, is <u>sober</u> when he returns, and he <u>owns up</u> to his misbehaviour.  He breaks the rule it is true, but does not commit a number of sins which the rule is designed to discourage.  He does not inflict his drinking or drunken self upon other members of the house, he does not put temptation in the way of others by bringing drink to the house or by encouraging other residents to drink, his behaviour in the house is not disruptive, and he shows due regard for the principle of open and honest communication by coming clean at the first opportunity.

Table 10:   Statements of hypothetical instances of misconduct at
a small alcoholism hostel.

1.  If a man drinks while he is away from the house at the
weekend, and comes back to the house sober on the Monday,
and tells the house that he has been drinking? ('drinks').

2.  If a man covers up for another resident who is drinking?
('covers up').

3.  If a man continually does not do his dishes and does not
wash up his cup, etc? ('dishes').

4.  If a man goes out and stays out late without informing
the house that he will be out until late ('out late').

5.  If a man appears to be very touchy and very irritable?
('touchy').

6.  If a man appears to be very anxious and very nervous?
('anxious').

7.  If a man is known to be gambling heavily? ('gambles').

8.  If a man declares that he is not interested in anyone
else or their problems? ('not interested').

Each resident was asked whether any action should be taken in this
event, what action should be taken if any should, and who should take
it (fuller details of the procedure are given in Appendix C). This
and other questions on rule-breaking were put to each resident at an
interview approximately 2 weeks after his admission, and again at each
of a series of successive interviews held at 4-weekly intervals thereafter. Each staff member in charge was asked the same set of questions,
once only, at the end of the study.

Table 11 shows the data obtained from a sample of resident interviews taken from the first 24-week part of the study and the last 24
weeks, for each house. (The sample was obtained by excluding 1st and
last interviews for each resident, and then taking one interview for
each resident at random). The Table also shows the responses of the
4 separate staff members. First of all it can be seen that there is
near-total concensus of opinion only for the last 6 months at House A.
Residents were then virtually united in their strictness. All but 1
of the 14 residents in the sample were of the opinion that the hypothetical offending resident should be asked to leave the house and to
terminate his period of residence there. The 1 resident who disagreed
was almost as strict, being of the opinion that he should be given one
more chance but should be asked to leave if the offence occurred again.
Interestingly enough, the staff member (A2) was more lenient still, and
felt that the offender should be censured only. The body of residents
therefore led the staff member, rather than the other way around, in
terms of adherence to a strict no-drinking rule.

Resident opinions on this issue were very different 12 months earlier. The staff member in charge at that time (A1) had the same view as the man who took over from him at the end of the year. However, although some residents had a stricter view, the majority were much less strict - 3 thought that the matter was one that should be dealt with by insisting upon discharge, 1 thought the matter should be discussed sympathetically but that no further action should be taken, 1 felt that some sort of action should be taken but he was uncertain what, and 3 felt that no action should be taken at all. The lack of consensus about appropriate action at House A at this particular time contrasts with the cohesion evident the following year. This was a significant fact which will be discussed again in Chapter 8.

At House B consensus was lacking during both periods. At both times only ½ the residents or less felt that discharge was an appropriate punishment. Unlike the position at House A, the 2 staff members in charge at House B had differing opinions. Staff B1 shared with ½ his residents the strict line that discharge was required, and ½ his residents therefore lagged somewhat behind him in terms of strictness. The position of staff B2 was the reverse. He felt that the matter merited sympathetic discussion only, and the majority of his residents took a harder line than he did himself.

The second question regarding the control of drinking behaviour concerned covering up for another resident who was drinking. In both houses, during both 6-month periods, opinions were represented covering the whole spectrum from those who felt that no action should be taken to those who felt that this itself should result in the offender being required to give up his membership in the community. However, along with the previous item on drinking this was an offence about which the majority always felt that action of some sort should be taken. At House A the view was on the whole less harsh about 'covering up' than about drinking itself. The same tendency was evident at House B in the last 24 weeks of the study period but the trend was, surprisingly, in the reverse direction at House B in the first 24 weeks. At this time there was a much more united feeling about the importance of not 'covering up' than about not drinking.

Other House Expectations

There are obviously many other expectations of appropriate conduct in a small alcoholism hostel besides those concerned with drinking. The remaining 6 statements were chosen on the basis of preliminary discussion with residents and staff. Statements 3 and 4 ('dishes' and 'out late') were designed to reveal expectations about everyday, 'domestic' conduct. The next pair ('touchy' and 'anxious') were designed to reveal some expectations about personal and social conduct, and the remaining 2 items ('gambles' and 'not interested') were to reveal expectations regarding behaviours which might be viewed as 'anti-therapeutic' or 'problem' behaviours.

On the whole, as judged by the proportions of residents holding the view that no action was required, these behaviours were considered less actionable than drinking or covering up for drinking. However, there is the suggestion of some differences between the 2 houses. The everyday domestic issues (not washing up and staying out late) split the residents at both houses, at both times, roughly into 2 halves - those who thought action should be taken and those who thought no

Table 11: Numbers of residents and staff taking different views on action that should follow 8 types of misconduct at Houses A and B (Figures = No. of residents taking that view; S = Staff member takes that view).

| ACTION: | HOUSE A | | | | | | HOUSE B | | | | | |
|---|---|---|---|---|---|---|---|---|---|---|---|---|
| | A | B | C | D | E | F | A | B | C | D | E | F |
| **'Drinks'** | | | | | | | | | | | | |
| Months 1-6 | 3 | 1 | 1 | S | - | 3 | 2 | 1 | - | - | 2 | 5S |
| Months 13-18 | - | - | - | S | 1 | 13 | - | - | 3S | 1 | 2 | 4 |
| **'Covers up'** | | | | | | | | | | | | |
| Months 1-6 | 3 | S | 1 | - | 2 | 2 | 1 | 1 | - | S | 1 | 7 |
| Months 13-18 | 1 | - | - | 3 | 2 | 8S | 2 | - | 1S | 3 | 1 | 3 |
| **'Dishes'** | | | | | | | | | | | | |
| Months 1-6 | 4 | 1 | - | 2S | 1 | - | 6 | - | - | 4S | - | - |
| Months 13-18 | 6 | - | - | 8S | - | - | 4S | - | - | 6 | - | - |
| **'Out late'** | | | | | | | | | | | | |
| Months 1-6 | 5 | 1S | - | 2 | - | - | 5 | 1 | - | 3S | 1 | - |
| Months 13-18 | 6 | - | - | 8S | - | - | 4 | - | S | 6 | - | - |
| **'Touchy'** | | | | | | | | | | | | |
| Months 1-6 | 6 | S | 2 | - | - | - | 7 | - | 3S | - | - | - |
| Months 13-18 | 6 | S | 7 | - | 1 | - | 7 | - | 2S | 1 | - | - |
| **'Anxious'** | | | | | | | | | | | | |
| Months 1-6 | 4 | S | 4 | - | - | - | 7 | - | 3S | - | - | - |
| Months 13-18 | 6 | S | 7 | - | 1 | - | 7 | - | 2S | 1 | - | - |
| **'Gambles'** | | | | | | | | | | | | |
| Months 1-6 | 4 | - | 1S | 3 | - | - | 8 | - | 1S | - | - | 1 |
| Months 13-18 | 5 | - | 6S | 3 | - | - | 10 | - | - | S | - | - |
| **'Not interested'** | | | | | | | | | | | | |
| Months 1-6 | 1 | - | 3 | 3 | - | 1S | 5 | 1 | 2 | 2S | - | - |
| Months 13-18 | 4 | - | 2S | 7 | - | 1 | 7 | - | 1S | 1 | - | 1 |

Key: A - Nothing should be done; B - Some action but don't know what; C - Sympathetic discussion only, etc.; D - Censure; E - One more chance before asked to leave; F - Asked to leave.

House A, Months 1-6, N = 8 Residents plus Staff member.
        Months 13-18, N = 14 Residents plus Staff member.

House B, Months 1-6, N = 10 Residents plus Staff member.
        Months 13-18, N = 10 Residents plus Staff member.

action was necessary. On the other hand, residents at House A were more likely than residents at House B to take a strict view of behaviours in the personal and social area, and in the 'anti-therapeutic problem' area. At House B at least 50% thought no action should be taken on any of these matters, and the percentage advocating no action reached 100% with regard to heavy gambling towards the end of the study. Staff at House B, in both years, felt that some action should be taken with regard to each of these matters. The particular significance of the residents' disregard for the staff view that heavy gambling was an important matter at House B at the end of the study will be discussed again in Chapter 8.

Residents at House A were much more likely to regard these matters as important. In particular they took a dim view of a resident

declaring his lack of interest in fellow residents or their problems.
In the last 24 weeks this was more frequently considered actionable
than any matter other than drinking and covering up for drinking. In
the 1st 24 weeks there was in fact more agreement that action should
be taken on this matter than there was agreement that action should be
taken about drinking-related issues.

Table 11 shows that these behaviours were rarely considered so
serious that the resident involved should be asked to leave, or even
given one more chance. Censure was more likely to be considered
appropriate, and even then only by some, for 'no interest' at House A
(in the first 24 weeks of the study), or 'domestic' offences at House
B (first and last 24-week blocks), and for all of these offences at
House A in the last 24 weeks.

A further interesting point concerns the relative positions of
staff and residents on these 6 issues. Whereas with regard to drinking offences residents were frequently more severe than staff, the
opposite was very definitely the case with regard to these other
behaviours. This was particularly true for both staff members in
charge at House B, and was almost equally true for staff A1. In all
these instances staff were well to the tough-minded end of the spectrum of views represented in the house at the time. Only in the
relatively strict atmosphere of House A at the end of the study did
the staff member in charge appear moderate in comparison with residents

Resident Involvement in Rule Enforcement

On the same occasions that questions were asked about appropriate
responses to hypothetical instances of rule-breaking, questions were
also asked about the locus of responsibility for making decisions
about the imposition of sanctions. Responses were taken to indicate
resident involvement only if real collective responsibility for taking
a decision was implied, and not merely if the consultation of residents followed by a staff decision was indicated. Decisions taken
jointly by staff and residents were therefore only considered as instances of 'resident involvement' if it was felt that decisions could
conceivably go against staff wishes.

The results showed that residents and staff, with the exception
of staff A1, were in principle in favour of real resident involvement.
At House A, in both years, only an exceptional resident was in favour
of exclusive staff decision-making and then only on isolated issues.
Those in favour of exclusive staff decision-making at House B were also
in a minority, but the minority was a somewhat larger one.

Some issues were more likely to be thought outside the residents'
sphere of competence than others. Particularly early on, House B
residents who thought something should be done about social-personal
behaviour ('touchy' and 'anxious') thought that staff should make
decisions, and staff tended to agree with them. Staff at House A were
also likely to think that these matters were best reserved for their
own decision-making, and staff A1 felt that a wide variety of other
issues should be dealt with on this basis also. Unlike other members
of staff, he was therefore in favour of much greater staff power than
was advocated by his residents, and some implications of this fact
will be discussed in Chapter 9.

## Matters Arising - Some Illustrations

Although there is an expectation of some degree of resident involvement in decision-making in all small therapeutically-oriented
hostels for alcoholics, the extent of this 'democracy' varies a great
deal from house to house and staff retain important elements of decision-making even in the most democratic establishments, such as
House G in the survey. At Houses A and B, where there was a higher
than average expectation of resident involvement, but which were nonetheless noticeably less democratic than House G, there was much room
for disagreement about the scope of resident and staff involvement and
many issues had to be individually negotiated. In many such instances
the reality is highly complex and may not correspond with preconceived
or stated notions.

Information on matters that arose and which tested the limits of
staff and resident power was obtained from a variety of sources
throughout the study at Houses A and B. Regular interviews with
residents constituted a major source of information. Interviews with
staff members in charge, held on alternate weeks, were another major
source. Other non-residents who were regularly involved, such as the
regular weekly visitor to House A and the project director at House B,
were also interviewed monthly. The cooks of the two houses were also
interviewed every 2 weeks, and other non-resident visitors such as
project social workers at House B were interviewed less often. In
addition, the research worker made observations during her regular
visits to the houses and subsequently dictated notes of these observations.

The following lists illustrate the range and variety of issues
which arose. The same, or similar, matters frequently recurred again,
often more than once:

House A During Staff A1's Time

How to react to a long-term resident who was now causing friction
in the resident group.
How to respond following the relapse and departure of a resident
who had been a central figure in the group.
Whether a re-application should be considered from a resident
recently discharged drinking.
How to cope with tension that had arisen between some of the
longer-term and some of the shorter-term residents.
Whether to allow the presence in group meetings of students on
placements at the house.
What arrangements should be made whilst major structural repairs
were carried out to the house.

House A During Staff A2's Time

Whether to extend the selection criteria to include women.
Whether to introduce a new selection system involving a 3-week
'probationary period'.
Whether to take any action following the staff member expressing
his dissatisfaction with the lack of a house 'program'.
Whether to support the idea of a joint house meeting with residents of House B.

How the residents should respond to the staff member being away a lot, on leave and helping out at another house.

## House B During Staff B1's Time

How a new cook should be selected.
Whether residents should contribute towards the buying of a new washing machine.
Deciding whose responsibility it is to deal with 'difficult' residents.
How to help overcome the problems that some longer-term residents have over leaving the house.
Who should answer the door to ex-residents or friends who have been drinking.
Whether staff should spend more time at the house.
Whether residents who do the cook's work when she is away sick or on holiday should be paid.
Whether, as the staff member supposed, cliques were developing in the house, and if so what should be done about it.
Whether enough food of the right sort was being ordered.
Whether it was right for a member of staff to have interviewed, in the house, an ex-resident who had been drinking.
Whether one resident should have special responsibility for handling visitors to the house.
Whether the referral procedure should be changed.
Whether residents should elect a representative to the project's management committee.
Whether, as several residents were demanding, each resident should have a key to his own room.
What the implications were of one of the current residents becoming employed on the staff of the project.

## House B During Staff B2's Time

The advisability of allowing ex-residents who had relapsed to stay at an alternative project house.
How to react to any ex-resident who was returning to the house rather more regularly than many thought correct.
How residents could make better use of their holiday times.
How to respond to the proposed raising of the house rents.
Whether the house meeting was primarily concerned with domestic house matters or with 'therapeutic' issues.
How much decision-making power residents had in the selection of new residents.
Whether residents should pay extra each week to have a colour television set.
Whether the leaving of a longer-term resident who had been group chairman would affect the house.
Whether residents should take part in the selection of new house staff, and if so how.
Whether the house should re-admit an ex-resident who had found living alone difficult despite remaining 'sober'.

Of these issues, which range from the purchase of a new washing-machine to the appointment of new staff, some required a simple Yes or No decision, others required a much more complex resolution, and some scarcely required a 'decision' at all. Two sets of issues, and their attempted resolution, will be described in greater detail. One occurred at House A and one at House B. The choice of these 2 particular matters is of course arbitrary to some extent, but they are illustrative of the complexity of decision-making and of the uncertainty over the limits of resident and staff responsibility, and were fairly typical of the way in which issues were discussed and resolved at the 2 houses. They were also chosen as matters that were sufficiently well-documented in interview and observation notes.

Whether a re-application should be considered from a resident recently discharged drinking (House A During Staff A1's Time).

The recently discharged resident (Andrew C) had been in House A for 4 months before being discharged for drinking. During his stay he had become one of the central figures in the resident group, not only because he was well-liked by staff and residents, but also on account of his hard work and success as editor of the house magazine. Such was his success that the staff member (staff A1 - referred to here as Colin S) had begun negotiations with the management body for the house magazine to have further financial support to allow for a national circulation. The magazine brought the house considerable prestige amongst local alcoholism agencies and this in turn reflected on Andrew C. However, the magazine apart, Andrew spoke little about his personal problems in group meetings and it seemed that he had few close friends in the house.

Later Andrew C started drinking secretly. After the event, other residents stated that they had suspected that something was wrong, but nothing was made public despite various rumours. Colin was unaware of Andrew's drinking. Finally Andrew disappeared for 2 nights before returning, clearly drunk, at midnight on the 3rd night. The residents permitted him to stay in the house that night because of the bad weather and his condition. He continued to visit the house over the course of the next 2 days. During this time he slept elsewhere and Colin S arranged for his admission to an alcoholism treatment unit in a psychiatric hospital. He was finally escorted to the hospital by a small party of house residents.

Two months later Andrew, encouraged by a resident who had been visiting him in hospital, re-applied to come back into the house. Colin S had also been visiting him there. Colin conveyed to the group the message that Andrew wished to come back because, although he (Andrew) felt that the group meetings had been of little real value to him, he valued the other residents' support. Colin had already arranged with Andrew that he might come to the next group meeting to discuss his possible re-admission, and he put this proposal to the group. Colin was undoubtedly keen that Andrew be re-admitted. His relationship with Andrew had been closer than with most of the other residents and he had strongly encouraged his magazine activities. He described their relationship as, "...quite a close working relationship". He also felt that he had come to know about Andrew's own problems and felt that returning to the house could be of great benefit to him.

With the exception of Andrew's hospital visitor (Norman B) the residents felt rather differently. In particular the group leader

and some of the more dominant residents (see Chapter 9 for a descripti
of the make-up of the resident group at this time) felt depressed and
hurt by the manner of Andrew's departure.  They had held him in high
esteem, had been shaken by his leaving, and they told Colin they were
not prepared to see Andrew or to consider him for re-admission.  Colin
recounted feeling, "Quite angry about it", and being "Strongly irritated", after the group meeting at which the issue was discussed.  The
issue was not reconsidered thereafter, and Andrew withdrew his request
for re-admission on hearing of the residents' response.

Residents and staff were clearly involved in a fine balance of
power.  The tradition of the house was strong enough to dictate that
Andrew had to leave the community following his drunken appearance at
the house and no 'decision' was involved.  However, to let Andrew stay
the night was by no means automatic and the remaining residents took
this decision upon themselves.  The group leader played a major part.
Thereafter, the decision to allow Andrew to visit the house for the
next few days appears to have been a joint staff and resident decision
fairly unanimously agreed to.  On the other hand, to back Andrew's re-
entry to the house was a staff and minority resident move and opinions
were very much divided.  Quite apart from the issue of re-admission,
there was discussion in a group meeting about whether some money shoul
be taken from the small group fund to buy Andrew some tobacco whilst h
was in hospital.  Two residents were in favour and 2 were particularly
against.  Their argument was that such a gesture should be held out to
all if it was to be made for one, and that Andrew's secrecy about his
drinking, his failure to 'open up' in group meetings, and their suspicion that he had walked off with magazine funds, scarcely qualified
him for special treatment.  When it came to voting (Colin S like every
one else had only 1 vote) the majority were against this suggestion,
and against considering Andrew C for re-admission.  The will of the
majority of residents was directly contrary to the will of the staff
member in this instance and the former imposed the final decision.

There was perhaps greater clarity about the division of responsibility for turning decisions into action.  It was, for example, Colin's
responsibility to refer Andrew to hospital, and the residents responsibility to let him in when he came back drunk, and during the next fe
days when he visited the house.  It was their responsibility, finally,
to accompany him to hospital.

How a new cook should be selected and, later, whether enough food of
the right sort was being ordered (House B During Staff B1's Time)

The background to the second of this pair of issues was the appointment of a new cook to House B 4 months earlier.  The previous cook
Pauline S, had been very popular with residents and, as the only femal
member of the community, had played a major role which seemed on occasions to be one almost of unofficial 'social worker'.

It did seem, however, that there had been a competitive element in
the relationship between Pauline and the staff member in charge (staff
B1 - referred to here as Robert S).  Residents would frequently ask her
advice and not infrequently would return to see her rather than anyone
else after they had left.  Robert S felt that this was improper and
expressed the view that she had been allowed too major a position in
the house in the past, before his own arrival.  It was noted that ther
was no occasion set aside on a regular basis for Robert and Pauline to
get together.

The residents had been particularly concerned that the new cook should be an adequate replacement and, in particular, that she should have no objections to the informal 'comings and goings' around the kitchen which had been so much a part of house routine. On account of this anxiety some residents put forward the idea that they should screen applicants for the job. Robert recounted that this attempt at greater resident involvement had been rejected on practical grounds, and also on the grounds that the cook was there to cook a meal only and hence, "It was no business of theirs whether she was their type of person or not".

A compromise was agreed in the house meeting; namely that the selection of the one most likely applicant should be the responsibility of staff but that this chosen person should then visit the house one evening and meet the residents informally before being appointed. Advertizing, interviewing applicants and making a choice of the most likely applicant were therefore staff responsibilities. In the event, residents reported to staff that they approved of the latter's choice, and with this feedback from residents staff took responsibility for making the appointment.

At the time the second issue arose, some months later, there had been growing dissatisfaction amongst the residents over what they saw as a decrease in the amount of food they were served. In particular, some residents were upset that chops rather than the traditional joint of meat had been left out for them one weekend. Accordingly, residents brought up the need to review the ordering of food at the next house meeting. Robert later told the research worker that residents had referred the matter to him in the mistaken belief that he, rather than the cook, controlled the ordering of food. Whilst it was his job to liaise with the cook, it was only his responsibility to order food if she was away.

Discussion at the house meeting centred around the position of the new cook (Joan S) as an integral part of the house, but as someone without the right to participate in the house meeting. The meeting took a decision to invite Joan S to future meetings. Ambivalence about her status as a full member of the community was enshrined in the decision to invite her only to the 1st ½ hour of each meeting to enable domestic matters which particularly concerned her to be discussed then. Robert was clearly unhappy about this decision and because there was an 'absence of concensus' the matter was passed over for further discussion at the next house meeting.

Joan told the research worker that she had been aware of the dissatisfaction about food amongst residents for a while. She had tried to meet complaints by altering orders, for example by making a different choice of fruit. However in her eyes the quantity of food ordered was not her responsibility and she claimed that she had been told by Robert to cut down on the ordering. As she put it, "I'm employed here". Her impression was that this had happened a number of times, that residents had put the matter to the house meeting, but that they had had no reply from the staff. Following further discussions in the house meeting, Joan was invited to come to meetings and did so. However the practice was discontinued within a matter of weeks, the general concensus being that, "There was nothing to discuss". Later on, after a number of misunderstandings between them, it was decided that Robert and Joan should have a regular ½ hour meeting once a month but again the practice was speedily discontinued.

Unlike the issue of re-application at House A, these matters had ne very obvious settlement. They ceased to be topics for debate in the house and the resident complaint did not recur during the period of the study in any very obvious form. It seems likely that while it lasted the issue had the effect of making the views of some residents known to staff, thereby imposing some constraints on the freedom of staff to make their own decisions about the ordering of supplies. This aside, the limitations of resident involvement in decision-making in this domestic area seemed clear. What seemed equally apparent was the potentia for misunderstanding and confusion of responsibilities in an area which despite its apparent triviality had undoubted capacity for causing trouble. For example, the cook and staff member received different messages about residents' feelings on the matter. It is also evident that such an issue was part of a number of much wider issues such as the role of the cook and the nature of the relationship between her and the staff member in charge.

## SUMMARY

### Similarities Between Houses A and B

Work

1. Outside employment was considered an integral part of everyday routine and neither house arranged a program of events which would interfere with daytime weekday work. In practice the proportion of residents in work varied from nearly all to a small minority. All residents were required to pay a fixed rent comparable to rents paid for lodgings elsewhere.

House Meetings

2. A single regular weekly evening meeting was held at each house. It was an important event, compulsory at one house and in effect compulsory at the other due to strong group pressure to attend.

Staff-Resident Contact

3. Staff reported spending an average of 40 hours a week at the house (nearer 30 at House B due to the staff member's responsibility for another hostel). These hours were put in almost entirely during weekday daytime hours. Staff rarely visited the house at weekends.

4. There were large differences between staff members in the amounts of time they reported being in contact with residents. Averages ranged from $3\frac{1}{2}$ hours a week reported by a staff member at House A, to 32 hours a week reported by one staff member at House B. At each house one staf member reported very much more time in contact with residents than the other. Of the 2 members of staff reporting relatively little contact (1 at each house), one had little but regular contact with all residents, whilst the other had uneven contact with residents with the result that some residents went without staff contact for 2 weeks or more at a time.

5. All 4 members of staff reported having more informal than private personal contact with residents, and in the case of the staff member reporting most contact with his residents, 5 times as much informal

as private-personal contact was reported.

## The Control of Drinking

6. Drinking was a serious matter for which the penalty could be discharge. However there was rarely complete consensus about how instances of drinking should be dealt with. Residents' opinions varied from those who felt that no action should follow to those who felt that a resident should be asked to leave. There was similarly strong feeling, coupled with lack of complete consensus, about residents covering up for others who might be drinking. Residents were often stricter in their views about drinking-related matters than were staff.

## The Control of Other Conduct

7. Residents' views were less harsh, and often less strict than those of staff, over such issues as residents failing to do domestic tasks, staying out late without informing others, being over-anxious or touchy and irritable with other residents, heavy gambling and declarations of lack of interest in others' problems. Although these matters were considered less important than drinking, there was again lack of consensus over how they should be handled.

## Resident Responsibility

8. The majority of residents at both houses thought that action over all these matters, if it was to be taken at all, should be taken by residents (with or without staff). The majority of residents were in favour of real resident involvement and not just consultation with residents followed by staff decision. With the possible exception of one of the members of staff at House A, staff shared this philosophy.
9. In practice a range of issues arose in the course of everyday management, ranging from the relatively trivial such as whether to purchase a new washing machine, to the relatively important such as the appointment of a new staff member. The limits of resident responsibility for making decisions on these matters were rarely clear and tended to be worked out afresh on each occasion.

Differences Between Houses A and B

## Work

1. Although unemployment was not much higher for House B residents, their opportunities were more limited and they were rarely able to obtain more than semi-skilled employment.

## House Meetings

2. At House A the regular weekly meeting was known as a 'Group therapy and business' meeting, whilst that at House B was known simply as a 'House meeting'. Thus at House A there was a greater expectation of self-disclosure, and meetings at House A were regularly, and measurably, more emotional. Staff at House A were also more emotional than at House B but differences were less marked than for residents (staff were consistently less emotional than residents at both houses). Staff at House A often took a back seat in discussion, whilst staff spoke

relatively much more at House B. A staff member was always the most voluminous speaker at House B meetings.

## The Control of Resident Conduct

3. Although residents were equally strict about drinking at the 2 houses, residents at House A were stricter over other conduct issues. For example, at least ½ House A residents thought that action should be taken over heavy gambling, whilst a minority (and at one time none at all) of residents at House B thought that action should be taken. A majority of House A residents, but only a minority at House B, took a harsh view of a resident declaring a lack of interest in others' problems. One of the results of this difference between the Houses was that staff at House B took a consistently stricter view than most residents over most of these matters.

## Resident Responsibility

4. At House B a larger minority of residents than at House A were in favour of staff taking decisions about sanctions for behaviour. This was particularly the case for 'personal-social' issues (a resident being over-anxious or touchy and irritable with others). Staff at House B were therefore almost always equally, if not more in favour of 'democracy' than most residents, whilst the opposite was the case for 1 of the 2 staff members at House A.

# Chapter 8

# Stability and Atmosphere and the Contribution of Individuals

...the main difficulty in developing the group is that of
creating a nucleus of residents who have been in the hostel
long enough to be settled, and who are keen to use the program...
The group atmosphere has fluctuated enormously, and residents'
allegiance has sometimes been completely non-existent.  In
particular, there has been a very destructive period in the
house, when a sub-group challenged the aims of the program...
(from an unpublished account of experience at a hostel for
adult ex-offenders, Jenkins and Harvey, 1974, p.22).

The previous 2 chapters have documented details of referral and
selection procedures,  characteristics of the resident intake population, and details of the houses' programs.  For the most part these
data have been presented and discussed as if the houses presented a
static, unchanging, picture.  In fact nothing could be further from the
truth.  If the present authors were convinced of only one thing during
the course of this research, it was the need to provide a more dynamic,
on-going, description of small hostels in order to give anything like an
adequate account of them.  Informal observations suggest that small
hostels are subject to decided 'ups and downs' reminiscent of the
'oscillations' which Rapoport (1956, 1960) considered endemic to all
sociotherapeutic institutions.  The particular intention of the first
part of this chapter is to document oscillations at Houses A and B in
terms of a variety of criteria, some relatively tangible such as turnover rate, others more subjective such as staff and resident regard for
one another.
The history of a given period at a house cannot be written without
emphasizing the roles played by certain key figures, or occasionally by
pointing to the failure of any one existing member to occupy a particular
role, the occupancy of which might have made a significant difference to
the course of events.  It is a psychological truism that one person's
contribution is the product of some interaction between relatively fixed
aspects of his behaviour (his personality) and the setting in which the
contribution is made.  It is thus impossible to know, at least from the
data available to us, to what extent one resident's or staff member's
behaviour in the hostel reflected his personality, or to what extent his
behaviour would be changed at a different house or in a quite different
environment.  What is a fact however, and what can therefore be studied,
is the existence of reputations which different members of a hostel community acquire with other members during the course of their stay.  It is
this which forms the subject matter of later sections of this chapter.

Small hostels for alcoholics constitute one, albeit rather special type of small group, and the body of research which exists on the operation of small groups (e.g. Douglas, 1970; Hare, 1962) suggests the regular emergence of individuals who have acquired particular reputations. It is for example only to be expected that certain individuals will come to acquire, in small hostels as in other small groups, reputations as 'leaders', that still others will acquire reputations as 'isolates', and yet others as 'deviants'.

It is clear too, from previous chapters, that staff members play a very central part in small hostels and that they reflect a variety of approaches, no doubt determined in part by differences in both temperament and training. The reputations which they acquire with other members of hostel communities are therefore of special interest. Also investigated in this chapter are the opinions which staff hold of different residents. How these compare with residents' reputations with their own peers may provide important clues to the degree of congruence or lack of it, between staff and resident values.

## THE HOSTEL ENVIRONMENT

### Stability of the Resident Group

A Decade in Perspective

Figures 13 and 14 show data, for Houses A and B respectively, for the whole of the periods during which the 2 houses have existed up to the time the present data were analyzed. The study is included towards the end of these 10 and 8 year periods, respectively. Three factors are shown in these figures:

1.  The number of residents living in the house at the end of each calendar month (the solid line).
2.  The total number of months in residence accumulated by all these residents up to that month (total 'accumulated months') – for example, if 6 men were in residence, 3 of whom had been at the hostel for 2 months, 2 for 4 months and 1 for 8 months, the total 'accumulated months' would be (3x2) + (2x4) + (1x8) = 22 (shown by the broken line).
3.  The number of residents leaving the house during that month (shown in numerals).

Whilst number of residents is probably a relatively superficial characteristic, numbers leaving shows variation in turnover, and total 'accumulated months' provides one indication of the decline and fall of relatively stable resident groups containing at least a proportion of members with relatively long periods of stay. The graphs have been plotted in such a way that where the 2 lines cross, current residents have an average length of stay of 6 months.

Oscillations are apparent in the data from both houses. At House A, after an unsteady start during which time the abstinence ethic became established, there was relatively little resident turnover for more than 2 years. Figure 13 suggests that the resident group built up during this time to a period of unrivalled stability between the summer of the 4th year and the spring of the 5th year. The same stability was not achieved at any time in the subsequent 6 years, and on 3 occasions, at roughly 2-year intervals, turnover increased and stability declined markedly. The most serious of these declines occurred during the study

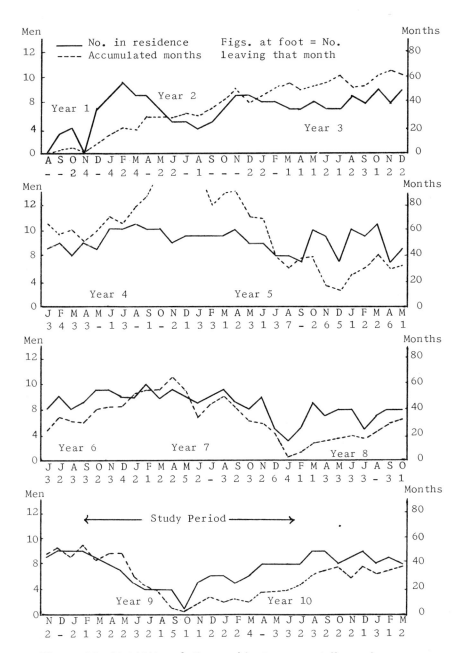

Figure 13: Stability of the resident group at House A over
10 years.

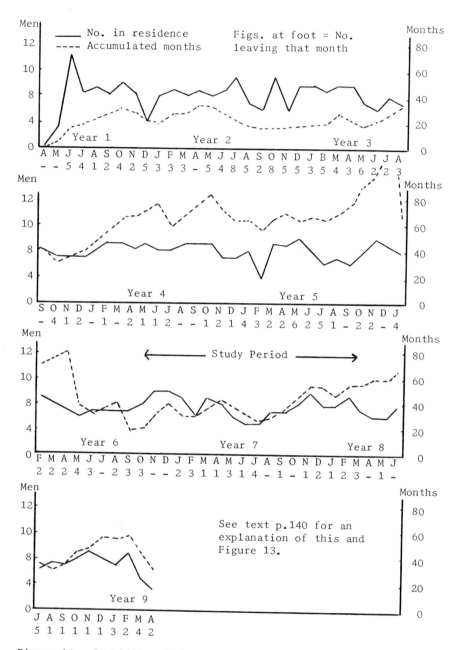

Figure 14: Stability of the resident group at House B over 9 years

period itself, reaching its nadir in the October of the 9th year when a single resident remained in the house. Each low point appears to have been the culmination of 9 to 10 months of steady decline, and in each case the subsequent accumulation of resident experience of the house seems to have been more gradual, and has scarcely been achieved after 12 months, when the next decline has set in.

House B also appears to have taken as long as 3 years to establish a stable resident group. Almost the whole of the first 2 years were characterized by extremely high resident turnover and the failure to build up a really stable group. Subsequently, around the middle of the 3rd year, resident turnover declined, a stable resident group was consolidated over a period of approximately 12 months, and was then maintained for fully 2 years before declining. As at House A, this stability has scarcely been achieved in the subsequent years. Policy on selection and other matters has undoubtedly been an influence. For example, in recent years men with greatest past experience of sobriety have tended to be directed to the project's House G, thus depleting House B of part of its most hopeful input. Nonetheless there have not been the dramatic declines that have characterized the recent history of House A, but nor has there been the establishment and maintenance of the type of stable group that characterized both houses in earlier times.

The Study Period in Detail

Figures 13 and 14 make it possible to see the time of the study in the more complete context of the history of each house over a longer period of time. The study caught House A at a period of steady decline culminating in what appears to have been the most serious crisis in its history, followed by the beginnings of a slow revival. It is less easy to characterize this time at House B. The early months of the study showed a moderately stable resident group, and the final 12 months showed a fairly steady increase in 'accumulated months' which was not maintained but declined sharply in the months following the end of the study.

Table 12 shows turnover figures for the study months at Houses A and B, respectively, in greater detail (as explained in Chapter 5, the study was divided into 18 4-week 'months' rather than into calendar months). Some of the constituents of oscillations in house stability can be discerned. At the beginning of the study both houses appear to have been relatively stable with sizeable groups of residents. Most of the residents were 'established' in the sense that they were present throughout the first month of the study, and therefore provided continuity from one month to the next. At House B this 'establishment', or continuity, was maintained throughout the study with the exception of a single 4-week period (month 7). At that time the comings-and-goings exceeded the establishment in size and, as Table 12 shows, stability in terms of total accumulated months reached its lowest ebb at around that time. However this trend was quickly reversed. Only a single short-stay resident left in the following 4 weeks, and no one left in the 4 weeks following that. During the rest of the study the leaving of some residents was always matched by the coming of others. Month 16 was particularly stable with no changes in the resident group over the 4 weeks.

The pattern at House A was quite different. For the first 9 months of the study leavings were not matched by an equal number of admissions,

Table 12:   Stability of the resident groups at Houses A and B
            over the 18 months of the study.

| | HOUSE A | | | | | HOUSE B | | | | |
| | Residents in Category | | | | | Residents in Category | | | | |
| Mth. | A | B | C | D | Tot. | A | B | C | D | Tot. |
|---|---|---|---|---|---|---|---|---|---|---|
| 1 | 9 | 1 | 1 | – | 11 | 6 | – | 3 | – | 9 |
| 2 | 7 | 1 | 3 | 1 | 12 | 6 | 2 | – | 1 | 9 |
| 3 | 7 | 1 | 1 | – | 9 | 7 | 1 | 1 | – | 9 |
| 4 | 6 | 1 | 2 | – | 9 | 5 | 1 | 3 | – | 9 |
| 5 | 4 | 2 | 3 | – | 9 | 5 | – | 1 | – | 6 |
| 6 | 4 | – | 2 | – | 6 | 5 | 1 | – | – | 6 |
| 7 | 3 | 1 | 1 | – | 5 | 3 | 3 | 3 | 1 | 10 |
| 8 | 2 | 1 | 2 | 1 | 6 | 6 | – | – | 1 | 7 |
| 9 | 1 | – | 2 | 1 | 4 | 6 | 1 | – | – | 7 |
| 10 | 1 | 3 | – | – | 4 | 7 | 1 | – | 1 | 9 |
| 11 | 2 | 3 | 2 | 1 | 8 | 7 | 1 | 1 | – | 9 |
| 12 | 2 | – | 3 | – | 5 | 7 | 1 | 2 | – | 10 |
| 13 | 1 | 3 | 1 | 1 | 6 | 6 | 3 | 1 | – | 10 |
| 14 | 3 | 4 | 1 | – | 8 | 6 | 1 | 3 | – | 10 |
| 15 | 4 | 2 | 3 | – | 9 | 6 | – | 1 | 1 | 8 |
| 16 | 6 | 2 | – | – | 8 | 6 | – | – | – | 6 |
| 17 | 6 | 1 | 2 | 1 | 10 | 5 | – | 1 | – | 6 |
| 18 | 5 | 2 | 2 | 1 | 10 | 5 | 3 | – | – | 8 |

A – Present at beginning and end of month; B – Arrived during
month and remained; C – Present at beginning but left during
month; D – Arrived and left during month.

and the resident group declined in size. What is even more apparent
from Table 12 is that the 'establishment' (those present at the beginning and end of a month) declined dramatically, both in overall
size and as a proportion of the total number of residents present in
the house at any time during the month. As these months passed the
comings-and-goings of new and old residents began to be a more prom-
inant feature of the house than the continuity provided by established
residents. From month 10 onwards the process was reversed, with gains
of new residents on the whole exceeding losses of old residents.

One way of making order out of the data presented in Figures 13 and
14 and Table 12 is to attempt some sort of categorization of the state
of stability of a house at any given time. The following represents
one such attempt although it is recognized that any such system of
classification is bound to be arbitrary to some extent:

1.  High level of stability: Characterized by a fairly full house, a
    relatively low turnover of residents, and a large total of
    'accumulated months' (as at House A between September of the 4th
    year and April of the 5th year, and at House B between May of the
    4th year and April of the 6th year). Although the data from House
    B show that such a state can be maintained for as much as 2 years,
    such a state seems bound to be in permanent danger of declining to
    a lower level of stability.

2.  Moderate stability: Characterized by intermediate levels of turn-
    over and 'accumulated months' which are maintained for at least 3
    to 6 months (as at both houses at the end of year 8 and the beg-
    inning of year 9). Such a state seems to be a common experience
    for houses of this size and type, and the future uncertainty which
    accompanies such a state epitomizes the uncertainty that seems to
    continually surround the question of stability.

3.  Increasing stability: Characterized by low or decreasing resident
    turnover, and increasing 'accumulated months' (as at House A during
    almost the whole of the 6th, 8th and 10th years; and at House B
    throughout the 3rd and 4th years). There are also relatively short
    periods of improving stability which are relatively short-lived.
    This was the case, for example, at House B just prior to the study
    and just after the study had finished.

4.  Declining stability: Characterized by increasing turnover, part-
    icularly the loss of 'established' residents, and a consequent
    decline in stability as indicated by total 'accumulated months'
    (as at House A between April of the 7th year and January of the
    8th year; and at House B between December of the 5th year and Sep-
    tember of the 6th year). While there are several examples, at both
    houses, of fairly dramatic and long declines often culminating in
    breakdown, there are also examples of short declines which do not
    result in a long-term shift to a markedly lower level of stability.
    This was true, for example, between months 3 and 6 of the study at
    House B.

5.  Breakdown in stability: Characterized by high resident turnover
    and low 'accumulated months', and sometimes by virtual emptying of
    the house (as at House A in December of the 5th year, January of
    the 8th year and October of the 9th year; and at House B in No-
    vember of the 2nd year). Given the uncertainty over the life of
    these 'experimental' projects backed by non-statutory organizations,
    it is not surprising to find that at these times there is usually
    some discussion of the possibility that the hostel might close
    permanently. This has not happened at House A or B to date, and so
    long as the house remains open things can only improve once a break-
    down point is reached. It does however appear that the community
    rebuilds relatively slowly when breakdown occurs.

### Resident and Staff Perceptions

    The following 4 variables were employed as measures of subjectively
perceived elements of oscillations in hostel atmosphere or climate:

(i)   Residents' assessment of atmosphere. At each of their monthly
    interviews with the research worker (the 1st approximately 2 weeks
    after admission) each resident was asked to discuss his current
    feelings of satisfaction or dissatisfaction with the house he was
    living in. The discussion was initiated by the research worker
    asking, "What is it like for you being at ------ House at the
    moment?" Replies were recorded in narrative form and the research
    worker immediately coded each resident's response, on a 5-point
    scale, taking into account both the content and tone of the res-
    ponse. (The scale ranged from +2, representing a very positive
    response, to -2, representing a very negative response). Scores of
    all residents interviewed at any one house during a single 4-week

period were averaged, and these averages were taken to represent the residents' assessment of atmosphere for that house for the month. At House A averages ranged from +1.40 for month 18 to -1.00 for month 10. At House B averages ranged from +1.75 for month 7 to +0.20 for months 16 and 17. (Further details of the method of questioning are given in Appendix C).

(ii)   Residents' assessment of staff. At the same interviews residents were asked 10 standard questions regarding their perceptions of the staff member in charge of the house at the time. Examples of these questions are, 'Is sufficiently sensitive and understanding?', 'Treats me like a child?', and 'Is always there when you need him?' Residents were required to reply, 'yes', 'uncertain' or 'no'. Favourable responses (a maximum of 10,'uncertain' responses being treated as unfavourable),were added for each individual resident, and scores of all residents interviewed during any one month at a house were averaged to produce a 'residents' assessment of staff' score for that house for the month. At House A average scores varied from 9.60 for the 18th month to 3.00 for month 10. At House B average scores ranged from 9.29 for month 4 to 4.50 for the 14th month. (The complete list of items which are taken from the scale published by Ellsworth, 1965, is shown in Table 15) later in the chapter.

(iii)   Staff assessment of atmosphere. At each 2-weekly interview with the research worker, the staff member in charge of a house was asked to discuss his perception of the current atmosphere. The discussion was initiated by the research worker asking, "What has the atmosphere been like in the last 2 weeks?" The discussion was tape-recorded and subsequently transcribed. The transcriptions were then content analyzed for favourable and unfavourable statements, and the number of the latter subtracted from the number of the former. The average of 2 scores (derived from 2 separate interviews, 2 weeks apart) was the 'staff assessment of atmosphere' score for that house for the month. At House A this score varied from +3.5 in the 1st month to -7.0 in the 15th, and at House B from +3.5 in the 13th month to -3.0 in the 3rd. (Some examples of staff responses are provided later in this chapter).

(iv)   Staff assessment of residents. During the same interviews staff members were asked to record their current perceptions of each resident in the house. Transcribed passages relating to each resident were subsequently rated on a 100-point scale: 100 represented a completely and extremely favourable comment; 0 represented a totally and extremely unfavourable comment. Inter-rater reliability was tested using 3 independent raters, both before the study started, and towards the end. On both occasions reliability was found to be very high. All staff assessments of residents made at any one house during a 4-week period were averaged to produce a 'staff assessment of residents' score for that house for that period. At House A average scores varied from 68.1 in the 16th month to 27.5 in the 10th and at House B averages ranged from 77.3 in the 9th month to 36.1 in the 2nd. (Examples of staff responses and their coding, and details of the reliability tests, are given in Appendix A).

Table 13 shows the correlations among these 4-monthly scores across the 18 months of the study for Houses A and B separately. Also shown

are correlations with 'accumulated months' (a variable described
earlier in this chapter) and with 'total staff time in contact with
residents' (a very variable quantity, described in Chapter 7). Table
14 shows the averages of all 6 variables for each of the 4 separate
staff 'regimes' at the 2 houses. Table 14 also indicates when differences between average scores for the 2 'regimes' at any one house are
statistically significant.

## Inter-Relatedness of Perceptual Variables

Inspection of these 2 tables reveals a number of things. Firstly
there is quite a strong relationship, at both houses, between the 2
resident perception measures. During periods when residents on the
whole said favourable things about the house atmosphere, they also said
more favourable things about the staff member in charge. Large differences between the 2 staff regimes at each house (Table 14) are probably the major contributors to these relationships. On the whole,
residents at House A had relatively unfavourable things to say about
the atmosphere, and about the staff member in charge under staff A1's
'regime', and relatively favourable things to say about both under
staff A2's 'regime'. The position was reversed at House B, residents
having relatively favourable things to say both about atmosphere and
staff B1 during months 1-11, and relatively unfavourable things to say
during the last 6 months under staff B2.

Table 13: Inter-correlations of staff and resident perceptual variables,
'accumulated resident-months' and staff-resident contact at
Houses A and B (N = 18 4-week 'months' in all cases. Correlations are Spearman's rank-order. Those for House A are
shown above the diagonal and those for House B below it.
Only those statistically significant at least at the 0.05
level are shown).

|   |   | 1 | 2 | 3 | 4 | 5 | 6 |
|---|---|---|---|---|---|---|---|
| 1 | Residents' assessment of atmosphere | | 0.66 | | | | 0.59 |
| 2 | Residents' assessment of staff | 0.67 | | 0.42 | | | 0.71 |
| 3 | Staff assessment of atmosphere | | | | | | |
| 4 | Staff assessment of residents | 0.75 | 0.59 | | | | |
| 5 | Total 'accumulated months' | -0.64 | -0.72 | | -0.48 | | |
| 6 | Total staff time in contact with residents | 0.53 | 0.62 | | 0.53 | -0.62 | |

The 2nd noticeable feature of these results concerns the overall absence of systematic relationships involving <u>staff</u> perception measures. At neither house was there any relationship between what the staff member had to say about the atmosphere and what he had to say on average about residents, and on the whole there was little or no relationship between what staff said and what residents said. The exception to this last statement involved 'staff assessment of residents' at House B. The latter variable was related to residents' opinions of atmosphere and staff, but principally on account of the relatively unfavourable remarks which staff B2 made about residents.

## Stability and Perceptual Variables

The question then arises of whether staff or resident perceptions are related to the stability of the house as indicated by 'accumulated months'. It might well be expected that stability and favourability of perceptions would go hand in hand. The results do not support this hypothesis. At House A there were no significant relationships between 'accumulated months' and any of the perceptual measures; and at House B correlations with 3 perceptual measures were negative, opposite to predictions. In other words, residents' and staff perceptions tended to be favourable when stability was low, and vice versa. Table 14

Table 14: Average values for each of 4 staff and resident perceptual variables, total 'accumulated resident-months' and staff-resident contact, for each of 4 staff regimes at Houses A and B.

|  |  | HOUSE A | | HOUSE B | |
|---|---|---|---|---|---|
|  |  | STAFF A1 (Months 1-11) | STAFF A2 (Months 13-18) | STAFF B1 (Months 1-11) | STAFF B2 (Months 13-18) |
| 1 | Residents' assessment of atmosphere | 0.27 | 1.21* | 1.32* | 0.47 |
| 2 | Residents' assessment of staff | 5.85 | 8.08* | 8.47* | 6.62 |
| 3 | Staff assessment of atmosphere | -0.04 | 0.16 | 0.75 | 1.83 |
| 4 | Staff assessment of residents | 49.8 | 49.6 | 60.3* | 46.7 |
| 5 | Total 'accumulated months' | 19.8 | 6.7 | 29.1 | 46.2* |
| 6 | Total staff time in contact with residents | 3.4 | 13.5* | 28.6* | 4.3 |

* Statistically significantly greater than corresponding average for the other staff regime at the same house.

suggests the reason for this anomalous finding. Stability ('accumulated months') increased towards the end of the study and reached its highest level in the last few months (although as Figure 14 shows, stability declined sharply just after the end of the study). It was during the same latter months of the study that resident perceptions, and staff perception of residents, were at their lowest. The lack of correlation between stability and perceptual measures at House A may also be understood more clearly by a more detailed consideration of the way these variables were changing over the months. The first 6 months of the study were the best as far as stability was concerned at House A (although as Figure 13 and Table 12 show, stability was declining during this period and afterwards) but resident perceptions of atmosphere and staff were relatively unfavourable. In contrast, during the last months of the study, under a new staff member, stability was relatively low (but increasing) and resident perceptions were relatively favourable. Hence favourable perceptions may be more reflective of the direction of change of stability than of its current absolute level.

Staff-Resident Contact and Perceptual Variables

Although they had not been anticipated at the outset, there were quite strong relationships between the resident perceptual measures on the one hand, and 'total staff contact with residents' on the other hand. Again, major differences between the 2 staff regimes at each house appear to be responsible for these relationships. It has already been noted in Chapter 7 (and is shown in Table 14 again) that there were significant differences between the amounts of contact with residents reported by the 4 different staff members. Staff A1 and staff B2 reported spending much less time in contact with residents than did the other 2 staff members, and it was during the former 2 'regimes' that resident opinions of atmosphere and staff were most unfavourable.

This relationship between the 2 resident perceptual measures (themselves correlated) and the amount of staff-resident contact reported by the staff member, occurred at both houses, and appears to have been a consequence of the change of staff member. If these 3 variables are rank ordered and plotted month by month for the 2 houses separately, dramatic shifts of all 3 variables occur at the points when staff change (a shift to a higher level at House A and to a lower level at House B). However it is noticeable that residents had relatively favourable things to say about the 1st staff member at House A and the 2nd staff member at House B during their first few weeks as staff members, even though resident opinions of these staff members declined thereafter and settled at lower levels.

INDIVIDUAL PERSONALITIES

Staff Reputations; Residents' Views

The results of the residents' assessments of staff are shown in greater detail, item by item, in Table 15. A number of features of these results are of interest. First of all, at House A, staff A2 received fewer 'uncertain' or negative appraisals by residents than staff A1 on 9 out of 10 items (statistically significant in 7 instances). The largest differences in resident perceptions of these 2 members of staff concerned the item, 'Let's the men get to know him', and

Table 15:   Residents' views on staff members in charge at Houses A and B (Proportions of occasions on which each staff member received positive as opposed to 'uncertain' or negative, appraisals).

| Item | Direction of scoring | HOUSE A A1 | A2 | HOUSE B B1 | B2 |
|---|---|---|---|---|---|
| 1  Is sufficiently sensitive and understanding. | + | 63 | 80 | 83 | 59 |
| 2  Treats me like a child. | – | 71 | 75 | 99 | 74 |
| 3  Is always there when you need him. | + | 51 | 85 | 75 | 44 |
| 4  Says one thing and does another. | – | 68 | 85 | 74 | 53 |
| 5  Is open and honest with me. | + | 76 | 83 | 89 | 68 |
| 6  Has little insight into your problems. | – | 51 | 78 | 67 | 44 |
| 7  Is friendly and approachable. | + | 87 | 98 | 93 | 89 |
| 8  Is unpredictable. | – | 80 | 73 | 80 | 65 |
| 9  Lets the men get to know him. | + | 22 | 75 | 97 | 80 |
| 10  Is domineering. | – | 78 | 93 | 94 | 89 |

the item, 'Is always there when you need him'.  Only $\frac{1}{2}$ of the resident responses towards staff A1 indicated the feeling that this staff member was 'Always there when needed', and less than $\frac{1}{4}$ of resident responses indicated that residents thought he 'let the men get to know him'. The only item more favourable to staff A1 was the item, 'Is unpredictable', but the difference was not statistically significant.

At House B, staff B1 received fewer 'uncertain' or negative resident appraisals than did staff B2 on every one of the 10 items (all statistically significant).  The largest, and most statistically significant differences concerned the 2 items, 'Is always there when you need him' and 'Treats me like a child'.  For the 2nd of these items, 'Treats me like a child', the difference at House B was attributable to the unusually favourable position of staff B1 who, unlike all other 3 staff members involved, was scarcely ever marked down on this account.

Resident perceptions of the degree to which staff were 'Always there when needed' was, therefore, a major discriminator between staff regimes at both houses.  This is in keeping with staff accounts of the amount of time which they spent in actual contact with residents. Staff B1 in particular spent a very great deal of time with residents, by his own account, and most of this time was spent in informal contact.  Apart from this, staff A1 emerged as having a reputation (relatively, in comparison with all 3 other staff members) for not 'Letting the men get to know him', and for being 'Domineering'.  Staff A2 had a particular reputation for being consistent in what he said and what he did (item 4), for having 'Insight into residents' problems' and for being 'Friendly and approachable'.  Staff B1 had a reputation for not 'Treating residents like children' and for 'Letting the men get to know him', whilst staff B2 was relatively often described as 'Saying one thing and doing another' and 'Unpredictable'.

### Resident Reputations; Residents' Choices

A sociometric method, based on the experience of preliminary interviewing and observation, was used to investigate reputations that residents acquired with each other.  At each of their monthly interviews with the research worker (the first held approximately 2 weeks after arrival) each resident was asked to nominate 3 fellow residents (2, if the total number of current residents fell to 5 or 6, and 1 only if the number fell to 3 or 4) in accordance with each of the following 3 criteria which were chosen from a larger number after piloting:

Contribution. Other residents were to be nominated who, it was felt, 'Contributed most to the house, made it a good place to live in'.

Social. Residents to be nominated with whom the respondent felt he would like, 'To go out in the evening or at weekends'.

Understanding. Residents to be nominated who were felt to be 'The most understanding'.

The first 2 criteria were designed to capture the 'task' and 'interpersonal' dimensions of informal group organization. These 2 dimensions have been repeatedly identified in small group research, notably by Zelditch (1955). Early discussions with residents at Houses A and B, and pilot work, suggested the importance of the 3rd 'understanding' or 'sensitivity' dimension.

Leaders and Isolates

For each criterion, a sociometric diagram was prepared based upon all nominations made by members of one house during each 4-week period. These data were examined for indications of the existence of 'leaders' and 'isolates'. The operational definition of 'leader' was someone who was the most frequently chosen resident in the house, according to that criterion (contribution, social or understanding), for 2 or more consecutive 4-week periods (it was allowable that one or more other resident(s) be chosen equally often). The operational definition of an 'isolate' was complementary, namely someone who had the least number of nominations (almost always none) for at least 2 consecutive 4-week periods.

The numbers of leaders (contribution, social and understanding) at each house during the study, as well as the months during which they held these positions are shown in Table 16. Complementary information on isolates is given in Table 17.

At neither house did any man who stayed for less than 12 weeks acquire any sort of reputation either as a leader or an isolate. This fact is largely a consequence of the operational definition of 'reputation' which has been adopted here. To meet the '2 consecutive periods' criterion a resident who stayed for a shorter period would have to have made a strong impression almost immediately upon arrival. Of the 18 men who stayed long enough to acquire a reputation at House A, 9 acquired some sort of specialist leadership reputation (6 as contribution leaders, 5 as social leaders and 5 as understanding leaders), 7 acquired a reputation as some sort of isolate (4 as contribution isolates, 4 as social isolates, and 5 as understanding isolates), and 3 acquired no specialist reputation of either kind. Only one House A resident had both types of reputation (Sam N, who had a reputation as a contribution leader in months 11 and 12 after having been an isolate by one or more criteria for the previous 4 months). With this single exception, leaders at House A were never isolates, nor were isolates ever leaders.

At House B, 13 men stayed long enough to acquire a reputation and all of them did in fact acquire some sort of reputation at some time.

Table 16:   Occupants of leadership positions at Houses A and B (Months during which positions were occupied).

| | Contribution Leaders[a] | Social Leaders[a] | Understanding Leaders[a] | Great Leaders[b] |
|---|---|---|---|---|
| **HOUSE A** | | | | |
| Simon J | | 1-2 | | |
| Scott E | 2-4 | | 1-3 | 3 |
| Dick D | 2-6 | 6-8 | 4-8 | 6 |
| Daniel R | | 4-5 | | |
| Sam N | 11-12 | | | |
| Daniel K | 11-15 | | 13-14 | |
| Ian T | 12-13 | 11-13 | 11-13 | 12-13 |
| Sid S | | | | 12 |
| Paul U | 16-17 | | 16-18 | 16 |
| Stewart Y | | 17-18 | | |
| Patrick Z | | | | 18 |
| **HOUSE B** | | | | |
| Joe D | 1-2 | 2-5 | 1-2,4-5 | 2 |
| Keith E | | 1-2 | | 1 |
| Andy F | 3-4,7-8 | 6-7 | | 7 |
| Pat C | | 5-6 | | |
| Ross G | 6-8,15-18 | 5-16 | 5-18 | 7-8,10,15-16 |
| Ron M | | 8-10 | | |
| Pat R | 11-13 | | | |
| Dick P | | 16-18 | | |

a   The most frequently chosen by that criterion for 2 consecutive months.
b   The most frequently chosen by all 3 criteria for that one month.

However, the division between those who acquired leadership status and those who became isolates was not as clear cut as at House A.  Eight residents became leaders of one specialized sort or another (4 contribution leaders, 7 social leaders and 2 understanding leaders), but only 3 of these avoided any sort of isolate status.  A total of 10 House B residents became isolates (8 contribution isolates, 6 social isolates and 5 understanding isolates).  Two men were both 'contribution leaders' and 'contribution isolates' (at different times), and 2 men were social leaders and social isolates at different times.  The only simultaneous combination of leadership and isolate status which occurred was a combination of 'contribution isolate' status and 'social leader' status.  This combined role was held by 4 House B men for a total of 7 months.  This comtination never occurred at House A and this may be an indication of an important difference between the houses.

Tables 16 and 17 suggest further differences between the houses which are consistent with informal observations.  Firstly, there was the prominence at House B of a 'great leader' (i.e. Ross G who had a rep-

Table 17: Occupants of isolate positions at Houses A and B (Months during which positions were occupied).

| | Contribution Isolates[a] | Social Isolates[a] | Understanding Isolates[a] | Total Isolates[b] |
|---|---|---|---|---|
| HOUSE A | | | | |
| William H | 1-4 | 1-4 | 2-4 | 1-4 |
| Norman B | 1-2,4-5 | | 2-4 | |
| Jimmy Q | | 2-4 | | |
| Arthur L | | 5-7 | | |
| Sam N | 7-8 | 7-11 | 8-10 | 8,10 |
| Walter V | 16-17 | | 16-17 | 17 |
| Arnold W | | | 16-18 | |
| HOUSE B | | | | |
| Hughie A | 1-5,7-14 | 6-7,9-10, 12-17 | 1-6,8-18 | 1,3,9-10, 12-14,17 |
| Pat C | 3-5 | | | |
| Andy F | 5-6 | | | |
| Ron M | 8-10,17-18 | 14-17 | 14-17 | 17 |
| Jim N | 8-10 | | | |
| Mike T | 8-10 | | 8-10 | 10 |
| Kevin L | | 13-16 | 11-12 | |
| Reg S | | 12-13 | 12-13 | |
| Dick P | 13-17 | | | 15 |
| Pat R | 15-16 | 15-18 | | 15 |

a  The least frequently chosen by that criterion for 2 consecutive months.
b  The least frequently chosen by all 3 criteria for that one month.

utation for leadership by all 3 criteria) and a 'total isolate'(i.e. Hughie A, who was 'isolated' by all 3 criteria) each of whom stayed for many months. These men had no equivalents at House A. The result is that House A was without a leader of a particular type, or without an isolate of a particular type, for a number of months, whilst House B was much less often without residents of established reputation.

Furthermore, leadership and isolate status at House B was much more apparent in day-to-day activities as witnessed by relative dominance in house meetings, for example.

Reputation and Group Participation

When an examination was made of the frequency with which leaders and isolates of different kinds achieved positions in the top ½ of the rank order lists for volume spoken and amount 'received' in house meetings, it was found to be the case that leaders at House B were consistently relatively highly involved in group meetings, both as speakers and receivers, and that isolates were fairly consistently under-involved. At House A the relationships between leadership and isolate status on the one hand, and involvement in group meetings on the other hand, were consistently less strong. The effect at House B can be largely attributed to the dominance of Ross G, and the withdrawal of Hughie A in house meetings. As Table 18 shows, when all participants in a house meeting were rank ordered in terms of the volume of their speech, Ross G was found to occupy ranks 2, 3 and 4 more frequently than would be expected by chance, and to occupy lower ranks less frequently than expected (it will be recalled from Chapter 7 that a staff member most frequently occupied the 1st rank in meetings at House B). On the other hand, as Table 18 also shows, Hughie A never occupied 1 of the top 4 rank positions in recorded house meetings although he would have been expected to do so, by chance, on roughly 11 occasions. He occupied relatively lo positions, of 6th rank or lower, more frequently than expected.

It might also be noted that there was a greater tendency at House B towards the emergence of social leaders, contribution isolates and understanding isolates. Each of these 3 positions was occupied virtually throughout the study at House B, but was occupied only a little more than ½ the time at House A.

### Resident Reputations; Staff Views

Table 19 shows how weak was the relationship between sociometric status and staff opinions. Residents who had 'leadership' reputations with other residents were, on the whole, no more likely than those who had 'isolate' reputations to receive favourable comments from staff. In fact, in a number of instances the relationship tended in the other direction. This was particularly the case for 'social leaders' and 'social isolates'; it was the latter who were somewhat more likely to receive favourable comments from staff. It was even the case for 'great leaders' and 'total isolates' at House A; again it was the latter who were somewhat more likely to receive favourable staff comments. On the other hand, 'great leaders' were more likely than 'total isolates' to receive favourable staff comments at House B, again largely because of the impact of Ross G and Hughie A.

Table 18: Contributions of a great leader and a total isolate to meetings at House B - a comparison of actual and expected rank order positions for volume spoken at 24 meetings

| Rank order positions | A Great Leader (Ross G) Expected | Actual | | A Total Isolate (Hughie A) Expected | Actual |
|---|---|---|---|---|---|
| 1 | 3.0 | 1 | | 2.8 | - |
| 2 | 3.0 | 7 | | 2.8 | - |
| 3 | 3.0 | 7 | a - Due | 2.8 | - |
| 4 | 3.0 | 5 | to tied | 2.8 | - |
| 5 | 3.0 | 1 | ranks | 2.8 | 3 |
| 6 | 3.0 | 2 | | 2.8 | 5.5[a] |
| 7 | 2.6 | - | | 2.6 | 3 |
| 8 | 1.8 | - | | 2.3 | 7.5[a] |
| 9 | 0.8 | 1 | | 1.1 | 2 |
| 10 | 0.5 | - | | 0.8 | 2.5[a] |
| 11 | 0.3 | - | | 0.4 | 0.5[a] |

Table 19:   Staff opinions of leaders and isolates at Houses A and B
(Proportions of all occasions on which staff comments on leaders and
isolates were above the median for favourability).

|  | HOUSE A | HOUSE B |
|---|---|---|
| Contribution leaders | 62 | 41 |
| Contribution isolates | 57 | 51 |
| Social leaders | 38 | 45 |
| Social isolates | 56 | 54 |
| Understanding leaders | 61 | 55 |
| Understanding isolates | 62 | 47 |
| Great leaders | 46 | 60* |
| Total isolates | 60 | 26* |

\* The difference between these 2 proportions is the
only statistically significant difference between
leader and isolate proportions in this table.

There must have been many occasions when staff made favourable
comments about relatively unpopular residents, and unfavourable comments
about those who were relatively popular.  A closer look at some of the
things which staff members said about their residents helps to explain
these apparent incongruities.

Using Different Criteria

On a number of occasions staff appeared to be using criteria which
did not enter into the sociometric task which was required of residents,
and upon which our definition of 'reputation' has been based.  For
example, staff were frequently concerned with the personal distress,
insecurity, anxiety or depression of residents.  In other instances
staff stressed events which were taking place outside the house.  For
example, over a period during which Walter V was both a 'contribution'
and an 'understanding isolate' staff A2 was of the following opinion:

Walter V is fairly quiet, he talks a bit about his work
situation, the sorts of responsibilities he has and how he's
coping with them, he doesn't contribute a great deal to the
group, but when he does make an observation it is an astute
observation. He seems quite stable, you can feel that this
is a good base for him.  He's constructive - on the face of
it he's often accused of not making much contribution, but I
think rather the reverse by the fact that he is a solid,
stable, responsible, character, he's probably making more
contribution than anyone else.  The fact that he's capable
of going out to work daily and leading a life outside is
certainly something which is an obvious target - I think
this is where some of the friction, if there is friction,
comes in between him and other people...

In other cases staff were particularly impressed with changes. For example, because of Hughie A's long-standing special role as an isolate, staff were particularly impressed by any change for the better. On one occasion, despite Hughie A's continuing 'isolate' reputation with residents, staff B1 said:

> Strength to strength - talks at meetings now - raises his points. Has made points that the carpet and the suite need cleaning, raised the matter as to how long we should keep people's gear for them, talked about the cook, etc. He has gone into hospital, largely on his own account, to have his teeth out. I took him in and left him there without any great signs of strain... He seems to be coping, smarter, cleaner and neater than he was. First of all, his length of time here has obviously had the greatest effect... the group now is a very tolerant sort of group, accepting, non-threatening. He feels part of the house now. He started to talk about alcoholism to me... and he says the right things. He isn't repeating what he's learned.

## Staff-Resident Strain

Incongruity was not always the result of staff and residents using different criteria however. There were several instances in which staff and residents simply had different opinions. In many of these cases the incongruity between staff opinion and reputation with other residents appeared to be of relatively little consequence. In other instances, however, the disagreement appeared more serious, and was sometimes symptomatic of strain in the house. This was particularly the case when staff had reason to hold other than a totally favourable impression of a resident who occupied a position of high status in the eyes of fellow residents. Dick D was a case in point. During month 5 he was both a 'contributions leader' and an 'understanding leader' and he was a 'social leader' in the following months. He also held the position of official 'group leader'. Staff A1, nonetheless, was concerned that his influence was not a wholly good one:

> ...last Monday night...I was going to bring up the question of how Dick D makes his money. I want to bring this up, we have to face the subject. Scott E is the only one in the group who ever makes an attempt to look at Dick's situation in relation to the group expectations. He finds himself on his own in this - Dick doesn't communicate, he doesn't communicate with me. If I ask him to organize something like the purchase of furniture, on behalf of the group, he goes off quite as an individual without bringing it up with the group at all.

One of the clearest examples of incongruity of this sort, and which was of some significance in the context of what was going on in the house at the time, was that of Dick P at House B. His role was a special one and deserves lengthier comment. He scarcely participated in meetings at all for his first 2 months and rapidly acquired a reputation as a 'contributions isolate' which he maintained until the end of the study. He regularly came in late from work, ate alone and otherwise kept to himself, continued to gamble (he had a known 'gambling problem'), and led an unusually full social life outside the house.

Staff B2 and the project director were both concerned about his gambling. Fellow residents on the other hand seemed to take his gambling relatively lightly. On occasions he placed bets for other residents. Staff B2 had an average amount of contact with Dick P during the latter's first few weeks in the house, but thereafter for the next 4 months they had virtually no contact at all. For his first 5 months in the house, staff B2 gave consistently unfavourable comments on Dick P. Sometimes these comments were mixed, but very often they were totally negative. The project director remarked that he was, "...surprised everyday that Dick is still there because he doesn't actually want to be there at all".

Some 3 or 4 months after his arrival at the house Dick P started to become more involved in house meetings. Whenever this happened, he appeared to be a fairly major focus of others' concern - his rank position for 'receiving' comments from others was fairly consistently higher than his rank order position for speaking. In several ways he became a central figure in conflicts surrounding the very purpose of house meetings. Staff B2 was aware of a 'very passive atmosphere' in the house at the time, and was conscious that Dick reflected a prevalent feeling that house meetings were relatively useless. It was put to the staff member by an ex-resident that it could be an advantage to have these issues raised, but staff B2 had expressed the reservation that:

> ...it would mean that a number of other people would identify with his view because they are unsure about how to use the house meeting effectively and have difficulty participating - so it is dangerous in that there is not a strong enough counter-argument, and that the counter-arguments to the whole business of the house meeting being useless will come from the staff, which is exactly the wrong place for the counter-arguments to come from.

In view of staff opinions about the importance of house meetings, and the evident strain between staff and residents over their purpose at House B, Dick's role at this time was clearly vital. Research notes described him as by now the most dominant resident in the house. He was popular and his popularity seemed to centre around gambling activities. His main complaint about meetings was that they were too long. He didn't see their purpose, and it was through his influence that the time of the start of meetings got put back from 7 to 8 o'clock. It was his view that a meeting should only discuss 'hole in the carpet' issues. He touched on a sensitive point when he claimed that the project director could swing a vote in the house, that the project director was ultimately the major decision-maker, and that residents did not have the final say. The research notes described 'low morale' in the house and prevalent heavy gambling in which Dick appeared to be the ringleader. Kevin L, who had been group chairman, left the house and staff saw the significance of this:

> Kevin had quite established himself and he was very much an alternative to Dick in terms of leadership or direction in the house meetings.

Dick had established his reputation as a 'social leader' by this time but staff continued to find him an enigma. It was not until the final month of the study, when Dick had been in the house for about 6 months, that staff seemed to come to terms with his status in the house. Staff B2 and Dick P had a small amount of contact during this period for the first time for several months, and for the first time staff comments were slightly more favourable than unfavourable. It was noticed that he had been particularly considerate to Hughie A who had refused to contribute to the extra cost of a colour television set. Dick seemed to be at pains to convince Hughie that he was welcome to watch the set even though he was not contributing financially to it. Dick was described by staff as, "warmer - more constructive". He was offered the group chairmanship but refused. He remained at House B for almost a further year after the end of the study, and was undoubtedly by most criteria one of House B's successes.

## Things Approved and Disapproved by Staff

The above extracts give a flavour of some of the staff comments about residents. A more systematic attempt was made to analyze staff comments by scruitinizing a proportion of particularly favourable comments, and a proportion of particularly unfavourable comments. The things which staff seemed to particularly approve of, and things of which they particularly disapproved, can be summarized under the following headings:

(a) Responsible Involvement.

All 4 staff members made many favourable comments of this type. They reported favourably upon the relatively high level of "responsibility", or "concern", or "involvement" which some residents displayed. Others were described as "putting in a lot", being "practically helpful", "playing their part". Others were described as "part of the house", a "pillar", "supportive", or just "doing things" around the house. Staff A1 described Scott E as, "a support for the standards of the house and the culture of the place". He felt Scott had, "got the best understanding of what being a group member and feeling the responsibility for other members of the group was all about".

'Responsible involvement' seemed to be more apparent by its presence than in it's absence. However, a small number of residents were described as "withdrawing", "saying little", "not giving", as being "no part of the house", having "nothing for the house" or being "anti-groups".

(b) Sociability.

Strongly related to 'responsible involvement', 'sociability' was more apparent in the negative than in the positive. Occasionally staff would describe a resident as "capable of relating", "socially good - entertaining" or just "likeable". More frequently staff would describe residents in terms such as "aggressive, argues, bitter", "cunning, manipulative, exploiting", or "attention-seeking, flamboyant, cock-of-the walk". Several were thought by staff to be "upsetting others", and occasionally a staff member would go so far as to predict that he, "could not get a group going" with a particular resident in the house. Social difficulties often took the form of specific untoward events, such as a resident "storming out" of an interview, or raising "difficulties over ex-residents". Pseudo-technical jargon was employed occasionally as when Sam N was described by staff A1 as "paranoid". Staff A2, perhaps because of his training, was particularly likely to use the term "psychopathic". After a particular resident had left the house after being accused of a "taking and driving away" offence, staff A2 said of him that he was a "typical psychopathic personality - totally without remorse - didn't profit from the experience at all". Another resident he said was, "demonstrating a total lack of remorse, a total lack of insight - psychopathic personality - a form of immaturity, semi-depressive, part of his emotional disorder".

(c) Sense, Insight and Openness.

A surprisingly large number of favourable comments by staff had to do with what might be called 'cognitive virtues'. Staff particularly valued "intelligence", "common-sense", "thoughtfulness", "insight" and "realism". They favoured residents who were "inquisitive", who "spoke sensibly" or who had "an appropriate attitude". They liked residents who were "forthcoming", "ready to talk about themselves" and who "used the group" or "brought up subjects". People were in favour who had plenty of "ideas" and who "saw things in their true context". Staff B1 described one resident as having "internalized useful concepts" and another, Ross G, as "probably the most thoughtful and insightful member of the group - certainly has a far better comprehension of the aims, ideals, theories behind the house than anyone else has". There were many more favourable than unfavourable comments under this heading although a few residents were described, particularly by staff A2, as "using covering up language", "having a glib use of words", "speaking at people" and "not good at looking at self".

(d) Outside Progress.

Many favourable comments had to do with the progress that residents were making, particularly at work, and sometimes in making contact with family and friends. Many negative comments were also of this type.

(e) Mental Health.

Many positive staff comments noted resident "happiness", "integration", "relaxation", "calmness and security", and "confidence", whilst a smaller number of negative comments noted that residents were "lonely", "low", "scapegoated", or "needs a psychiatrist".

(f) Miscellaneous.

The occasional resident was disapproved of on account of "gambling", "pill-taking" or for "borrowing money". Perhaps most interesting of all was the rarity of any reference to drinking. Staff B1 described one resident as "determined to stop drinking", and another as "saying the right things about alcoholism". Of another resident he said, "he has never really intended to stop drinking". There were scarcely any other references to drinking at all, except following a resident's departure and his known, or assumed, return to 'drinking'.

SUMMARY

Similarities Between Houses A and B

Fluctuations in Stability.

1. An examination of numbers of residents, lengths of stay and rates of leaving for the study period and throughout the history of the houses, shows that rapid turnover creates a continual problem of maintaining both quantity and quality of membership. These are necessary to create and maintain a nuclear 'culture-carrying' group with some continuity from month to month.
2. There were marked fluctuations in the stability of the resident

group at both houses. The state of stability of the house varied from one of low turnover with a relatively large number of long-staying residents, to a state of decline characterized by high turnover. The latter can result in a crisis which, on account of small numbers and loss of morale, may even threaten the continued existence of the hostel. It may take many months, or even 2 to 3 years, to build up a strong stable resident group when a hostel is opened, and may take many months to restore stability after a crisis.

## Perceived Atmosphere

3. At both houses the favourability of residents' perceptions of house atmosphere was associated with the favourability of their perceptions of the staff member in charge. The 2 staff members with a positive reputation (1 at each House) were those who reported spending much more time with residents.
4. Staff perceptions of house atmosphere were not related to their perceptions of residents, nor were they on the whole related to residents' perceptions of atmosphere or staff. Neither residents' nor staff ratings of atmosphere were related to the stability of the resident group. However it is possible that an unsatisfactory perceived atmosphere is predictive of a later decline in stability.

## Resident Reputations

5. With very few exceptions, there was little relationship between the popularity of a resident with other residents and the favourability of staff comment about him. In particular, residents who were socially popular tended to receive less favourable staff comments. Sometimes this discrepancy between staff and resident opinions was of little consequence, but at other times it was indicative of strain and lack of consensus about house ideals and goals. Staff particularly approved of residents who displayed 'responsible involvement' in the house and 'sense, insight and openness' about their problems; and they particularly disapproved of residents who were unsociable or socially disruptive.

## Differences Between Houses A and B

## Fluctuations in Stability

1. Although in recent years neither house has maintained high levels of stability as attained in its early years, the stability pattern has been different at the 2 houses. House B has maintained a moderate level of stability, whilst House A has fluctuated more dramatically, declining to crisis point at roughly 2-year intervals. A major crisis occurred in the middle of the study itself.

## Reputations

2. At House A there was a relatively sharp division between residents who were popular (by 1 or more criteria) with fellow residents, and those who were unpopular. This division was less sharp at House B. In particular there was a number of residents who had reputations for making little contribution to the running of the house, but who had high social reputations.

3. There was little continuity of resident leadership at House A
during the study, and those who briefly held the position of 'great
leader' (popular by several criteria) were not specially approved of
by staff. At House B on the other hand, there was continuity of
resident leadership throughout most of the study in the form of 1 man
who also met with strong staff approval.

# Chapter 9

# A Description of 10 Months
# at Houses A and B

...the well-being of the hostel does not depend purely on
the personality of the man in charge, at any rate insofar
as personality is regarded as some fixed and unalterable
thing. But it is noticeable that when things were going
wrong, all those concerned blamed the warden and his alleged
personality defects (Sinclair, 1971, p.112, writing of
hostels for juvenile probationers).

This chapter attempts to put some flesh upon the bones of previous
chapters by providing a narrative account of events which occurred
over a period of some months at the 2 houses. The selection of potential new residents, characteristics of actual residents and staff,
the conduct of group meetings and the operation of the drinking rule
are all topics which arise and which illustrate research material
presented in earlier chapters. The narrative accounts are particularly
relevant, however, to the matters raised in the previous chapter. It
is hoped that they will convey to the reader the reality of changes in
stability and atmosphere, as well as the key influence of individual
people, in small hostel communities like Houses A and B.
    During the course of the study the research worker (S.O.) spent a
considerable amount of time at Houses A and B and was able to make
many observations, and form many impressions, beyond the more formally
collected research data. These observations and impressions were discussed with, and recorded by, another research worker (J.O.) at a regular weekly meeting throughout the study. The accounts given below are
based very largely upon these research notes. The accounts concern the
same block of 10 4-week 'months' (roughly 9 calendar months), during
which time the stability of the resident group at House A declined from
a relatively high level to breakdown point, whilst stability at House B
fluctuated but was maintained.

Decline - Months 1 - 10 at House A

    The staff member (Colin S) had taken up his post in the previous
Autumn and had inherited a well-established group of residents. Howeve
by the start of the study a number of residents who had been in the
house for some months were thinking of leaving. It was also immediatel
clear that the group was not totally cohesive and supportive. In particular, a clique of relatively well-educated and professionally trained
men, self-styled the Saville Row group, stood out from the others.
Prominent in this group was Brendon A who had recently resigned his

group leadership preparatory to his leaving the house, and who appeared to an outsider to be gossipy and to have a mocking sense of humour. The latter he directed towards members outside the 'upper class' clique, and in particular towards Norman B who was a rather sensitive, new resident and who was clearly upset by it. He had an isolate reputation, both by the contributions and understanding criteria. He was a tense man, whose status in the group had always been low, and who seemed to occupy almost a 'scapegoat' role. He attempted to contribute but things always seemed to go wrong for him. On one occasion he repainted one of the communal rooms in the house and, instead of receiving praise for his work, received irritated comment that he had done it for his own motives without the group really wanting the job done. He took responsibility for the regular visitors' meeting which involved him in making a short introduction to the house for visitors, and in reading the 'house charter'. He was highly anxious when doing this, did it badly, and on one occasion walked out in a panic.

Other members of the in-group included Andrew C who was distinguished from the others principally by his considerable involvement in editing the house magazine. However it was noticeable that whilst Andrew was so effectively task-involved, he had few strong emotional links with other residents, was lacking in spontaneity, and scarcely ever made personal remarks in group meetings. His facade appeared scarcely punctured at all. The current group leader, Dick D, was also a member of the in-group. As described in Chapter 8, he was one of the two 'contribution leaders' at House A in the first half of the study, but he progressively withdrew from house activities during this time and was by no means wholly approved of by staff.

Only one man, Scott E, appeared to stand between the 'in' and 'out' groups and was respected by both. He had a reputation for his 'contributions' and also for being 'understanding'. He was well-respected for the part he played in domestic activities and for his energetic visiting of other facilities such as the reception centre. In the context of the declining stability of the house, he was the most articulate about the commitment which he felt to the house, and the way he felt this should be expressed by taking an active part in domestic arrangements as well as in group meetings. He particularly expressed the view that the house was a democratic community which should be run, "for the men by the men". His 'disorderly' departure some months later was probably a significant event in the decline of the house. Scott E and Dick D were in fact the only two 'contribution leaders' at House A between months 1 and 10.

Around this time a member of the 'out-group', Phillip F, had left after a relatively brief stay. The research worker had felt that he was someone who was easily hurt, he had been much criticized for disturbing his room mate by snoring, and the attitude of most other residents towards Phillip and this 'problem' had seemed to be somewhat uncaring. He had come back to the house after his departure, 'maudlin drunk', and had had to be turned away.

Colin S's personality started to emerge. He was described by several of the residents as being an effective administrator but not the kind of man who 'Let the residents get to know him' (this was a standard questionnaire item and not a spontaneous remark and has thus been put in single rather than double quote marks). There was the suggestion that he was not a potent force who would bring about changes in the house, but on the other hand he was capable of introducing ideas without appearing to dominate. A party was held for the purpose of saying a

belated farewell to the previous staff member who had taken up the post
of senior social worker with the same organization; Colin S, although
his senior in years, was therefore responsible to him. The party was
probably also a testing time for many of the residents, and it was
noticeable that most of the Saville Row clique were ill-at-ease and
failed to mix. Their behaviour seemed to be in marked contrast to
their normal, somewhat dominating, behaviour within the house. Scott
and Norman were also ill-at-ease and had disappeared early. Colin had
found Scott upstairs on the verge of tears saying that it was "superficial, meaningless" and that he himself was on the verge of mental
illness. Norman too had felt unhappy and excluded.

An additional important feature of the house climate at this time
concerned the issue of alcoholics 'returning to social drinking'. The
latter issue divided the 'in' and 'out' groups. The former maintained
that once they had worked through some of their problems, and time had
been allowed to elapse, they could experiment successfully with 'normal' or controlled drinking. The out-group were unhappy about this and
critical of it. It is of interest that the residents of House B, who
got to know of this attitude on account of an article written by one of
the Saville Row clique members in the House A magazine, were even more
outraged and indignant.

That was the situation at House A as it appeared to the research
worker during the first month of her observations. Around the end of
that month the situation was changed by the admission to the house of
a young man, Dave G. He was talkative and forthright, critical of the
'social drinking' idea, of the exclusiveness of the house preached by
the Saville Row group, and of what he saw as the unhelpful criticality
of some residents. Scott also spoke strongly at the group meeting at
which Dave had expressed these ideas, and himself spoke of people
wearing 'masks' and the dangers of people losing their individuality
by their conformity to the house norms. In fact Dave G quickly came to
occupy a dominant position in group meetings - he only relinquished
the position of most voluminous speaker just before he left. On the
occasion mentioned he spoke almost 3 times as much as anyone else,
and although the meeting was a particularly emotional one, he was one
of the most emotional participants. A great deal of what other participants said was directed at him. Because many remarks in all meetings were recorded as directed towards the group as a whole, it was
unusual for any participant to 'receive' more than he 'gave'. However,
on this occasion Dave not only received more than he gave, but received
more than 4 times as many comments as anyone else in the group.

Dave proved to be a challenge to the establishment of the house in
more than one way. He brought down his girl-friend to London, arranged
a flat for her, and started to see a great deal of her, all without
consulting 'the group'. He invited her to the house to visit and some
consternation was expressed about "ladies using the loo". There was
mention of the flouting of "commonsense rules". Dave G bought himself
a small car and he was told by a number of other residents that he was
"doing things too quickly". He, in his turn, was critical of the pass-
iveness of the group ("You just sit and watch T.V.") and was critical
of the way the group approached its members' problems ("Attacking to
destroy, not to build up", was how he described it). The research worker
felt his role in the house to be crucial - he appeared to be able to
see through the rather empty atmosphere which existed.

A number of 'senior' residents announced their intentions of moving
on to one of the self-contained flats in the 'three-quarter-way house'

across the road from House A. The former group leader, Brendon A was
amongst these. So was Andrew C who continued with his major involvement in the magazine, and continued to be in many ways a 'model' resident, although he sat rather sullenly in the corner in group meetings
and revealed himself not at all. The much-respected Scott was heavily
involved in outside activities such as the reception centre 'encounter
groups' for recruiting and inducting potential new residents and in
activities designed to improve facilities for homeless people.

Research notes for the 2nd and 3rd months are full of Andrew's
unexpected departure and its aftermath. Everyone was very shocked,
not least Colin S. The expression, "As Andrew used to say", was heard
more than once at this time. His courteousness was now spoken of as
"a veneer", it was felt that he had "not progressed", and that the
house had not helped him. It emerged that he had been preoccupied
with personal problems.

Departures from the house, some of them planned, but others like
that of Andrew unplanned and unexpected, were not being made up with
the same number of new residents, although 2 new residents did come to
the house during months 2 and 3. Morale was low and more open criticism
of Colin began to appear at this time (He was not someone that they
could 'easily get to know', he was not 'around the house enough' and he
showed 'insufficient insight into their problems'). He himself expressed regret at being caught up in administration, much of it petty
("replacing bath mats and tooth-paste for example!"). More fundamental dynamic issues seemed to be being put aside. For example, the
question of return to social drinking remained unchallenged, with the
result that staff and residents alike appeared somewhat confused about
goals. The group leader, Dick D, was reputed to be engaged in 'deal-
ings' of suspect legality, but he remained unchallenged on this. The
regular house visitor, Kate S, expressed concern about the house; she
felt strongly that the house was losing its central purpose, and that
it was no longer adhering to the ideals of the 'therapeutic community',
to which she felt the previous staff member had adhered strongly. The
residents' views on the whole were much more charitable. One resident
described Colin as "kind but aloof", and more than one commented that
he allowed the group to have "a life of its own", and that he didn't
"impose himself upon it".

During the following few weeks a number of individual problems
were frequently mentioned in the research notes. For example, Dave G
continued to present a threat. Other residents felt that he took advantage of them, that he should ask before he did things and not present ultimatums. As one resident put it, "It's your attitude which is
wrong". Another resident, William H, had been a focus of concern for
some time. He had been in the house for several months, since before
the beginning of the study, his physical health was poor and he had not
worked for some months. He was generally uninvolved in the group to
the point of failing to do his bit by way of domestic duties, and had
clearly been allowed to occupy a special deviant role in the group for
some time. He was a social isolate. On account of his professional
background, he was reluctant to get "just any job" and it was felt that
he should be given a period of time in which to find a job or else
leave the house. The group debated whether this period should be 1 or
2 months and the latter was decided upon.

Towards the end of month 3 Dave G left and later phoned the house
to say he had been drinking. The brevity of Dave's stay in the house,
and his failure to permanently influence the group, are undoubtedly of

great significance in the history of the house during this period. The group was in decline, badly needed new leaders, and many of its attitudes may well have been maladaptive. Whatever they have to say about Dave personally, the events of this period appear to demonstrate the failure of the house to contain a potentially very contributory member.

A few weeks later Simon J, one of the more popular members of the Saville Row set, announced his intended departure and made it known that when he left he would certainly be attempting 'normal weekend drinking'. At about the same time a rift appeared between Colin S and the majority of residents over the issue of whether Andrew C should be allowed to return to the house. When the decision went against him (see Chapter 7 for a fuller account of this issue) Colin gave some thought to his own role. He subsequently appeared to be asserting himself more and the residents reacted by uniting in some resistance to what they saw as his "new authoritarianism".

Scott, described by the research worker as "the only strong point in the house" had been elected some weeks previously as the deputy group leader. Indeed he appeared to have the greatest authority in the house. He took a strong and attacking line in group meetings but seemed constructive. Norman B, and also Daniel K, a relatively new resident, appeared upset by this type of meeting and Scott took time in between meetings to explain why he saw the need for it. The group feeling was good during this period. A new resident, Arthur L, joined the group. He was a little older than many of the others and had a background of considerable involvement in Alcoholics Anonymous. A young female student was also attached to the house around this time and appeared to be rather more available to residents than Colin S.

During month 5 the house suffered a severe set-back when Scott left the house in an unplanned and stormy fashion. He returned to the house drunk and insisted on confronting the group with his critical opinions about the group and several of its members. His opinions later appeared in the form of an article in the house magazine. Like Andrew C before him, Scott was much missed by the group and his words were quoted long after he had left. Daniel K also left at about this time and it emerged that he had been concealing drinking for at least 2 weeks before his departure.

Two new residents, Fred M and Sam N, appeared on the scene at around this time. The latter appeared to adopt a fairly attacking posture from the beginning. He was referred to the house from the nearby assessment centre, and whilst there had written a critical article in the house magazine about the referral process to House A. There was a suspicion in some minds that this had influenced the decision to accept him despite an initially negative view of his application. Both of the new residents remarked on the lack of humour and warmth in the house.

The research notes described a "sad scene" at the house at this stage. There appeared to be a division between the newcomers and the slightly longer-stay residents with Arthur L lying somewhere between the 2. Of the longer-stay residents, William H had recently left, Dick D, still the group leader, was spending long hours working away from the house and appeared to be withdrawing from his involvement, and another long-staying resident left at about this time to go to a bed-sitter in the 'three-quarter-way' house. The process of disintegration of the established house group and the consequent increasing proportion of residents who were relative newcomers was therefore continuing at a fast pace at this stage. Sam N was adopting a role which many were inclined to describe as "destructive". He became an increasing focus of the concern of both staff and residents. Expressions such as "paranoid" and "over-aggressive" were being used to describe him. Other residents described him as "argumentative" and "given to reacting too extremely". An issue arose over the possible selection to the house of a potential resident whose work had been in the police force. Sam was adamant that this should not be allowed, and was concerned at the same time with what he saw as the "takeover" of the house by the assessment centre and by the probation service (the organization and method of referral to the assessment centre was changed around this time so that referrals should come almost exclusively from the probation service).

Colin was "putting his money" on Arthur L at this time. In itself this was an indication of the position the house had reached as Arthur had only been in the house a relatively short time and seemed as yet to have little grasp of what the house was for.

In the next few weeks much attention was paid to trying to encourage referrals to the house and everyone was agitated about their slowness. Colin was away during this rather crucial period and Arthur acted as unofficial social worker in obtaining background details about prospective residents. Fred M left the house after a very brief stay and antagonism between Sam on the one hand, and Arthur and Robert P, on the other hand, was noticed by a psychiatrist who attended the group meeting on one occasion around this time. Dick D, who had his time taken up with heavy work commitments and was keeping the house magazine going, resigned as leader, and Arthur took over. However the latter appeared uncertain of himself and there was clear friction between he and Sam.

In month 7 the senior social worker's criticisms of Colin S were expressed directly to him and there was mutual antagonism. The essence of the criticism seems to have been that Colin S was not putting enough effort into make the house a truly 'therapeutic community'. A complicating factor was that his responsibilities had been enlarged to include the direction of the assessment centre.

A week or two later the ex-policeman came up for his group selection interview. Meanwhile Sam had continued to express his prejudice about the matter and Arthur had expressed his determination to deal with the matter more rationally. In the event Arthur started to drink in the house shortly before the selection interview was due and only appeared at the interview long enough to put his head around the door before disappearing. His subsequent departure seemed attributable both to his conflict with Sam over the selection issue and a number of other matters, as well as to recent personal family troubles. Dick D had also left the house by this time and Sam took over as group leader. That such a relatively new resident, whose reputation with both staff and fellow residents contained distinctly unfavourable features, should become group leader at this time, was a live illustration of the disintegration of 'the group'. Two new men joined. Kenny Q had a long prison record, had a reputation for being wildly aggressive when drunk, and spoke frequently of violence. The other new resident, Alan R, was described as a "loner".

Another week later it was reported that both Kenny Q and Robert P had "gone drinking". Sam had had to deal with the situations that had arisen and had in effect had to evict Kenny. Coincidentally with this further collapse of the group structure, the very fabric of the house was dealt a severe blow. Dry rot was discovered throughout a large

part of the front of the house and extensive repairs were initiated
with extreme rapidity by the organization responsible for the house.
Scaffolding was erected and the front face of the house was virtually
removed. It became impossible to lock the house. By an unfortunate
twist of circumstance, Kenny had obtained employment with the builders
who were working on the house and Sam was scared of some physical reprisal from him. Kate S was critical that Colin S seemed insensitive
to Sam's realistic fears on this count. Residents were reduced to 2,
Sam and Alan R. The latter slept temporarily in the assessment centre
whilst Sam slept alone in the house. Referrals appeared to have "dried
up" and Colin described the house as "not a hostel at all". One new
resident came but stayed only 3 days telling Colin S that he found Sam
"autocratic". Colin declared an embargo on new residents. He attempted
to keep the group going by holding daily meetings with the 2 remaining
residents but he complained that Sam, "had no concept of the house".
A fortnight later Alan R had also gone. Colin described the atmosphere
as, "disturbed, truncated and chaotic". He told the research worker
that the house was "officially closed". Tensions were high and both
Sam and Colin S felt unsupported. Colin was very depressed with events
and Sam was frightened and unwell. In theory Colin S had had the benefit of a 'support group' throughout, but he clearly felt that it had
failed to fulfil its supposed function. In their turn several of the
support group felt that he had failed to use them to the full.

As a postscript to a description of this period of several months
of decline, it should be said that a long period of revival began
almost immediately and was under way by the time Colin S left House A
2 months later.

### Containment - Months 1 - 10 at House B

Despite his relative youth and very different social background,
Robert S seemed to identify well with the residents at House B from
the beginning. He said he wanted to conduct things on a normal, social
level, and he considered the residents not to be disordered or disturbed purely on account of their drinking problems. He appeared to be
popular with residents, and the only criticism was that he seemed to
have 'little insight into residents' problems'. The research worker
predicted that if he had any difficulties they would be with the organization that ran the house and not with the residents themselves.

There was relatively little turnover to disturb the resident group
at the beginning of this period and the house was settled enough for
Robert S to feel that he could leave the house for a week and yet not
feel over-concerned about it. The naturalness of the conversation in
the house, in comparison with that prevailing at House A, was noted.
The house took a regular daily paper and there was much discussion
about current events. The house had also recently bought its own radio
(House A in contrast did not have a communal radio or newspaper).
There was noticeably much 'chatter' in the kitchen. The atmosphere was
such that residents were well able to tolerate, indeed to nurture,
Hughie A (the 'total isolate' - see Chapter 8), whose participation in
the house was felt to be below expectations and whose behaviour was, on
occasions, strange. For example he would sit with his head sideways
during meetings, not talking and not looking at anybody. He was not
one for pleasantries and if given anything would tend to snatch it and
rush away. He had great difficulty making relationships with other
people without being abrupt and aggressive. For many weeks he would

talk at length only with the cook. At another time he was fairly close
to Mike B and Pat C who shared his rural Irish background, whilst at
other times his pattern consisted of repeatedly attempting friendship
with new residents who arrived at the house (see Figure 15 for example).
These attempts nearly always failed and he would return to his isolated
position. He was an individualist and described himself as a "rough
diamond". He was the only resident to resist certain changes in domestic policy; for example he was the only one against the renting of a
colour television set which required increased payments by residents.

A major factor in the good atmosphere at the time was the contribution of 3 main figures in the resident group, Joe D, Keith E, and
Andy F, whose temperaments seemed to be complementary to one another
rather than conflicting. Robert S described Andy particularly as "an
ascending star". Although he was not working because he was waiting
for a medical appointment, he appeared to be making excellent progress
and was very much involved in the domestic routines of the house.
Indeed one of the first new residents at House B during the study had
left after only 2 weeks saying that Andy was in effect, "running the
house". Keith E had supported Andy saying that this was just an excuse.
Several residents had felt that the departing member had been very nervous during his brief stay and had been obsessed with working all hours.
It was thought that the fact that these 3 'leaders' had formerly been
members of the same 'drinking school' lent considerable stability to
the house. The sharing element of the 'skid row ethic' was noticeable
in little things. For example Andy was kept going in cigarettes by the
others while he was not working, and another resident was given his fare
to work when he was short of money. On the other hand, the non-interference element of this ethic was also apparent and was confusing for
staff. Robert S (as well as the project director who retained involvement during this time through his regular attendance at house meetings)
doubted the 'commitment' of residents to the house, and tried to discuss in the house meeting why residents were not more involved in out-
going leisure activities. Several residents responded that they thought
of the house as a "home" and that while they were out at work during the
day they preferred to "put their feet up" in the evening.

Two residents who had been particularly friendly, both before coming
to the house and during their stay in the house, left at around the same
time. The remaining residents were not surprised nor much disturbed.
Staff, however, tried to raise the question of the difficulty that residents might have in leaving the house and the resulting sudden 'disappearance' of many residents. They threw out the challenge that there
might be other residents in the house who were "thinking of leaving".
There was little response from residents in the house meeting and the
subsequent discussion concerned more domestic issues.

Turnover remained relatively low. Only a few residents left during
months 1 and 2, and 3 new residents joined the house. One of these was
Ross G, a long-established 'skid row' drinker who was well known to many
of the existing group. He was much respected by men both inside and
outside the house and was later to become a 'great leader' at House B.
Staff too considered him to be a highly intelligent man whose occupational potential had never been realized. By way of contrast, another
new resident, Patrick H, admitted to being conscious of the difference
between his own background and that of most of the other residents.
For example he had very few convictions whilst the majority of other
residents had many.

The house seemed to be "jogging along". Hughie's behaviour appeared a little more normal although 1 or 2 other residents expressed some resentment that they were required to treat him as a special case.

In months 3 and 4, although the resident group contained a stable nucleus of 6 men, the atmosphere seemed to deteriorate. There were signs of a new, and growing conflict amongst residents particularly around the assertiveness of Joe D, one of the longer-established and more dominant residents  Gambling activities had begun to increase and a number of residents including Hughie A, and Pat J, and even Andy F, sustained heavy losses. In month 4 residents organized themselves to redecorate the house one weekend, with everyone in the group playing their part. At the next house meeting some dissatisfaction was expressed towards Robert S and the project director who were accused of spending insufficient time at the house. When staff asked what more residents wanted, the latter denied that they wanted more time from the staff, but it did emerge that they would appreciate more interest in their efforts, particularly their efforts of the previous weekend.

Overall, residents were growing more critical of Robert. A number said they found he was 'not around when they needed him', that he had 'little insight into their problems', and that he 'tended to say one thing and do another'. Even so Robert recorded spending an average of over 6 hours a day at the house during this period despite his additional responsibility at House G. The housekeeper (Joan S) complained that she was not receiving her wages regularly at the time agreed and that she was not being consulted on a number of domestic matters including the ordering of a new cooker.

Although the atmosphere had degenerated somewhat over these few weeks, it began to pick up at the beginning of month 5. There was notable solidarity around the news of the death of an ex-resident who had been well known to many residents and to project staff for many years, and who was greatly respected. Over this time all residents and staff gave great support to each other and their attendance at the funeral created a strong sense of group cohesion. At the end of this period residents were noticeably less critical of staff.

The homely, 'fireside' atmosphere of the house was challenged by the arrival of a new resident, Phil K, who seemed to get out of the house a lot, had many friends and was thought to be a "womanizer". He confided in Joan S that he was not really an alcoholic but had merely had some difficulty getting on his feet again after his wife's death. She described his as "cocky". He did not stay long however, returning one night with a woman friend and leaving early in the morning. Patrick H left at about the same time and Joe D was at pains to find out whether Phil had "led him astray". Robert and Joe disagreed on the propriety of this investigation and Joe left a few days later. The feeling in the house about Joe's dogmatic manner was such that no one seemed particularly upset by his departure. His leaving left 3 Irishmen and 2 Scotsmen in a group that was, to quote the housekeeper "a cosy small group".

Keith E had also left the house a few weeks earlier and Ross G had emerged as Joe's and Keith's successor as 'leader' in the house. Numbers of residents remained at 5 for a while but 3 new residents then joined the group over a period of a few weeks.

There were indications that Robert felt over-burdened at this stage, particularly on account of his extra responsibilities at House G. He had made it known that he intended to leave in a few months time and had written a document, and spoken about, the multiple roles and role confusion involved for the staff member in charge of such a house.

The project director seemed worried about the situation at the house. Robert had made it known that he thought there should be 2 members of staff for House B and G, whilst his senior thought that when the house was going well it needed no staff at all. The research notes described an absence of any sense of a vibrant ethic - the house seemed to be quiet and "drifting".

Robert went on holiday for a week in month 7 and described what he found when he returned as the "collapse of House B". Four residents had left, all during his week of absence. There had apparently been strongly-felt religious and political differences amongst the residents and it had come to the point where one man, a relatively new resident, had refused to sit down to eat with Andy. Other residents had found the former's behaviour strange; he had appeared detached and forgetful and tended to make irrelevant contributions to house meetings. He returned very aggressive after he left. Two other men had left after relatively brief stays in the house. In one case it seemed that his personal problems, which were thought to be multiple, had not been discussed and he said he had found it difficult to identify with the 'skid row' men. The other "should never have come", according to the director of the project, as he had been drinking since his referral from the assessment centre. Pat J was the last to go. The research worker's notes suggested that he had been "neglected", that he had been "slipping away" for a long time, not attending meetings, and had been seen very little around the house. In fact Joan reported that she had seen very few people at all around the house in recent weeks.

The house went through a bad patch with increased criticism by residents of the staff and of the house itself. There also seemed to be friction between Robert and the other staff of the overall project, with a certain degree of demoralization within the project regarding the functioning of House B. Robert and the project director made several attempts to introduce organizational changes. A volunteer from amongst the residents was asked to organize arrangements for visitors in the house, a role that had been performed by staff previously, and Ross reluctantly agreed to take the task on. The idea was also introduced that the occasional visit of residents to prospective residents at the 'quarter-way house' should become more regular and formalized, and the idea was rather passively accepted. The atmosphere seemed "subdued". There were continued misunderstandings between Robert and Joan, and it was about this time that the idea of a regular ½ hour weekly meeting between the 2 of them was mooted. The notion was soon abandoned (see Chapter 7 for a fuller discussion of these issues). Robert was sensitive to the unenthusiastic feeling in the wider project regarding the house and accused the project director of writing an annual report without mentioning the house. He seemed to feel unsupported.

Despite these various inter-staff problems, the resident group itself appeared to have found its equilibrium again quickly. Despite the several departures in month 7, 3 new residents had arrived in the same month and remained, and turnover during month 8 was confined to a single resident who came and left very quickly. Nearly all residents were working and they had become noticeably less critical of staff. In month 9, Robert made public his intention of taking up another post elsewhere, but despite this and continued inter-staff tension the atmosphere in the house continued to improve. A single new resident came and stayed and one left. Everyone was working by this time and several individual residents had developed definite pride in newly acquired

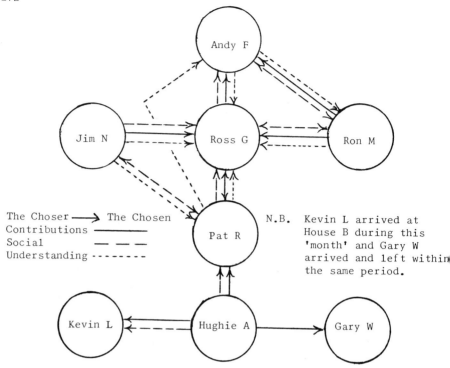

The Choser ——→ The Chosen
Contributions ————
Social — — —
Understanding ----

N.B.  Kevin L arrived at
House B during this
'month' and Gary W
arrived and left within
the same period.

Figure 15:  A sociogram showing the positions of a 'great leader'
and 'total isolate' (House B, Month 10).

possessions.  Ross in particular had consolidated his position as a
'leader' with a high reputation amongst both residents and social
workers.  Indeed he was helping one of the project staff with her work
at this time and later on became a paid employee of the organization.
The importance of Ross G in the history of House B over this period was
evident.  He had been well-known and had a high reputation amongst the
men in the house, project staff, and the local 'drinking schools'.  He
had a reputation as a man of high intelligence and compassion.  He
remained quietly unobtrusive during his first few weeks at the house and
then, almost unwillingly it seemed, became the unofficial leader.  Residents and staff maintained their respect for him and he retained his
position until he left.  He was very conscious of this position and
seemed to make efforts to ensure that he did not dominate excessively.
His position, as well as that of others, including Hughie A, the 'total
isolate', is illustrated in the sociogram (Figure 15).
There appeared to be definite cohesion at this time around the
general feeling of sharing and the maintenance of an orderly and harm-
onious house.  There was an established group of 6 men and this nucleus
was augmented by the arrival of a new resident (Kevin L) who had had
several months experience as a House B resident on a previous occasion.
A staff member who covered for Robert while he was away on holiday at
this time found the house well integrated, if lacking excitement or
"sparkle".  It was felt that the house was strong enough to continue
for a time without any member of staff having special responsibility

for it in the interim between Robert S leaving and a new staff member taking over.

## SUMMARY

### Similarities Between Houses A and B

A detailed narrative account of 9 months at Houses A and B suggests the importance of both staff behaviour and the size and composition of the resident group as determinants of the state of a hostel at any given time. At any one time the resident group was composed of those who had entered, and who had remained. Whilst the hostels had some control over who was admitted in the first place, they seemed to have relatively little control over who remained. A close examination of the events of these periods demonstrates the difficulty of attributing cause or blame to either residents or staff alone. Rises and falls in stability and atmosphere appeared to be the result of a concatenation of events which often seemed beyond the control of staff. Nevertheless staff were very frequently blamed for untoward events.

### Differences Between Houses A and B

At the beginning of this period both houses were in a state of at least moderately high stability. The subsequent course of events was quite different however; stability steadily declined at House A to a point of near total disorganization, whilst House B maintained its stability despite some minor fluctuations. There were a number of differences between the houses, each of which could have provided a partial explanation of the different course of events:

(a) Firstly, there were evident strains and divisions within the resident group at House A at the beginning of that period, whilst the
resident group at House B was comparatively stable and lacking in
strain. There was a feeling that the resident group at House A
was uncaring in the way it handled individual problems. Furthermore, there was a strong challenge to the abstinence ethic of the
house.

(b) Secondly, staff time in contact with residents, and residents'
opinions about the staff, although moderately high at the very
beginning, rapidly declined at House A. Although some decline from
a high level of staff-resident contact at the beginning of a regime
was a characteristic of all 4 members of staff, staff B1 maintained
a high level of availability and was on the whole well-liked.

(c) Thirdly, residents who left were not balanced by new residents arriving at House A, whilst the balance was maintained at House B.

(d) Fourthly, at House A a number of major contributors, or 'leaders',
amongst the resident group left sooner than was expected, and in
an unplanned and disorderly way, whilst the 'leadership' was maintained at House B in the form of at least one resident highly respected by both staff and residents.

(e) Finally, there were accidental factors. It was, for example, most
unfortunate that major repairs to House A were required and the
number of places available in the hostel cut, just at a time when
the house needed a fresh input.

Because these various factors operated together it is of course impossible to say which, if any, were truly causative. It seems most likely that each made a contribution and that in the end each factor reinforced the others to produce a vicious downward spiral of increasing momentum at House A. For example, inter-resident strains and the departure of particularly 'hopeful' residents may have contributed to staff withdrawal, which itself then militated against revival of good feelings.

# Chapter 10

# Progress, Departure and Afterwards

Success is the consequence of correlative smaller achievements.
In other words, success is a rehabilitative process rather than
an outcome (Blumberg et al, 1973, p.184, writing of programs
for skid row alcoholics in the U.S.).

...you think, oh dear, why couldn't he have stayed a wee bit
longer, thinking maybe that would have been the answer. But
nobody can explain these things. We can't get into other
people's minds. I'd be disappointed if any of them left. I
don't want any of them to leave (The cook at House G, quoted
in a recent annual report).

After the more detailed consideration of the social structure and
relationships at Houses A and B (Chapter 9), this chapter will briefly
consider some questions to do with the short term effects of the
houses. There is no pretence that the results constitute an 'evaluation'; there is no satisfactory baseline against which to compare
the progress of men subsequent to their entry to a house, no satisfactory alternative besides which these small hostels can be compared,
and no systematic long-term follow-up was attempted. On the contrary,
the contents of this chapter reflect what these authors consider the
equally useful aim of describing some aspects of residents' progress
whilst in a house and details of the timing and nature of their departures. There has been confusion and controversy, for example in the
field of after-care for the mentally ill, over the related matters of
a hostel's purpose, the ideal and actual lengths of stay of residents,
and their subsequent destinations. In the fields of hostel provision
for ex-offenders and drug addicts there has also been concern over high
rates of early leaving, and departures associated with re-conviction
or relapse (Chapter 4). This chapter will consider these general questions in the light of data from Houses A and B.

What then are the immediate results of exposing residents to the
types of routine described in Chapter 7? What changes take place during
a resident's stay? How do residents and staff view a resident's progress? How long do resident stay? How do they leave, and do they maintain contact afterwards? These are the main questions to which this
chapter is addressed.

### Resident Progress

The indefiniteness of the aims of most alcoholism hostels (see

Chapter 2) makes it difficult to assess whether or not they are achieved, but an attempt was made in the studies of Houses A and B to
monitor some aspects of the progress of individuals in the course of
the regular interviews with each resident and with each staff member
in charge. Amongst prior expectations, derived from a relatively
straight-forward model of what constitutes rehabilitation, were the
following: that good health, employment, contact with friends and family, involvement in group meetings and out-going and other leisure
activities would all increase with time since entry to the house; that
the passing of time would be associated with an increasing sense of
satisfaction and achievement, that the passage of time would similarly
be associated with a declining sense of upset and frustration; and that
with time staff would come to hold an increasingly favourable impression
of each resident. The questions asked of staff and residents are shown
in greater detail in Appendices A and C.

The data on resident progress were summarized by plotting the proportion of residents at Houses A and B who were in work, in contact
with family, reporting achievements, etc., at successive monthly or 2-
weekly intervals after entry. After about the 5th or 6th month these
graphs became erratic and difficult to interpret owing to the smallness of the numbers of residents who remained for 5 or 6 months or
longer. Even before that point it was not clear whether apparent trends represented real increases or decreases or whether, because a large
number of residents left within the first 1 or 2 months, they represented the effects of selective recruitment to longer-stay groups. For
this reason trends were also examined which were based upon data from a
small handful of 'contant' residents at each house whose progress was
followed over at least 3 or 4 months from the time of their entry.
These plots helped to suggest whether real increases or decreases had
occurred. The resulting graphs were too numerous and detailed to present here, but the results can be summarized under the following headings.

## Improvements in Health and Work

The only prior expectations about progress which received confirmation at both houses were those to do with employment, health and
involvement in meetings. Only 1 in 5 residents at either house were in
work by the time of their 1st interview 2 weeks after entry. The proportion increased steadily thereafter, so that a majority of those in
their 3rd month at House A were employed, and the same were true at
House B by the 5th month. The progress line was particularly erratic
at House B owing to a considerable turnover in employment amongst residents. Many residents, about ½, reported feeling ill or 'under the
weather' during their first 2 or 3 months but the proportion feeling ill
declined thereafter. Almost ½ the residents at House B were being prescribed psychoactive drugs of some kind during their 1st month but the
proportion in this category declined steadily to approximately 1 in 10
by the 5th month.

## Increasing Involvements in Group Meetings

The hypothesis about increasing involvement in meetings was con-
firmed at House A. New residents were likely to say (and to 'receive')
relatively little during their 1st month but involvement increased
sharply in the 2nd month. However the trend was, if anything, reversed

after that. A similar trend was apparent for the 'constant' group of 8 residents at House B but there was no trend for the total sample. This is partly explained by the fact that several new residents who stayed only briefly at House B spoke, and 'received', comparatively much in their 1st recorded meeting. It was new residents who received relatively little attention in the 1st recorded meeting who stayed longest.

Uncertain Trends

In several other instances trends were uncertain and difficult to discern, or there appeared to be no particular trend at all. This could be said of contacts with family and friends, use of outside professional support, involvement in out-going leisure activities (types of leisure activity are summarized in Table 20), the experiences of achievement, the favourableness of staff comments, and (at House A only) the amount of staff-resident contact. The general picture here is one of patterns of behaviour established early, within the 1st month of residence, and on the whole maintained thereafter. If there were gains accumulated by a large proportion of residents over a period of months in these areas, then the data do not reflect them.

Half or more of residents at both houses had contact with family members, whether parents, brothers or sisters, wives or children, within the 1st month of their residence, and when this was the case contact was usually maintained throughout the period of residence. Residents were relatively unlikely to make new family contacts after the 1st month although 3 residents at House B did so (in their 3rd, 5th and 7th months respectively). More residents at House A than at House B had contact with friends outside the house, but unlike contacts with family members, these were more frequently discontinued and there were no very obvious trends over time. As a consequence of the policy of maintaining a link between a resident and the project's own referring social worker, a high proportion of residents at House B maintained a supportive contact of this kind, whilst the same was only true of a minority of residents at House A. Again there was no very obvious trend over time and a number of longer-stay residents maintained this link 6 months or more after their admission to the house.

At neither house did staff make the progressively more favourable comments about residents that had been anticipated. At House B staff comments bore no relationship whatsoever with time in the house, and at House A there was even a tendency for staff to make more unfavourable comments as time went by.

Most evenings and all weekends represented time to be filled, and although occasional house parties (at House A) and visits to the cinema, theatre or the coast were arranged, on the whole residents had to rely on their own initiative for entertainment. Forming friendships and developing interests and hobbies were considered to be consistent with regaining social competence and were therefore generally approved. Table 20 shows that residents at both houses were involved in a range of leisure activities. Activities were often solitary - many residents did a lot of lone walking for example. Although the range of activities was similar for the 2 houses certain activities were characteristic of one house or the other. For example, at House B a number of men enjoyed watching football and betting was popular, whilst in House A a number of residents enjoyed sketching or using the local record library. Inside the houses, House B had its own snooker table and dart board

Table 20: A summary of the leisure activities reported by residents at Houses A and B (Total numbers of residents ever reporting an activity in each category).

|  | HOUSE A | HOUSE B |
|---|---|---|
| **Social-formal** |  |  |
| House committee or other house business | 3 | 4 |
| Encounter group recruitment | 3 | - |
| Local alcoholism committee or public meeting | 3 | - |
| Other (visit probation officer, church, funeral) | - | 3 |
| Any 'social-formal' activity | 7 | 6 |
| **Social-informal** |  |  |
| Visit to, or activities with, friend(s) | 12 | 9 |
| Visit to family member(s) | 4 | 4 |
| Visit to social club | 2 | 4 |
| Visit to resident(s) of another alcoholism facility | - | 5 |
| Dancing | 3 | - |
| Other (teaching English) | 1 | - |
| Any 'social-informal' activity | 19 | 13 |
| **Solitary-out of house** |  |  |
| Walking, window-shopping etc. | 12 | 9 |
| Cinema | 7 | 5 |
| Spectator sport | - | 6 |
| Betting or bingo | 1 | 3 |
| Book or record library | 2 | 2 |
| Any 'solitary-out of house' activity | 17 | 16 |
| **Solitary-in house** |  |  |
| Domestic (gardening, cooking, decorating etc.) | 5 | 3 |
| Television | 5 | 8 |
| Snooker or darts | - | 6 |
| Reading or crossword | 6 | 4 |
| House matters (magazine, arranging for visitors etc.) | 4 | - |
| Drawing, sketching | 1 | - |
| Any 'solitary-in house' activity | 12 | 10 |
| Any leisure activity | 23 | 20 |
| Total residents interviewed | 27 | 20 |
| Total number of interviews | 79 | 101 |

whilst residents at House A spent time working on their house magazin
The majority of residents at both houses went out for their entertain
ment at least once in a while, but the proportion who went out alone
rather than in company was higher at House B. Most residents seemed
have adopted a pattern of leisure activity during their 1st month and
no obvious trends over time were discernible.

Table 21 shows that the major sources of feelings of achievement
were the attainment of 'sobriety' (frequently mentioned at both house
but more frequently at House B), an increase in physical and mental

Table 21:  Summary of pleasing and upsetting events and sources of feelings of achievement and failure reported by residents at Houses A and B (Number of occasions events in each category were mentioned).

| | Pleasing Events | | Upsetting Events | | Achieve- ments | | Failures | |
|---|---|---|---|---|---|---|---|---|
| HOUSE: | A | B | A | B | A | B | A | B |
| Health and feelings of well-being | 15 | 10 | 7 | 10 | 22 | 14 | 15 | 7 |
| Sobriety and drinking | – | 4 | – | – | 19 | 33 | – | 3 |
| Outside employment | 11 | 10 | 4 | 2 | 12 | 10 | 7 | 5 |
| Finances and possessions | 1 | 5 | – | – | 4 | 1 | – | 1 |
| Family, home | 12 | 14 | 7 | 5 | 1 | 6 | 3 | 2 |
| Friend(s) outside the house | 3 | 6 | 3 | 3 | 3 | 2 | 3 | – |
| A resident leaving | – | – | 9 | 7 | – | – | – | 2 |
| The house or fellow resident(s) | 19 | 10 | 30 | 10 | 14 | 6 | 16 | 1 |
| Outside events (inc. social club activities, getting a flat, and betting losses) | 3 | 8 | 2 | 6 | 4 | 2 | 1 | 2 |

health and feelings of well-being (frequently mentioned at both houses but more frequently at House A), satisfactory achievements and relationships within the house itself (more frequently mentioned at House A), and work achievements.  Under the 'sobriety' heading were statements such as "Went out alone in the city, met some interesting people in pubs but did not drink" (House A), "Still at --- and sober" (House B), and "I have achieved sobriety, I feel terrific and I'm eating well" (House B).  In the second category (health and well-being) were statements such as, "Getting off drugs prescribed - now sleeping regularly and naturally" (House A), "I feel I cannot do any more than I am, I seem to have strength" (House A), "I have got my teeth fixed and now I have ordered my glasses" (House B), and "I'm keeping dry and I feel more relaxed and the atmosphere is easy" (House B).  In the house/ residents category came statements such as "Possibly I'm going to be asked to be group leader, I feel complimented" (House A), and "I am in the encounter group and my activities are paying off as I feel that people respect me" (House A).  And about work, statements such as the following were made, "I feel pleased I have jumped over a number of obstacles at work" (House A), "I have had 2 offers of a job which is unusual in my trade" (House A), and "I feel I have achieved something through work - I proved I can work when ready" (House B).  At both houses the achievement rate was high during the first few months and this sense of achievement began early.  There was no discernible trend over the first few months but a definite suggestion of a decline at

both houses thereafter in the rate at which achievements were reported
by the minority of residents who stayed for 5 months or more.

Increasing Upset and Feelings of Failure

Finally in a number of respects trends were detected which were
opposite to those anticipated. For example, the majority of men reported particularly pleasing events in their 1st month but the proportion of residents reporting such events declined at both houses between months 1 and 4, with a corresponding increase in the proportions
of residents reporting particularly upsetting events (always more frequently reported at House A). Similarly, feelings of failure and feel
ings of being 'under the weather' tended to increase over time at
House A, and although there was a suggestion that feelings of failure
declined in the first few months at House B they increased at the 6th
and 7th months.

Events mentioned as being particular sources of pleasure fell, as
can be seen from Table 21, predominantly in the family, employment,
health and well-being, and house and residents categories. As was the
case with sources of feelings of achievement, the house and its resid
ents provided a more frequent source of pleasure to residents at House
A than to those at House B. Family, employment and health can also co
stitute sources of upset for residents at either house. So too can th
event of a former fellow-resident leaving the house (e.g. "I feel very
put out by --- leaving, I feel there has been some deception" - said b
one resident at House A). What particularly distinguished the 2 house
was the frequency of upsetting events to do with the house itself and
with fellow residents. House A produced many more of these although
this category constituted the largest even at House B. Examples are,
"There is an anti-community feeling in the house" (House A), "The warden - I'm very disappointed in him" (House A), "I don't feel appreciat
for the work I've done in the house" (House B), and "I'm finding that
everyone is a con and I think the warden is being short-sighted" (Hous
B). Residents at both houses expressed feelings of personal failure
over jobs and over self-change although feelings of failure were expressed more frequently at House A. Examples of self-change failures
were, "I feel I failed in that I still feel very intolerant, although
I'm working at it, the trouble is I've always been like this" (House A
and "I'm conscious of the setbacks of my last slip, I feel I haven't
really changed as much as I thought" (House B). Again what principall
divided the 2 houses was the house/residents category. Whilst this wa
the most frequently occurring 'failure' category for House A residents
only 1 statement in this area was elicited from 1 resident at House B.
Examples are, "I have not written my article for 'Achievement'" (House
A), and "I feel there is very little feedback in the group, I feel per
haps I have spoken a wrong" (House A).

Although no predictions were made about staff-resident contact and
time in the house, there was a very marked decline in contact over tim
at House B which was not anticipated. Both staff members at House B
(there was no trend at House A) tended to give more than their usual
amount of time to residents who were in their 1st months in the house,
and were less and less likely to do so as residents became more 'senio
The increasing likelihood of a resident finding work is probably a
major reason for this trend.

Length of Stay

The distributions of lengths of stay of men entering Houses A and B during the study period are shown in Figure 16. The most striking aspect of these histograms is the concentration at the left-hand, short-stay end. The largest proportion of residents at both houses (40% - 50%) left within the 1st month of their residence, and ½ of all residents at both houses had left within 5 to 6 weeks. Only a minority (21% at A and 29% at B) stayed for as long as the 5 months which was the shortest length of stay stated to be ideal at any of the 11 London survey hostels. Only approximately 1 in every 8 residents (1 in every 9 or 10 at A, and 1 in every 5 or 6 at B) stayed for as long as the 9 months which was more usually stated by staff as being ideal. Five men

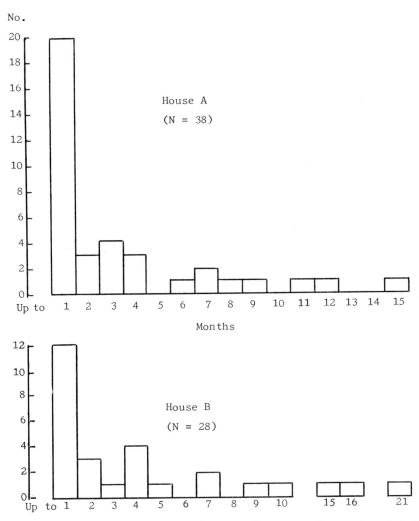

Figure 16: Lengths of stay of Intake Sample at Houses A and B (in months).

stayed for 12 months or more and the longest duration of stay was 21 months (House B). The whole length of stay curve was shifted slightly towards the longer-stay end for House B in comparison with House A, but the difference is slight and the general shape of the profiles is remarkably similar.

How representative are these profiles for these 2 houses? Figure 17 shows length of stay histograms for all the residents admitted from the time of each house's inception up to the beginning of the study period. The profiles are remarkably similar to one another and to the 2 study period profiles presented in Figure 16. The largest proportions of residents left Houses A and B within a month of arrival (40% - 60%), and only a minority have stayed for the 'minimum ideal' time of 5 months (27% at A, 16% at B). A handful only, less than 1 in every 12 at either house, have stayed for a year or more, and the occasional resident (1 at House A and 2 at House B) has stayed for 2 years or more.

Overall then, the study period emerges as fairly typical in the history of the 2 houses, in this one respect at least. There is, however, a slight suggestion that the study period may have been a relatively 'bad' period for House A, and a relatively 'good' period for House B. At House A the study median length of stay was between 4 and 5 weeks, compared with an overall pre-study median of 6 to 7 weeks, whilst at House B the study median of 6 weeks compared favourably with the overall pre-study median of 3 to 4 weeks.

## Ways of Departing

During their 2-weekly research interviews, each member of staff was asked to describe the circumstances surrounding the leaving of any recently departed resident. Informal information on the matter obtained from residents, or from other staff or regular house visitors, was also recorded. The type of information provided by staff about the departure of residents could be classified in a number of different ways. The method which seems most appropriate to these data is shown in Table 22.

### Planned and Orderly

Firstly it was apparent that only a small minority of departures (4 out of 39 at House A, and 4 out of 29 at House B) had a planned and orderly appearance in keeping with the rehabilitative aims of the 2 houses. From House A, 2 men left to take accommodation in the house of independent 'flatlets' which was situated almost opposite House A, in the same street, and which was managed by the same organization. Another resident left to take his own flat. All 3 of these men had been at House A for 6 to 7 months at the time of their departure. One further resident at House A left in an orderly, planned fashion but after only 5 weeks in the house. He worked for the Territorial Army and was offered a place on a residential course which required his leaving the house. The question of his possible return to the house at a later date was left open but in the event he did not re-apply. From House B, 4 residents left in a planned and orderly fashion after being at the house for between 15 and 24 months. One left having obtained his own accommodation, a 2nd left to take up a place in the house of 'three-quarter-way' flats organized by House C, and the 3rd left to take up residence in the project's own flats. The 4th took up residence at House G.

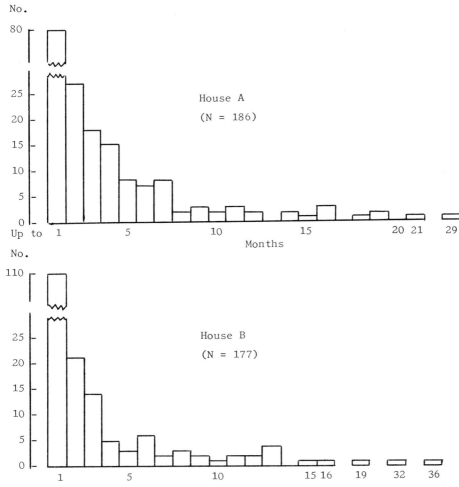

Figure 17: Lengths of stay of all House A residents admitted during the first 7 years, and all House B residents admitted during the first 5 years (in months).

Another 5 residents (3 at House A and 2 at B) left in a fairly orderly way but with the stated, or assumed, intention of resuming drinking. One resident left House A after only 1 week at the house telling the staff member in charge that he felt he was too young for a place like House A and was too young to stop drinking. He set off to seek work at a coastal resort. Another resident left after 4 months to share a flat with his girlfriend having made no secret of his intention to attempt 'social drinking'. His departure was well arranged in advance. The same was not true of the 3rd resident who also left House A after 4 months. He left to take a flat with a friend having expressed a strong, and uncontrollable compulsion to drink in the week prior to his departure. At House B,1 resident left after 6 months to take a living-in-job in a hotel. Staff and residents alike felt that such a move was tantamount to resuming heavy drinking although his departure from the house was an orderly one. The final case was that of a res-

Table 22: Ways of departing from Houses A and B (Departures of Intake Sample* outside brackets, departures during 18 4-week study months inside brackets).

|  | HOUSE A |  | HOUSE B |  |
|---|---|---|---|---|
| Drinking or drunk - left reluctantly | 8 | (7) | 4 | (4) |
| Drinking or drunk - left voluntarily | 5 | (5) | 10 | (9) |
| Left after dispute or tension - soon 'drinking' | 6 | (5) | 2 | (1) |
| Disappeared without warning - soon 'drinking' | 6 | (4) | 0 | (0) |
| Disappeared without warning - assumed 'drinking' | 7 | (6) | 7 | (7) |
| Orderly but with intention of drinking | 3 | (3) | 2 | (2) |
| Planned and orderly | 4 | (6) | 4 | (1) |
| Total departures | 39 | (36) | 29 | (24) |
| Total residents | 37 | (34) | 28 | (23) |

* Plus one resident at each house who had no intake interview.

ident who left, apparently on good terms with other residents, bound for a port to obtain work as a seaman. Staff and residents were left confused, as he had previously phoned up the project's director announcing his departure and saying that he had been drinking. One theory was that he had not in fact been drinking but had felt that this was one way of excusing his departure.

Drinking or Drunk

The remaining large majority of departures were disorderly and/or unplanned and were all associated with 'known' or 'assumed' drinking. At House A, ⅓ of all departures, and at House B, just under ½ were associated with drinking or drunkenness that was obvious to staff or other residents, or which was announced by the individual himself. In a number of instances (8 at House A, 4 at House B) the offending resident was reluctant to forfeit his membership and staff and/or other residents were obliged to 'turn him out'. The actual circumstances of these cases varied considerably. Some men were extremely drunk and obstreperous, while others disputed the right of staff and other residents to put them out. Several made a nuisance of themselves by returning repeatedly during the course of a single day or over the course of 2 or 3 days. Others, whose behaviour was not too disruptive, were allowed to stay overnight and were made to leave the following morning. One resident at House A returned and was allowed to stay on 2 successive night after it had become obvious to all that he had resumed drinking. He himself denied it.

In at least 2 further instances remaining residents had additional fears which were not in the event realized. For example at House A, when for a variety of reasons (see Chapter 9) the house was reduced to only 2 residents, one man failed to return one night and the single survivor locked himself in his bedroom fearing a reprisal for having discussed his suspicions with the staff member. At House B one resident created considerable bad feeling by declaring his expectation that other residents would support, against the views of the staff, his right to return to the house when drunk. There was a fear amongst the other residents that he might return to the house with a number of drinking friends.

A good deal of unpleasant disruption occurred in several instances. One man was described as "explosive and bitter - really angry and serious about things" when he returned drinking, and one man at House A was reported to have "shouted obscenities". In other cases departure followed a period of tension involving the individual concerned. One man at House B was reported to have been irritable and difficult for some time before drinking. He was said to have done a number of childish, spiteful things such as hiding the snooker balls and tipping ink on the staircase.

In other instances (more frequently at House B than at House A) a resident left quite voluntarily, making it known, if it were not already obvious, that he had been drinking. It was not unusual for residents at House B to leave in a quite non-disruptive fashion. Two residents phoned up the house to apologize for drinking and to say that they would not be returning. Another informed the house via another resident, and another did not return to the house but contacted one of the project's social workers. One resident went drinking with another one evening, returned to the house for the night, but slipped away before other residents were awake the following morning. Another House B resident returned for the night but left quietly the following morning handing his keys to another resident. Of one further resident it was just said that he "left quietly". This manner of leaving rarely occurred at House A although one resident did return to the house to hand in his key. He was reluctant even to enter the house although he was finally persuaded to do so by the group leader. Although it was agreed that he should leave, other residents were very sympathetic and discussed the possibility of having him back.

There was a more disruptive quality to the other 3 departures at House A which fell in this 'drinking but voluntary leaving' category. One resident, who had become tense in the house particularly over the group leader's behaviour, returned one evening and announced that he had been drinking. He then attended a group meeting specifically called by the staff member to discuss the incident. He was verbally aggressive towards almost all other residents in the meeting and was particularly accusatory against the group leader and 2 others. Another man stayed away on 2 consecutive nights, returning during the day, and slept in the house on the 3rd night. The following morning he was seen by the staff member and admitted that he had been drinking and should leave. Another House A resident was missing when it came time for the weekly group meeting. The staff member went to get him. He sat silently in the meeting for 10 minutes and then announced that he had been drinking. There followed a long discussion about him and his drinking. He accepted an invitation to stay the night but left the following morning.

After a Dispute

In a number of other instances, rather more frequently at House A, men left after a dispute or after a period of tension in the house. In such cases it was generally assumed that the person involved would be drinking either at the time of his departure or within the following few hours, and in most cases there seemed to be some confirmation of this expectation. For example, one resident at House A (Dave G, whose reputation is described in greater detail in Chapter 9) had been much criticized for his behaviour which was felt not to be in keeping with most of the other residents. He had been spending nights away from the house at his girlfriend's flat and was working unusual hours. Other residents had seen little of him in the days before he left. Within only a few days of his departure he was making tearful phone calls to the house and reported that he was drinking, threatening to commit suicide if he wasn't helped. Another resident had gambled with the money due to the house as rent for the week prior to his departure and on the day he left had gone out to collect his 'giro' cheque and had not returned. It was assumed that he was both drinking and gambling heavily, and indeed he did later phone the house to ask for further help on account of his drinking.

Another House A resident (Norman B) had been behaving strangely for some days before he left, and was suspected of taking 'pills'. He had also clearly been anxious about his job as organizer of the visitors' meeting and had 'broken down' when he had last been asked to introduce the house to visitors. He disappeared from the house, assumed drinking, and was later known to have been admitted to an alcoholism treatment unit in a mental hospital. In another instance tension had built up in House A around the personality of one particular resident. The staff member had a long session with him. He left the house the same day and was later seen drinking. He was next heard of at an out-of-London reception centre. In another case, one resident had become so agitated in the course of a particularly tense house meeting that he had hit another resident in the eye. He was clearly upset by his own behaviour, later apologized, and despite the attempts of other residents to persuade him to do otherwise, left. He was later reported drinking and was subsequently known to have been admitted to hospital for detoxification.

Perhaps the greatest tension of all surrounded one House A resident (Sam N) who was the sole surviving member of an earlier group despite being unpopular with 2 successive staff members. The new staff member felt that there was little hope of building a cohesive group with this resident still in the house and in the event almost all other residents left. He was finally discharged from the house to a mental hospital.

At House B one resident left after becoming noticeably tense, irritated and upset. He declared that he could no longer, "stand the four walls of the house". He left, and later gave his keys to another resident whom he met in the street. Subsequently he phoned the housekeeper, admitted he had had "a couple of pints", and asked her to meet him for a drink.

One of the 2 longest staying residents of all (Hughie A, 21 months at House B) had, almost throughout his period of stay, been afforded the protection of a special, rather deviant position as someone from whom full participation and co-operation could not always be relied upon (see Chapter 8). Periodically his behaviour would deteriorate to a troublesome level and this had occurred again just prior to his leaving the house. He finally left declaring that he was going to live with his sister. Another resident met him in a pub subsequently and reported that he had had "2 pints of beer".

Disappeared Without Warning

A very large number of residents (13 at House A and 7 at House B) simply 'disappeared' from the house without any explicit warning or explanation. Again the assumption was that in all these cases drinking had been resumed. The amount of evidence for this was highly variable. In some cases ex-residents returned to the house some days later obviously drunk. In other cases they phoned the house later, or occasionally wrote to say that they had started drinking again and wanted further help, or else were receiving it elsewhere. In most cases there were subsequent reports of admission to hospital, another hostel or a reception centre. In other instances the ex-resident had simply been 'seen'. In one case, for example, an ex-resident had been seen drinking publicly, on a number of occasions, and in a variety of locations in the south-east London area. On one occasion he was reported to be "going blind" and on another occasion to be "demented". Another resident was simply seen on one occasion on a bus, and the uncertainty which surrounds ex-resident drinking status is epitomized in the report that he was "sober but possibly drinking".

In some cases the assumption of resumed drinking may have been incorrect. One resident was known to have stayed at the reception centre shortly after leaving the house and was subsequently readmitted to House A. There was in fact no evidence that he had been drinking in the meantime. One resident at each house simply disappeared and was never heard of again, and one resident left House A because he "could not stand" another resident. He kept in contact with the staff member for 2 months during which time he recounted that he had his own flat, was working and not drinking. Only 2 months after leaving did he report drinking again. Even where there is fairly good evidence that some drinking has been resumed by an ex-resident, it is nonetheless quite uncertain how soon drinking is resumed, how heavy it is, how severe its effects, and how long it lasts.

In at least 3 cases the disappearance of a resident was associated with loss of money or personal possessions from the house.

## Information about Ex-Residents

### Further Contact with tne Hostel

During the course of the study an ever-growing list was compiled consisting of the names of ex-residents who had been present during the study period. Staff members were asked every 2 weeks, and other staff or house visitors were asked monthly, for any information they had received, either directly from the ex-residents or otherwise, about the whereabouts and drinking status of each ex-resident. No further systematic follow-up enquiry was attempted.

In fact there were very few residents (only 3 at House A and 1 at House B) about whom no one, known to the research team, had any subsequent information. A more systematic follow-up enquiry might well have made it possible to trace even these few individuals. Nearly all residents at both houses (28 at A, 20 at B) had some sort of contact with staff, remaining residents, or others connected with the house, within 1 month of their departure. Occasionally this contact amounted to nothing more than being 'seen' on a single occasion, but in most cases definite contact was made with the house either in person or by letter or telephone, or else the ex-resident's location at another hostel, or alternative helping or penal agency, was known. However, with the exception of the occasional resident who took accommodation in a flat managed by the same organization that ran the house he had left, or in one managed by a similar organization, and the 2 residents (1 from each house) who took up jobs on the staff of the organization running House B, contacts were sporadic. Undoubtedly the probability of contact with an ex-resident declined as time since departure increased.

Way of Departing and Subsequent Progress

The circumstances under which a resident leaves a small alcoholism hostel bear an uncertain relationship to subsequent events. Certainly the lives of those few residents who left in a 'planned and orderly' fashion were not all entirely trouble-free after they left. Two residents at House A moved to a flat across the road. Part of the idea of locating these flats so close to House A was the hope that the ex-resident would be a frequent visitor to the house, and would possibly benefit himself and current residents of House A in the process. One of these 2 ex-residents came back to House A only infrequently and staff A2 was disappointed on this account. He started drinking about 2 months after leaving the house and was required to leave his flat. Subsequently he was admitted to the 'quarter-way-house' which was part of the House B organization, and later he was admitted as a resident of House C. The other resident who left for one of these flats was described before he left as "lethargic" (by staff A2). The latter felt that his going to one of these flats was a sign of "dependency". Several months later he had not visited House A once, even at Christmas time, and was described by staff A2 as "very miserable - not going out - not getting up at weekends". Nonetheless he remained a resident in this flat for several months, apparently not drinking.

Another House A resident who left in a reasonably orderly and planned way had not been popular in the house before he left. He was considered dictatorial, self-centred, and unpleasant towards the first woman resident of the house. A few weeks after his departure the staff member received a phone call from his employer enquiring of his whereabouts. He was subsequently heard of at a psychiatric alcoholism treatment unit, and later at the reception centre.

Soon after leaving to live on his own after a long and distinguished period of residence at House B, one ex-resident was thought to be becoming a 'compulsive gambler' and it was thought that living on his own was impossible for him. Although there was no evidence that he had been drinking since leaving House B, he was readmitted to the house and after staying there for a further several months, he moved to a 'group home'. Two of the most obviously successful histories following admissions to one of these houses were those of 2 House B residents who left the house in a planned and orderly way. However it is notable that both used hostel accommodation for many further months, one in a flat operated by the House C organization and the other at House G.

Just as there were some men whose departure was smooth but who subsequently had a troubled history, there were others who left House A or B under a cloud but who subsequently did well elsewhere. One obvious example was a man who left House A after drinking and after a stormy group meeting, and subsequently spent periods at the reception centre and living at House G, before taking up his new career as a worker in the alcoholism field. The other man left House B after drinking having

been there for little more than 2 weeks.  Following a period in a hospital alcoholism treatment unit he was referred to another hostel where
he stayed for over 6 months and later also took up a job as an alcoholism worker.

A small number of other ex-residents appear to have settled later.
For example, 2 ex-residents of House A were known to be living in their
own flats some months later, one having been readmitted to House A for
a period in the meantime, the other having spent some time at another
small hostel.  One ex-resident of House B settled in one of the project's flats following a further period of residence at the house.

Further Agency Contacts

After leaving House A or B the majority of ex-residents continued
to make the rounds of hospitals, courts, prisons, reception centres,
lodging houses, and hostels large and small, as they had done before
their admission.  Table 23 shows the numbers of ex-residents known to
have been the patients, clients or subjects of a variety of institutions and agencies after leaving House A or B.  These figures almost
certainly represent under-estimates owing to the informal, and accidental nature of the follow-up on which they are based.  Furthermore,
the only contacts noted are those reported to have occurred up to the
June, 12 months after the last intake to the study.  Many ex-residents
were known to have stayed at a Government reception centre and quite a
number had been in a mental hospital or prison, some more than once.
Many (14 at House A, 15 at House B) had had a further period of residence at a small hostel for alcoholics.  Two ex-residents of House A
had had a further period of residence at the same house, and the same
was true of 7 ex-residents of House B.  Eight further ex-residents

Table 23:  Numbers of study period ex-residents of Houses A and B
known to have subsequently been the residents, patients, clients or
subjects of a variety of agencies and institutions.

|  | House A |  | House B |  |
| --- | --- | --- | --- | --- |
| Psychiatric hospital | 9 |  | 6 |  |
| General hospital | 3 |  | 1 |  |
| Hospital of either type |  | 11 |  | 7 |
| Returned to same alcoholism hostel | 2 |  | 7 |  |
| Another alcoholism hostel | 12 |  | 12 |  |
| Any alcoholism hostel |  | 14 |  | 15 |
| Prison | 4 |  | 9 |  |
| Court | 2 |  | 3 |  |
| Reception Centre | 16 |  | 9 |  |
| Prison, Court or reception centre |  | 21 |  | 15 |
| Any of these agencies or institutions |  | 29 |  | 23 |
| Total ex-residents |  | 37 |  | 29 |

of House A and 1 at House B had re-applied to the house, or shown an interest in coming back to the house, but had not been readmitted. Overall, no fewer than 29 of 37 ex-residents of House A were known to have been in subsequent contact with one or more of these institutions or agencies, and 4 others had applied to come back to House A. The comparable figures for House B were 23 of 29 ex-residents in contact with one or more institution or agency, and 1 further ex-resident who had re-applied to come back to House B.

## A Note on Drinking Outcome

It will be recalled that a few days after coming to one or other of the houses, roughly ⅓ of all residents (39% at A, 29% at B) claimed to have maintained a period of at least 3 months of continuous abstinence from alcohol at some time in the recent past, whilst living outside an institutional or other special environment which prohibited the use of alcohol. A further ⅓ (32% at A, 36% at B) claimed at least 2 to 3 weeks continuous abstinence (see Chapter 6). What is of present interest is that the proportions of residents remaining in Houses A and B for 3 months or more (39% at A, 50% at B), and for 3 to 12 weeks (37% at A, 29% at B) are not very different from the percentages claiming comparable periods of abstinence in the past, and that residents claiming longer periods of abstinence in the past are somewhat more likely to stay longer at House A or B (the numbers are too small to allow statistical significance). The overall effect is that only ½ or less (34% at House A, 46% at House B) are clearly shown to have achieved longer periods of abstinence with the support of House A or B than without it, and there is also a minority (26% at House A, 25% at House B) who claim longer periods of abstinence in the past. The unverified, self-report, nature of information on previous abstinence should of course be borne in mind in the interpretation of these figures.

A final word is in order about the possibility of 'controlled' or 'normal' drinking by former residents of alcoholism hostels. The general assumption was that the future drinking indulged in by ex-residents would be 'uncontrolled' in nature. Indeed there was much evidence to support this notion in many cases. Nonetheless there were occasional reports of continued drinking which was not uncontrolled. For example, it was staff A2's opinion that one ex-resident, who was now living approximately 50 miles from London, had been on a bender at Christmas time but was otherwise indulging in "controlled drinking". There were several similar reports of House B ex-residents. For example one man was described as "sober" on a return visit to the house but it was thought that he was "probably social drinking". Another ex-resident after coming out of prison, was reported by a project social worker who was in touch with him to be "drinking mildly". The same social worker spoke of "controlled drinking" in relation to yet another ex-resident of House B. Finally, a House B ex-resident who joined the project team gave his opinion that another ex-resident was now "drinking moderately".

## SUMMARY

### Similarities Between Houses A and B

Progress in the House

1. At both houses the likelihood of a resident being in employment,

feeling in good health, and contributing to group meetings increased within the first few weeks of arrival at the house.

2. The level of felt achievement in the areas of sobriety, health and well-being, outside employment, and involvement in the house were high within the first few weeks. However, on the whole, feelings of achievement and satisfaction tended to decline thereafter, and feelings of upset and failure tended to increase. Some residents made progress in contacting family or friends, and in recreational and leisure activities, but there was no general progressive trend as residents remained for longer periods of time.

Length of Stay

3. The largest proportion of residents (40/50%) left within the 1st month and only a minority (20/30%) stayed for 5 months or more. Most departures were therefore premature. These figures were fairly representative of the total histories of the 2 houses.

4. A minority of residents stayed for much longer; 5 for 12 months or more, and 1 for as long as 21 months.

5. Only a minority (between $\frac{1}{3}$ and $\frac{1}{2}$) of residents achieved longer periods of abstinence during residence than they claimed in the recent past before coming to the house, whilst about $\frac{1}{4}$ claimed longer recent periods of abstinence outside the hostel than they achieved during their stay there.

Manner of Leaving

6. Only a small minority (around 10/15%) left in a planned and orderly manner. Of the others, a large number left after drinking ($\frac{1}{3}$ / $\frac{1}{2}$). Others left after a dispute or tension in the house, or disappeared without warning. Another small number left in an orderly way but with the intention of resuming drinking.

7. In many instances uncontrolled drinking was obvious soon after the resident had left, and in other cases it was assumed to have occurred although the evidence for it was variable. It was generally assumed that drinking indulged in during residence and by ex-residents would be uncontrolled in nature, and no account was taken of the possibility that drinking might sometimes be controlled or limited.

Information about Ex-Residents

8. No systematic follow-up was attempted but nearly all residents had some contact with staff or remaining residents shortly after leaving, and some were in contact for much longer. Some longer-stay residents needed continuing support after they left. Like other hostel organizations, those running Houses A and B had started to provide accommodation, and in one case 'New Careers' also, for some ex-residents.

9. Length of stay and manner of leaving had little relationship with subsequent progress.

10. Even without systematic follow-up it was known that most ex-residents sought further help from the same or another small alcoholism hostel, or had some subsequent contact with some penal, treatment or helping agency. Many (40/50%) were known to have had a further period

of residence at a small alcoholism hostel.

## Differences Between Houses A and B

### Progress in the House

1. At House B, staff tended to spend less time with residents as time passed (there was no trend at House A). At House A, staff tended to give less favourable accounts of residents as time passed (there was no trend at House B).

2. 'The house' or 'other residents' were mentioned more frequently at House A than at House B as sources of pleasing events and feelings of achievement, but were also more frequently mentioned at House A as sources of upsetting events, and particularly of feelings of failure. 'Sobriety' was more likely to be mentioned as an achievement at House B than at House A.

### Manner of Leaving

3. At House B, men were more likely to leave voluntarily after drinking or to disappear without warning and without giving definite evidence that they were drinking. At House A, men were more likely to leave reluctantly after drinking, to leave after a dispute or tension in the house, or to disappear without warning but giving clear evidence that they were soon drinking.

### Information about Ex-Residents

4. After leaving House A, men were more likely to be known to have used hospital services than men at House B, while the latter were more likely to be known to have been in prison, to have appeared in court, or to have stayed at a reception centre. These differences parallel differences in experience prior to staying at House A or B (Chapter 6).

# Chapter 11
# Recommendations

> Historically, research in the mental health field has often
> not been used by mental health administrators to alter their
> existing programs; research and service usually proceed along
> parallel lines, neither one affecting the other very much.
> ...unused research material accumulates at an ever-increasing
> rate... (Fairweather et al, 1974, p.5).

A strong argument exists (see Chapter 4) for concluding that small
alcoholism hostels have made a positive contribution towards a humane
and effective response in this specialized area of social problems.
Nevertheless, the major conclusion of this account of research is the
highlighting of a number of serious operational difficulties which
limit the potential of the small alcoholism hostel as an effective
entity. Some of the main difficulties have been discussed already in
Chapter 4. They include the following: lack of clarity about the hostel
program; about the locus of decision-making in the hostel; about length
of stay and goals; the difficulty of maintaining a stable culture over
any length of time; the dislocation of the rehabilitation process when
residents leave; rigidity in the methods employed for controlling drinking (all being abstinence oriented); under-emphasis on providing new
resources for residents, particularly for those residents with long-
term needs for sheltered housing and work; and poor working conditions
for staff.

The following very general recommendations are made in the light of
this evaluation. This is not the place to make more detailed or specific recommendations which might be inappropriate in local circumstances or might be overtaken by rapidly changing ideas. More general recommendations, on the other hand, may assist in influencing the broad
direction of thinking. The following are presented roughly in order of
importance with the most important first.

The Need for Continued Innovation

There are at least 2 major reasons why variety and further innovation should be encouraged. The first consists of the list of problems
that beset those that run small hostels for alcoholics (see above and
Chapter 4). Whilst many will continue to wrestle with these problems
in the small hostels that already exist or in others like them, others
should be encouraged to try new forms of response which may not share
these same difficulties. The second reason for insisting that small
hostels do not become the sole, routine form of provision for 'alcohol-

ics' who are temporarily homeless or who have been homeless for a long time, is the evident heterogeneity of the population in need (see Chapter 3). Different people are likely to prefer, and to benefit from, different forms of provision.

It would therefore be quite inappropriate if thinking was limited in the next decade by the 'experiments' of the last one, or if systems for financing, accommodating and staffing new projects forced these to set in a mould which has been too hastily prepared. Variety should be encouraged in the form of different hostel sizes, mixes of 'alcoholics' and other 'problem' and 'non-problem' people, selection and discharge policies, drinking goals, and types of internal organization, to name only a few sources of potential variation. Of equal, if not greater importance, is the future development of forms which fall outside the definition of 'hostel' altogether. Some of these will be seen as adjuncts to the 'small hostel', whilst others will be alternatives to it. One such development was briefly discussed at the end of Chapter 4. Others are yet to be conceived.

To date the balance in alcoholism hostels has been towards the socialization task - getting residents to think and act appropriately. This balance should be redressed by greater awareness of the need to concentrate on the provision-of-new-resources aspect of social influence (see Chapter 2). Hostels need not be incompatible with a more effective 'push' in the areas of social contact and recreational facilities, but more particularly in the areas of housing and employment. There will undoubtedly be further advances on housing but there is much room for experiment in the special provision of vocational guidance, retraining, and employment itself. Individual non-statutory organizations may be too small to think of providing these facilities alone, an they may have to be provided on a consortium basis, or else more systematic use will have to be made of the resources that already exist.

Reducing the Dislocation on Departure

For those who intend to continue to grapple with the difficulties of running small hostels for alcoholics, the dislocation which occurs in the rehabilitation process when most residents leave (Chapter 10) is likely to continue to be the principal failing and the one that requires most thought and attention.

There is room for radical re-thinking about the beliefs which staff hold and which they encourage residents to hold about the nature of 'alcoholism', about the expectations which staff and residents hold concerning the future drinking habits of residents, about the handling of drinking incidents in hostels, and about lengths of stay and readmission policies. There is at present a depressing uniformity on these matters (see Chapter 4) and a very real danger that entrenched attitudes will prevent the innovation which is necessary to overcome a weakness which could prove fatal to the alcoholism hostel movement.

A way needs to be found to break the conspiracy of silence that exists inside alcoholism hostels over questions such as the future drinking of residents and the possibility of unplanned or premature departure Much more time needs to be devoted to preparing residents for these eventualities so that progress is not totally lost when they occur. Hostels must try and arrange for the continuity of care which at present they are largely failing to provide.

Advanced Consideration of Hostel Philosophy

Lack of clarity, contradictions, and misunderstandings over goals and methods often seem to be the rule rather than the exception in small hostels. Frequently there is conflict over quite basic issues, and this involves residents, staff, ex-members of staff, committee members, referral agents and others. These conflicts often stem from failure to recognize the obvious fact that different types of hostel are possible. Despite present uniformity in some respects, there is even now much variation in other ways, particularly in terms of internal organization and especially on the matter of resident decision-making.

The range of options open to those who plan and run alcoholism hostels should be recognized, and deliberate choices from amongst these options should be made and adhered to. Most important is the basic philosophy of the hostel. Is it to be 'democratic', using a general 'therapeutic community approach' and involving its residents in decision-making as much as possible? Or is it felt that residents require a firm helping hand from staff? Do residents require some form of group psychotherapy? Is the hostel 'transitional', intended as a halfway house, or is it anticipated that some residents will wish to stay more or less indefinitely? These are amongst the fundamental matters which must be agreed about and made fully explicit if confusion and conflict is to be avoided. Special attention needs to be paid to these matters when new staff are recruited. At such times it needs to be decided whether a staff member is to be appointed whose training, experience, and attitudes will make him likely to carry on established tradition, or whether he is to be given a free hand to develop his own regime which may well differ considerably from that of his predecessor.

Planners should be aware of the significance of structural variables such as the size of the hostel, the ratio of staff to residents, and whether staff live in or not. Decisions on matters such as these should be taken in the light of the agreed philosophy. It should be recognized that a hostel is not just 'a hostel' but is one of a particular kind. There must be all-round agreement on what kind it is, and policy decisions on a whole range of matters should be consistent with this.

Conflict frequently crystalizes around the question of the selection of new members, and such conflicts involve referral agents and prospective residents. Practice usually represents a compromise: whilst the hostel continues to be selective in the interests of cohesiveness and beneficial social influence within the house, it tries at the same time to preserve an image as a public service which operates with only the minimum of necessary selectivity. A great deal of confusion and misunderstanding could be avoided if those responsible for hostels were more explicit in their approach to referral and selection. One solution would be to acknowledge the uncertainty of selection procedures and hence to adopt a policy of being unselective, or of taking unselectively from selected referral agents. For those wishing to remain selective, and this will probably be the majority, there is a need to argue the case for selection far more cogently than is usually done. Referral agents need to understand the hostel's need to take care in establishing and maintaining a 'culture' of a particular type, and the reasons why selection criteria may change from time to time. Fostering this understanding is a time-consuming business. Ideally there should be regular communication and mutual visiting between hostel staff and existing residents on the one hand, and prospective residents and referral agents on the other.

## Control of the Social Influence Process

Staff and managers should be more aware of the group dynamics of a small socializing system with high turnover (see Chapters 2, 8 and 9). The inherent instability of such a system, and the difficulty of creating a group of beneficial influence, are likely to remain cardinal features of small alcoholism hostels. However, these problems are so central to the efficiency or inefficiency of a hostel that much thought should be given to producing partial solutions to them. How can those who run hostels come to feel that they have more power to control and facilitate the development and maintenance of groups that have a good influence?

In view of the undoubted importance of group composition, one way of gaining more control over group processes might be to obtain the services of ex-residents, ex-residents of other hostels, senior residents who might otherwise be leaving, or others whose character and values would assist the development of cohesiveness around the approved ethic. This 'planting' of culture carriers might be particularly important when group composition was otherwise lacking. Even if deliberate 'manipulation' of group composition in this way was impossible, there should at least be a greater awareness of fluctuations in stability and atmosphere so that trends can be discerned and any available appropriate action taken, or at least inappropriate action avoided. If there is to be any injection of 'technology' into the running of small hostels, it is likely to be in this department, drawing on findings in the social psychology of small groups and organizations.

In view of the special role which staff play in the social influence process in most small alcoholism hostels, functioning would be improved by relieving the isolation which many staff members feel whilst at the same time taking care not to reduce their autonomy. Although it may be too early to stipulate conditions relating to appropriate staff training, there would be benefit in laying down some guidelines for the facilitation of the support and continued education of hostel staff. In view of the tensions which very frequently arise in the course of work in small hostels, thought might be given to allowing for a regular review of the work satisfaction of all hostel staff, and even for the arrangement of independent investigation and advice in the event of local disputes. Such arrangements might be made conditions for the granting of financial assistance.

## Future Research

Although it is probably unrealistic to call for individual organizations to 'build research in' to all new or existing ventures, grant-giving and management bodies have a role to play in stimulating necessary future research. Large grant-giving bodies, such as Government departments or large charitable trusts, should sponsor research in collaboration with interested University departments. Meanwhile, all grant-giving and management bodies should require that records be kept to some minimum standard in order to facilitate monitoring and any future research that might be carried out.

Finally, research workers themselves could take more of an interest in this field. Alcoholism itself represents an intriguing puzzle for psychology and the social sciences, defying exact definition or reliable attempts at prevention or treatment.  Small hostels, quite apart from their current prominence in stated policies for residential care, embody both the small group processes about which social psychologists have had so much to say in the past, and some of the aspirations of those who would seek alternative forms of domestic arrangement other than the nuclear family.  As the present authors can testify, alcoholism and the small hostel or halfway house in combination present a range of phenomena irresistable to the social scientist.

## Appendix A - The Staff Interview

Except where indicated, each section of this interview was administered to all the following members of staff: the staff member in charge at the house (every 2 weeks), the senior social worker or project director (every 2 or 4 weeks depending upon the amount of their contact with the house), regular visiting staff (occasional interviews), and the cook at House B (every 2 weeks). The cook and the cleaner at House A were less involved with the residents and were interviewed informally only.

### Section 1 - Referrals (Staff in charge and senior staff only)

Staff were provided with forms on which they were instructed to record the details of each referral made. The information required was the name of the man **referred**, his date of birth, the name of the referring agent and agency, dates of **selection** interviews with staff and with existing residents, the outcome of the referral, and reasons for termination of the referral process if the referral did not result in admission. At each interview with the staff member the research worker checked that these forms were being completed, and asked for clarification of detail if any was needed.

### Section 2 - House Membership (Staff in charge only)

The research worker updated her list of current and ex-residents by asking for names and dates of admission of all newly admitted residents, and for the dates of leaving of all recently departed residents. In the case of recent departures staff were asked to describe the circumstances surrounding departure (whether the departure had been planned, or announced, whether it had been voluntary or not, whether it was associated with drinking or disruption, the attitude of fellow residents, etc.).

### Section 3 - Staff Availability

Staff were provided with forms, to complete between interviews, detailing the times which they spent at the house itself. The forms were of grid design with rows representing each of the 7 days of the week and columns for each hour of the day. At each interview with the staff member the research worker checked the completion of these forms and asked for clarification where necessary.

## Section 4 - Staff Contact with Residents

Each staff member was asked to consider in turn each man who had been resident in the house at any time since the previous interview with that staff member. In each case the staff member was asked to estimate the amount of time which he or she had spent with that resident. Three separate estimates were required: the amount of time spent on <u>house business</u>, the amount of time spent in <u>formal-personal</u> contact, and the amount of <u>informal</u> contact (fuller details of these 3 categories of contact are provided in Chapter 7).

## Section 5 - House Issues

At each interview with the research worker the staff member in charge was asked to choose and to talk about one 'issue' that had arisen since his last interview. The research worker probed to discover whether different opinions had been held on this issue, whether any decision was required and if so whether one had been reached, and who had made the decision. All other staff members were asked to talk about the issue which had been raised in the research worker's interview with the staff member in charge. All of these interviews were tape-recorded and later transcribed. Examples of 'issues' raised by staff members in charge, and an example of how one issue was dealt with at each house, are provided in Chapter 7.

## Section 6 - Staff Assessment of Residents

Each staff member was asked to comment upon each man who had been resident in the house at any time since the last interview. The initial question was general (e.g. "How is --- getting on?", "What do you feel about --- now?") and the research worker was otherwise as non-directive as possible. All these comments were tape-recorded and later transcribed.

Transcriptions were later rated on a 100-point evaluative (favourable-unfavourable) scale (also described in Chapter 8).

The following is an example of a comment rated as extremely favourable (90):

---is making good progress again, he is very determined to stop drinking. I found out that he had got an unbelievable history of not drinking in the reception centre, and he had 14 weeks in the reception centre earlier in the year. He is very determined, sensible and sensitive. He is a lot better since he started work, he is a lot more forthcoming, and I think that the early days when he was very quiet and morose and unemployed were worth it. I think he got to grips with something then.

The following is a passage rated as extremely unfavourable (10):

---is tending to withdraw from the group, it has been suggested that he has problems in relation to a married woman and that he is not prepared to communicate this to anyone else. He has tended to go to his own bed rather than making some excuses. In the group he is still very verbal although not much to say, he is used to using a lot of words, saying virtually nothing.

Inter-judge reliability tests were performed on these ratings after piloting and before their use in the study proper. Each of 3 judges rated each of 24 staff comments. Rank-order correlations between each pair of judges were 0.90, 0.91 and 0.97. This exercise was repeated on a 2nd set of 24 comments towards the end of the study. Correlations of the same order were produced.

Section 7 - Staff Assessment of Atmosphere

Staff responses to the single question, "What has the atmosphere been like in the last --- weeks?" were tape-recorded and transcribed, and the transcriptions were content analyzed for positive and negative statements (see Chapter 8).

Section 8 - Information on Ex-Residents

The research worker maintained an ever-growing list of former residents who had left the houses during the time of the study. Each staff member was asked if he or she had received any news of each man on this list. If fresh information was provided, details,including the source of information, were noted.

## Appendix B - The Initial Resident Interview

Detailed instructions to the interviewer are omitted here and the layout has been condensed. In the actual interview schedule terms such as 'weeks', 'friends' and 'hostels' were defined more carefully, and the interviewer was instructed to probe and check information in certain places.

## Section 1 - Recent Social History

Number of weeks in prison in the previous 12 months?
Number of weeks as an in-patient in hospital in the previous 12 months?
Number of weeks as a resident in an alcoholism hostel in the previous 12 months?

(The next 3 questions refer to the most recent 12 accumulated months living outside prison, hospital or alcoholism hostel).

Weeks in these 12 months living with family member(s) or with friend(s)?
(Coded: None = 0, 1 - 13 = 1, 14 - 26 = 2, 27 - 39 = 3, 40+ = 4).

Weeks in these 12 months living in reception centre, lodging house(s) or hostel(s) with dormitory accomodation, 'skippering', 'sleeping rough', sleeping out etc?
(Coded: None = 0, 1 - 9 = 1, 10 - 29 = 2, 30+ = 3).

Weeks worked (incl. part-time work)?
(Coded: 0 - 9 = 0, 10 - 26 = 1, 27 - 39 = 2, 40+ = 3).

Penultimate (to exclude bias on account of a single isolated recent contact) contact with any family (incl. phone, 2-way correspondence)?
(Coded: None in the last 12 months = 0, 4 - 12 months ago = 1, 1 - 3 months ago = 2, within last 30 days = 3).

## Section 2 - Recent Drinking History

(Answers to the next 9 questions were coded twice. Once for _ever_: never = 0, 1 - 5 times = 1, 6+ times = 6. Secondly for _recently_: not in the last 12 months = 0, in the last 12 months but not in the last 4 weeks nor in the last 4 weeks outside an institution = 1, in the last 4 weeks outside an institution = 2, in the last 4 weeks = 3, in the last week = 4).

"Have you, on waking in the morning after drinking the night before, been unable to stop yourself shaking so much that it was difficult to do things like lifting a cup of tea to drink?" (Tremor)

"Have you, the morning after drinking the night before, been unable to remember anything which happened over a period of an hour or more of the previous evening or day, although you knew that you must have been behaving fairly normally at the time?" (Amnesia)

"Have you, either whilst you were drinking, or within a day or 2 after stopping drinking, seen or heard quite clearly something

or somebody which you knew was really not there?"
(Hallucinations)

"Have you been convicted of a drunkenness offence: that is,
drunk or drunk and disorderly or driving under the influence
of drink?" (Drunkenness offence)

"Have you, as a result of drinking, been physically aggressive
towards some other person; a member of your family, a friend
or acquaintance or perhaps a complete stranger?" (Aggression)

"Have you been convicted of an offence other than a drinking
offence?" (Other offence)

"Have you drunk some crude spirit, methylated or surgical
spirit, even if only a small quantity?" (Crude spirit drinking)

"Have you felt so low in spirits that you have tried to take
your own life?" (Suicide attempt)

"Have you attended meetings of Alcoholics Anonymous?" (AA
attendance)

Longest unbroken period of total abstinence outside prison,
hospital or alcoholism hostel in the most recent 12 months
outside an institution?
(Coded: less than 24 hours = 0, 1 - 17 days = 1, $2\frac{1}{2}$ - 12
weeks = 2, 13+ weeks = 3).

Residence in alcoholism rehabilitation hostel, prisoners'
after-care or probation hostel?
(Coded: Never = 0, yes but never longer than 4 weeks = 1,
longer than 4 weeks = 2).

Hospital treatment for alcoholism?
(Coded Never = 0, out-patient only, less than 4 visits = 1,
out-patient only, more than 4 visits = 2, in-patient but
never more than 4 weeks = 3, in patient more than 4 weeks = 4).

Psychiatric treatment not for alcoholism?
(Coded: Never = 0, out-patient only = 1, in-patient = 2).

Most recent drink before commencing present hostel residence?
(Coded: Same or previous day = 0, 2 - 7 days before = 1,
8 - 14 days before = 2, 15 - 28 days before = 3, 29 - 42 days
before = 4, 43+ days before = 5).

Section 3 - Previous Social History

(Several questions in this section constitute the scale of previous social stability described in greater detail in Table 5).

Country of birth?

Age left childhood home?

Age completed full-time education?

Nature of highest status job held? (Coded later in accordance
with the Hall-Jones scale of occupational prestige).

Longest continuous employment with one employer? (Coded in
months).

Longest continuous period of time living at one address since leaving childhood home? (Coded in months).

Age at first conviction of any offence other than a drunkenness offence?

Age first stayed at a reception centre, or in a lodging house or hostel with dormitory accomodation, or 'slept rough', etc.?

Section 4 - Demographic

Age?

Date of birth?

Full name? (plus any aliases or nicknames).

## Appendix C - The Subsequent, 4-Weekly, Recurring Resident Interview

As outlined in Chapter 5, the first of these interviews was conducted approximately 2 weeks after a resident's arrival at the house. Detailed instructions to the interviewer have been omitted from this Appendix.

### Section 1 - Events and Satisfactions Since Previous Interview

Any illness since last interview?

Feelings of being 'under the weather' or particularly tense or anxious?

Taking any prescribed drugs?

In, off, or out of work?

Work satisfaction? (Coded on a 3-point scale; satisfied, neutral or qualified, not satisfied).

Source of finances?

Satisfaction with present financial situation? (Coded on a 3-point scale; satisfied, neutral or qualified, not satisfied).

Number of evenings out in company?

Number of evenings out alone?

Nature of leisure time activities?

Anything happened which has caused upset?

Anything happened which has been particularly pleasing?

Anything happened which represents a personal achievement?

Anything happened which was particuarly disappointing and represented a personal failure? (Answers to this and the previous 3 questions each coded on 3-point scales; little, moderate, or extreme upset, pleasure, achievement or failure).

Any contact with any family member?

Satisfaction with recent family contacts? (Coded on a 3-point scale; satisfied, neutral or qualified, unsatisfied).

Any contact with friend(s)?

Satisfaction with recent contacts with friend(s)? (Coded on a 3-point scale; satisfied, neutral or qualified, unsatisfied).

Any contact with outside source of help?

Satisfaction with recent contacts with outside source(s) of help? (Coded on a 3-point scale; satisfied, neutral or qualified, unsatisfied).

### Section 2 - Views on Handling of Hypothetical Instances of Misconduct

The interviewer presented each of 8 hypothetical instances of misconduct in turn (details are provided in Chapter 7, Table 10) and in each case asked the 1st of the following 3 questions, followed by the 2nd and 3rd questions if applicable:

A     "Should anyone in the house do anything about it?" (Coded: no, nothing you can do, shouldn't be a rule, individual problem, doesn't matter = 1; only sympathy, friendly advice, etc. = 2; should be discussed only = 3; depends on individual, frequency of misconduct, motive, etc. = 4; don't know, uncertain, etc. = 5; yes something should be done = 6).

B     "Who should decide what should be done? Where and how should the ultimate decision be taken?" (Coded: staff alone = 1; staff and group leader or chairman together = 2; group leader or chairman alone = 3; staff and residents jointly but staff should have last say or special responsibility = 4; group leader or chairman with all other residents but group leader or chairman should have last say or special responsibility = 5; joint decision of staff and all residents = 6; residents as a group without staff = 7; not applicable because of answer to question A = 8).

C     "What ought to be done to the resident concerned?" (Coded: should be asked to leave = 1; one more chance before being asked to leave = 2; should be spoken to, confronted, tackled, lectured, etc. = 3; sympathetic discussion in meeting, group should find out cause, group should advise, etc. = 4; should have private talk with a staff member or group leader or chairman, etc. = 5; don't know, uncertain, etc. = 6; not applicable because of answer to question A = 8).

## Section 3 - Sociometric Choices

Each resident was asked to nominate up to 3 other people (2 if the total number of current residents was only 5 or 6, 1 if the total was only 3 or 4; staff were not excluded) in accordance with each of the following 3 criteria:

1     "If you were to go out in the evening or at weekends with someone, with whom would you most like to go?" (Social).

2     "Who contributes most to the house, makes it a good place to live in?" (Contribution).

3     "Who seems the most understanding about other people's problems?" (Understanding).

## Section 4 - Residents' Assessments of Staff

Each resident was asked to respond 'yes', 'no', or 'uncertain' in reply to each of 10 statements pertaining to his perception of the staff member in charge. These items were selected from a scale devised by Ellsworth (1965) and are shown in Chapter 8, Table 15.

## Section 5 - Residents' Assessment of House Atmosphere

This section was also administered at the time of the initial resident interview. The following 2 questions were asked of each resident and responses were recorded verbatim:

1     "What is it like for you being at --- House at the moment?"

2   "I wonder if you could suggest one thing that could be changed or improved to do with the house?"

The following additional question was asked if the 2nd question met with no response:

3   "Could you mention anything that you are disappointed with or not happy about?"

Responses were subsequently rated on a 5-point scale which is described in Chapter 8.

Appendix D - Interaction Recordings of House Meetings

The technique of interaction recording was designed to monitor the following three variables:

1    The volume of speech contributed by each participant.

2    The volume of speech received by each participant.

3    The level of emotionality of each contribution.

Each participant was assigned a number and a row on the sheets of graph paper on which the research worker made her recordings. Successive entries were made in successive columns; thus the passage of time was represented by movement from left to right across a single sheet of recording paper, and from sheet to succeeding sheet.

The speaker determined the row in which the entry was made. The entry itself consisted of a symbol indicating the level of emotionality of the speaker's utterance (Alpha, Beta or Gamma), followed by the number of the person to whom the speaker directed his utterance ('0' if it was unclear to whom the utterance was directed, or if it was directed to the whole group or to no one in particular). Hence a new entry was made whenever there was a change of speaker, or a change in level of emotionality, or a change in the direction of an utterance. A unit was therefore, for these purposes, a speech of constant level of emotionality delivered by a single speaker in a single direction. Hence length of time was not a determinant of a unit.

As described in Chapter 7, the symbol Alpha was used for utterances judged to be unemotional, Beta for utterances judged emotional in content but which were unaccompanied by non-verbal indications of emotion, such as tone of voice, posture or gesture, and Gamma was reserved for utterances judged emotional both in content and non-verbally. The following are single examples of each coding:

Alpha:    In relaxed and easy tones, one resident said, "I thought I would tell the group that I'd been thinking of getting a job around Charing Cross. I tried it before and think this would be the kind of thing I want".

Beta:     The group leader, ---, had been provoked by earlier remarks and said, "It isn't only my opinion but the whole group's, and I am the group leader". There was however nothing in tone of voice, gesture or posture to indicate emotion.

Gamma:    A normally quiet man, ---, suddenly sat forward clutching the arms of his chair, moved his body aggressively in the direction of the previous speaker, and said, "I'm not going to put up with you...".

After piloting, and before the application of the technique in the study proper, 1 meeting at each house was recorded independently by 2 research workers. This allowed a rough test of reliability. At both meetings the 2 judges agreed well on the rank ordering of individual participants both for volume spoken and volume of speech received (rank order correlations of +0.90 or higher). They also agreed fairly well on the overall level of emotionality of the 2 meetings, but agreed less well on the rank ordering of participants in terms of proportions of emotional utterances.

Appendix E - The Rapid Survey of London Alcoholism Hostels

Section 1 - Basic Information About the Hostel

This information was obtained from the staff member in charge. Except where indicated answers to all questions were recorded verbatim and later typed. Detailed instructions to the interviewer have been omitted.

When was the house established?

By whom?

With what purpose did the house originate?

Was there a particular group(s) for which the house was intended?

Has the group changed?

If yes, how does the present group differ from the original group?

For what reasons are some groups now excluded (if any)?

For what reasons are some groups now included (if any)?

What are the requirements for selection of residents?

For what reasons would a prospective resident who fulfilled these selection requirements be rejected?

How is a prospective resident selected?

By whom are prospective residents referred to you?

How many residents are there at present? Is this average, more or less than normal?

Of your present residents, how many are: 20 or younger, 21 - 30, 31 - 40, 41 - 50, 51 - 65, 66 and over?

Of your present residents, how many have been in: a psychiatric hospital, a prison, destitute/reception centre/common lodging houses, in other hostels, in this hostel, previously?

Does the house have any legal responsibility for any residents? If yes, how many?

Who is the management committee of the house? What is the nature of their responsibility to the house? Do they visit the house regularly?

Who is on the staff of the house? (In each case record title, professional qualifications or training, number of years of experience, length of time in present job, hours per week).

How many staff are on duty at any one time? Is there any time when there are no staff on duty?

How many wardens have there been since the house originated?

What is the average length of stay of assistant staff?

What kind of staffing problems have you had?

Are the staff resident or not? Who is resident? Who is not resident?

Do you have any voluntary help?

Do you have any visiting professional staff such as psychiatrist, probation officer, social worker?

Could you briefly describe the building, including age, size, layout, and who owns it?

How satisfactory is this building? What changes would you like to make?

How many bedrooms/dormitories are there?

How many rooms are there for general use?

Are any rooms closed to residents?

Is there an office for staff use?

What recreational facilities does the house have?

What is the principle source of funds? Are there any conditions to be met in order to receive this support?

Is there a Home Office subsidy?

Does anyone pay rent? If yes, is there a set rent or does it differ for individuals? If set, what is the rent per week? If it differs what is the range? For what reasons does it differ?

What proportion of the total operating expense is covered by rents?

Are any residents employed in the house? If yes, how many? What is the nature of their work?

Do residents help out by doing some domestic duties in the house which would otherwise require hired labour? Is this work formally assigned, informal and at residents own initiative, other?

What is the general nature of the work of those that are employed outside the house? What proportion of residents are not in any employment at present? Why?

Does anyone in the house arrange jobs or job contacts for residents?

Is employment outside the house compulsory, encouraged, or not emphasized?

Do residents do voluntary work outside the house? Is this encouraged by the staff?

What is the length of time which you would prefer a resident to stay?

What is the actual length of stay? (range and average).

Who decides when a resident is ready to leave?

Do any residents stay indefinitely? (more than 2 years).

What proportion of residents leave before they are considered ready to leave?

When residents leave can you briefly describe where they move to?

Is there any follow-up of residents who leave?

Are ex-residents encouraged to visit the house?

What is the policy concerning an ex-resident's re-entry into the house?

Does the house have any written rules? If so what are these? Or does the house have any unwritten but understood rules? If so what are these?

Can you describe briefly how these rules are enforced?

Could you briefly describe what the house is attempting to achieve?

How does the house achieve these aims?

How satisfied are you that the house is achieving these aims?

What changes would you like to make?

Is there any provision to have therapy outside the house?

Can you briefly describe your relations with your local community?

What community facilities are used by the residents such as educational, recreational facilities, social agencies or employment agencies?

In conclusion, is there anything else about the house that you would like other people in the field to know about?

Section 2 - Views on Handling of Hypothetical Instances of Misconduct

Of the 8 hypothetical instances of misconduct (see Chapter 7, Table 10, and Appendix C, Section 2) used at Houses A and B, 4 ('drinks', 'dishes', 'not interested' and 'anxious') were put to the staff member in charge, 1 or 2 assistant staff members and 2 or 3 residents. Questioning was the same as described in Appendix C, Section 2.

Section 3 - 16-Item Decision-Making Inventory

The same staff members and residents were asked to respond to each of 16 items, each pertaining to everyday life in the hostel (shown in Chapter 3, Figure 4). They were asked who made decisions on these matters and replies were coded as indicating decision-making solely by staff, solely by residents, or jointly by staff and residents.

# REFERENCES AND AUTHOR INDEX

(Page nos. at the end of each reference are the pages of this book upon which the reference occurs).

Alcoholics Recovery Project (1973).  Third Report on the Alcoholics Recovery Project, A.R.P., London.  (p.121).

Apte, R.Z. (1968).  Halfway Houses: A New Dilemma in Institutional Care.  Occasional papers on social administration, no. 27, Bell, London.  (pp.iv,1, 8-12, 27, 33, 49-52, 55-9, 70-4, 89).

Archard, P. (1975).  The Bottle Won't Leave You: A Study of Homeless Alcoholics and their Guardians.  J. Bellers Press, London. (p.93).

Bahr, H.M. (1973).  Skid Row: An Introduction to Disaffiliation. Oxford University Press, London and New York.  (pp.78-9).

Bales, R.F. (1950).  A Set of Categories for the Analysis of Small Group Interaction.  American Sociological Review, Vol. 15, pp.146-59.  (p.iv).

Bartak, L. and Rutter, M. (1975).  The Measurement of Staff-Child Interaction in Three Units for Autistic Children.  Chapter 8, In: Tizard, J. et al (Eds.).  (pp.49, 57).

Barton, R. (1959).  Institutional neurosis.  Wright, Bristol.  (p.2).

Blumberg, L., Shipley, T.E. and Shandler, I.W. (1973).  Skid Row and its Alternatives: Research and Recommendations from Philadelphia. Temple University Press, New York.  (pp.43, 47, 67, 69, 76, 83, 175).

Brown, J.S. (1965).  Sociometric Choices of Patients in a Therapeutic Community.  Human Relations, Vol. 18, pp.241-51.  (p.56).

Camberwell Council on Alcoholism (1974).  Alcoholism Facilities in England and Wales.  C.C.A. Journal on Alcoholism, London.  (p.16).

Caudill, W. (1958).  The Psychiatric Hospital as a Small Society. Harvard University Press, Cambridge, Mass. (p.58).

Central Council for Education and Training in Social Work (1973). Social Work: Residential Work is a Part of Social Work.  Report of the Working Party on Education for Residential Social Work, CCETSW Paper No. 3.  (pp.8, 23).

Clark, D.H. (1965).  The Therapeutic Community - Concept, Practice and Future.  British Journal of Psychiatry, Vol. 111, pp.947-54. (p.7).

Clark, D.H. (1974).  Social Therapy in Psychiatry.  Penguin Books, Harmondsworth, Middlesex.  (p.2).

Collier, D., Walsh, J. and Oki, G. (1970).  Bon Accord: Milieu Therapy for Public Inebriates.  Addiction Research Foundation, Toronto. (pp.iv, 40).

Collins, B.E. and Raven, B.H. (1969).  Group Structure: Attraction, Coalitions, Communication and Power.  In: G. Lindzey and E. Aronson (Eds.).  The Handbook of Social Psychology.  Addison-Wesley, Reading, Mass. (2nd Ed., Vol.4).  (p.29).

Cook, T. (1975).  Vagrant Alcoholics.  Routledge and Kegan Paul, London. (pp.41-2, 67, 78-9, 86, 88-9, 93).

Cook, T., Morgan, H.G. and Pollak, B. (1968).  The Rathcoole Experiment: First Year at a Hostel for Vagrant Alcoholics.  British Medical Journal, Vol. 1, pp.240-2.  (pp.iii, 46, 80, 93, 119).

Cook, T. and Pollak, B. (1970).  In Place of Skid Row: The First Three Years of the Rathcoole Experiment, May, 1966 - May, 1969.  NACRO Papers and Reprints, No.4.  National Association for the Care and Resettlement of Offenders, London.  (p.93).

Corden, J., Hogg, D., Wells, T. and Willson, A. (1974).  Teetotal Democracy.  New Society, 31st January, pp.258-259.  (pp.40, 66, 80).

Davis, W.E. (1973). The Irregular Discharge as an Unobtrusive Measure of Discontent Among Young Psychiatric Patients. Journal of Abnormal Psychology, Vol.81, pp.17-21. (p.75).

Department of Health and Social Security (1973). Community Services for Alcoholics. D.H.S.S. Circular 21/73. H.M.S.O., London. (pp.17, 22).

Durkin, E. (1971). Hostels for the Mentally Disordered. Young Fabian Pamphlet, No. 24. The Fabian Society, London. (pp.70-3, 75).

Douglas, T. (1970). A Decade of Small Group Theory, 1960-1970. Bookstall Publications, London. (p.140).

Edinburgh Corporation (1974). 1 Thornybauk, 'The First Year'. Edinburgh Corporation Social Work Department. (pp.66-7, 82, 86, 90).

Edwards, G. and Guthrie, S. (1966). A Comparison of In-Patient and Out-Patient Treatment of Alcohol Dependence. Lancet. pp.467-8. (p.16).

Edwards, G., Hawker, A. and Hensman, C. (1966). Setting up a Therapeutic Community. The Lancet, ii, pp.1407-8. (pp.iii, 39-40, 82, 88, 91-2).

Edwards, G., Hawker, A., Williamson, V. and Hensman, C. (1966). London' Skid Row. The Lancet i, pp.249-252. (p.15).

Ellsworth, R.B. (1965). A Behavioural Study of Staff Attitudes Towards Mental Illness. Journal of Abnormal Psychology, Vol. 70, pp. 194-200. (pp. iv, 5, 95, 146, 205).

Etzioni, A. (1964). Modern Organisations. Prentice-Hall, Englewood Cliffs, New Jersey. (p.5).

Fairweather, G.W. (Ed.) (1964). Social Psychology in Treating Mental Illness. Wiley, New York. (p.7, 56).

Fairweather, G.W., Sanders, D.H. and Tornatsky, L.G. (1974). Creating Change in Mental Health Organisations. Pergamon, New York and Oxford. (p.193).

Fletcher, J.C. (1970). Mental Health Hostels: Progress and Problems. Buckinghamshire County Council, Department of Health and Welfare, Aylesbury, Bucks. (pp.70-2, 74).

Gilbert, D.C. and Levinson, D.J. (1956). Ideology, Personality and Institutional Policy in the Mental Hospital. Journal of Abnormal and Social Psychology, Vol. 53, pp.263-71. (p.5).

Glaser, D. (1964). The Effectiveness of a Prison and Parole System. Bobbs-Merrill. (pp.36,43).

Goffman, E. (1961). Asylums: Essays on the Social Situation of Mental Patients and Other Inmates. Anchor Books, Doubleday and Co., New York. (pp.2-3, 48).

Grygier, T. (1975). Measurement of Treatment Potential: It's Rationale, Method and some Results in Canada. Chapter 7, In: Tizard, J. et al, (Eds.). (pp.36-7, 46).

Hall, J. and Jones, D.C. (1950). Social Grading of Occupations. British Journal of Sociology, Vol. 1, pp.31-55. (p.108).

Hare, A.P. (1962). Handbook of Small Group Research. Free Press, New York. (p.140).

Heal, K., and Cawson, P. (1975). Organisation and Change in Childrens Institutions. Chapter 4, In: Tizard, J. et al, (Eds.). (pp.57, 59).

Helping Hand Organization (1972). Annual Report, 1972. The Helping Hand Organization, London. (pp.91-3).

Hewett, S., Ryan, P. and Wing, J. (1975). Living Without the Mental Hospitals. Journal of Social Policy, Vol. 4, pp.391-404. (pp.8-10, 28, 56, 71).

Hinton, N. (1970). Hostels - New Approaches. NACRO Papers and Reprints, No. 5. National Association for the Care and Resettlement of Offenders, London. (p.69).

Home Office (1971). Habitual Drunken Offenders. H.M.S.O., London. (pp.iii, 17).

Hunt, W.A. and Matarazzo, J.D. (1970). Habit Mechanisms in Smoking. In: W.A. Hunt (Ed.). Learning Mechanisms in Smoking. Aldine, Chicago. (p.85).

Ingram-Smith, N. (1967). Alcoholic Rehabilitation Centre of the West London Mission. British Journal of Addiction, Vol. 62, pp.295-305. (pp. 65-6, 78, 88).

Jacobs, R.C. and Campbell, D.T. (1961). The Perpetuation of an Arbitrary Tradition Through Several Generations of a Laboratory Microculture. Journal of Abnormal and Social Psychology, Vol. 62, pp.649-658. (p.32).

Jellinek, E.M. (1960). The Disease Concept of Alcoholism. College and University Press, New Haven, Conn. (p.15).

Jenkins, D. and Harvey, J. (1974). Two Years On, 1972-74: Ellison House, A Discussion Paper. Unpublished report. (p.139).

Jones, M. (1952). Social Psychiatry: A Study of Therapeutic Communities. Tavistock, London. (Published as, The Therapeutic Community. Basic Books, New York, 1953). (pp.6, 119).

Jones, M. (1968). Beyond the Therapeutic Community: Social Learning and Social Psychiatry. Yale University Press, Newhaven and London. (pp.6, 119).

Keller, O.J. and Alper, B.S. (1970). Halfway Houses: Community Centred Correction and Treatment. D.C. Heath, Lexington, Mass. (pp.8-13, 28-9, 32-4, 36).

Kiesler, C.A. (1969). Group Pressure and Conformity. In: J. Mills (Ed.). Experimental Social Psychology. Collier-Macmillan, Toronto. (p.iv).

King, R.D., Raynes, N.V. and Tizard, J. (1971). Patterns of Residential Care: Sociological Studies in Institutions for Handicapped Children. Routledge and Kegan Paul, London. (p.14, 57).

Larkin, E.J. (1974). Three Models of Evaluation. Canadian Psychologist, Vol. 15, pp.89-94. (p.69).

Leissner, A. (1971). St. Martin of Tours House. In: Explorations in After-Care. Home Office Research Studies, No.9. H.M.S.O., London. (pp.66-7, 75).

Lewin, K., Lippitt, R. and White, R.K. (1939). Patterns of Aggressive Behaviour in Experimentally Creative Climates. Journal of Social Psychology, Vol. 10, pp.271-99. (p.34).

Meacher, M. (1972). Taken for a Ride: Special Residential Homes for Confused Old People: A Study of Separatism in Social Policy. Longman, London. (p.74).

Moos, R. and Houts, P. (1968). Assessment of the Social Atmospheres of Psychiatric Wards. Journal of Abnormal Psychology, Vol. 73, pp.595-604. (p.iv).

Mountney, G.H. (1965). Local Authority Psychiatric Hostels. British Journal of Psychiatric Social Work, Vol. 8, pp.20-6. (p.72).

Murray, E.J. and Cohen, M. (1959). Mental Illness, Milieu Therapy, and Social Organisation in Ward Groups. Journal of Abnormal and Social Psychology, Vol. 58, pp. 48-54. (p.56).

Myerson, D.J. and Mayer, J. (1966). Origins, Treatment and Destiny of Skid Row Alcoholic Men. New England Journal of Medicine, Vol. 275, pp. 419-425. (pp.iii, 69, 76).

National Institute of Mental Health (1975). Halfway Houses Serving the Mentally Ill and Alcoholics, United States, 1971-1973. Mental Health Statistics Series A, No. 9. NIMH, Rockville, Maryland. (pp.8, 12, 16-8, 21, 23).

National Institute of Mental Health (1972). Directory of Halfway Houses for the Mentally Ill and Alcoholics. NIMH, Rockville, Maryland. (pp.16, 18, 23).

Ogborne, A. and Collier, D. (1975). The Drinking Habits of Residents of a Program with a Controlled Drinking Option. Substudy 720. Addiction Research Foundation, Toronto. Unpublished Research Study. (pp.40-1, 82).

Ogborne, A.C. and Smart, R.G. (1974). Halfway Houses for Skid Row Alcoholics: A Search for Empirical Evaluation. Substudy 632. Addiction Research Foundation, Toronto. (pp.76-7, 83, 100).

Oki, G. (1974). Alcohol Use by Skid Row Alcoholics: Part 1 - Drinking at Bon Accord. Substudy 612. Addiction Research Foundation, Toronto. (pp.40, 82).

Orford, J. (1974). Simplistic Thinking About Other People as a Predictor of Early Drop-out at an Alcoholism Halfway House. British Journal of Medical Psychology, Vol. 47, pp.53-62. (p.ii)

Orford, J. and Edwards, G. (1977). Alcoholism: A Comparison of Treatment and Advice. With a Study of Influence of Marriage. Maudsley Monograph Series. Oxford University Press, London. (p.16).

Orford, J. and Hawker, A. (1974a). A Note on the Ordering of Onset of Symptoms in Alcohol Dependence. Psychological Medicine, Vol. 4, pp.281-288. (p.ii).

Orford, J., Hawker, A. and Nicholls, P. (1974). An Investigation of an Alcoholism Rehabilitation Halfway House: I Types of Client and Modes of Discharge. British Journal of Addiction, Vol. 69, pp. 213-224. (pp.ii, 75, 83, 87, 109).

Orford, J. and Hawker, A. (1974b). An Investigation of an Alcoholism Rehabilitation Halfway House: II The Complex Question of Client Motivation. British Journal of Addiction, Vol. 69, pp.315-323. (p.ii).

Orford, J., Hawker, A. and Nicholls, P. (1975a). An Investigation of an Alcoholism Rehabilitation Halfway House: III Reciprocal Staff-Resident Evaluations. British Journal of Addiction, Vol. 70, pp.23-32. (p.ii).

Orford, J., Hawker, A. and Nicholls, P. (1975b). An Investigation of an Alcoholism Rehabilitation Halfway House: IV Attractions of the Halfway House for Residents. British Journal of Addiction, Vol. 70, pp.279-286. (pp.ii, 47).

Orford, J., Oppenheimer, E. and Edwards, G. (1976). Abstinence or Control: The Outcome for Excessive Drinkers Two Years after Consultation. Behaviour Research and Therapy, Vol. 14, pp.409-18. (pp.40, 85).

Owen, D. (1965). English Philanthropy, 1660-1960. Oxford University Press, London. (p.17).

Pattison, E.M., Coe, R. and Doerr, H.O. (1973). Population Variation Among Alcoholism Treatment Facilities. International Journal of the Addictions, Vol. 8, pp.199-229. (p.99).

Pearlin, L.I. and Rosenberg, M. (1962). Nurse-Patient Social Distance and Structural Context of a Mental Hospital. American Sociological Review, Vol. 27, pp.56-65. (p.5).

Pittman, D. and Gordon, S. (1962). The Revolving Door. Newhaven Press, Newhaven and New York. (p.15).

Polansky, N.A., White, R.B. and Miller, S.C. (1957). Determinants of the Role-Image of the Patient in a Psychiatric Hospital. In: Greenblatt, M., Levinson, D.J. and Williams, R.H. (Eds.). The Patient and the Mental Hospital. Free Press, Glencoe, Illinois. (p.36).

Polsky, H.W. (1967). Cottage Six: Social System of Delinquent Boys in Residential Treatment. Wiley, New York and London. (p.48).

Rapoport, R.M. (1956). Oscillations and Sociotherapy. Human Relations, Vol. 9, pp.357-373. (pp.42, 139).

Rapoport, R.M. (1960). Community as Doctor: New Perspectives on a Therapeutic Community. Tavistock, London. (pp.iv, 6, 30, 56, 119, 139).

Raush, H.L. and Raush, C.L. (1968). The Halfway House Movement: A Search for Sanity. Appleton Century Crofts, New York. (pp. 4-5, 8-9, 10-4, 16, 18, 31-2, 51-2, 54-7, 75).

Redl, F. (1959). The Concept of a 'therapeutic milieu'. American Journal of Ortho-psychiatry, Vol. 29, pp.721-736. (p.13).

Rigby, A. (1974). Alternative Realities. Routledge and Kegan Paul, London. (p.54).

Rothwell, N.D. and Doniger, J. (1963). Halfway House and Mental Hospital - Some Comparisons. Psychiatry, Vol. 26, pp.281-288. (p.14).

Rubington, E. (1970). Referrals, Past Treatment Contacts and Lengths of Stay in a Halfway House. Quarterly Journal of Studies on Alcohol, Vol. 31, pp.659-668. (p.iii).

Rubington, E. (1973). The Halfway House for Alcoholics. Addictions, Vol. 20, pp.18-31. (p.76).

Rush, B. (C.1785). An Inquiry into the Effects of Ardent Spirits Upon the Human Body and Mind. Reproduced in, Quarterly Journal of Studies on Alcohol, 1943, Vol. 4, pp.321-41. (p.15).

Secord, P.F. and Backman, C.W. (1974). Social Psychology. McGraw-Hill, New York and London (2nd Edition). (p.33).

Shandler, I.W. (1972). The Housing and Treatment of the Public Inebriate. Paper delivered at Conference on Alcohol Abuse and Alcoholism, Maryland. (pp.88-9).

Sinclair, I. (1971). Hostels for Probationers: A Study of the Aims, Working and Variations in Effectiveness of Male Probation Hostels, with Special Reference to the Influence of the Environment on Delinquency. Home Office Research Studies, No. 6, H.M.S.O., London. (pp.iv, 8, 27, 33-6, 42-3, 49-50, 59, 69-70, 75, 83, 162).

Sinclair, I. (1975). The Influence of Wardens and Matrons on Probation Hostels. Chapter 6, In: Tizard, J. et al (Eds.). (p.75).

Sinclair, I. and Snow, D. (1971). After-Care Hostels Receiving a Home Office Grant. In: Explorations in After Care. Home Office Research Studies, No. 9, H.M.S.O., London. (p.83).

Smart, R.G. (1974). Outcome Studies of Therapeutic Community and Halfway House Treatment for Addicts. Substudy No. 600. Addiction Research Foundation, Toronto. (pp.83, 89).

Smith, G. (1970). Social Work and the Sociology of Organizations. Library of Social Work. Routledge and Kegan Paul, London. (p.27).

Sobell, M.B. and Sobell, L.C. (1973). Individualized Behaviour Therapy for Alcoholics. Behaviour Therapy, Vol. 4, pp.49-72. (p.40).

Spencer, J. and Grygier, T. (1951). Cited by Sinclair, I., 1971. (p.69).

Sullivan, C.E., Grant, M.Q. and Grant, J.D. (1957). The Development of Interpersonal Maturity: Application to Delinquency. Psychiatry, Vol. 20, pp.373-385. (pp.89-90).

Tidmarsh, D., Wood, S. and Wing, J.K. (1972). Camberwell Reception Centre: Summary of the Research Findings and Recommendations. Department of Health and Social Security, London. (p.i).

Tizard, B. (1975). Varieties of Residential Nursery Experience. Chapter 5, In: Tizard, J. et al (Eds.). (pp.35-6, 49).

Tizard, J. (1975). Quality of Residential Care for Retarded Children. Chapter 3, In: Tizard, J. et al (Eds.). (p.14).

Tizard, J. (1976). Psychology and Social Policy. Bulletin of the British Psychological Society, Vol. 29, pp.225-34. (p.76).

Tizard, J., Sinclair, I. and Clarke, R.V.G. (Eds.). (1975). Varieties of Residential Experience. Routledge and Kegan Paul, London. (pp.4, 14, 35, 48, 57, 76).

Turner, M. (1972). Norman House. In: S. Whiteley, D. Briggs and M. Turner. Dealing with Deviants. Hogarth, London. (pp.52-3, 56).

Vaughn, C.E. and Leff, J.P. (1976). The Influence of Family and Social Factors on the Course of Psychiatric Illness: A Comparison of Schizophrenic and Depressed Neurotic Patients. British Journal of Psychiatry, Vol. 129, pp.125-37. (p.76).

Whiteley, S. (1972). Henderson. In: S. Whiteley, D. Briggs and M. Turner. Dealing with Deviants. Hogarth, London. (p.7).

Wilbur, B.M., Salkin, D. and Birnbaum, H. (1966). The Response of Tuberculous Alcoholics to a Therapeutic Community. Quarterly Journal of Studies on Alcohol, Vol. 27, pp.620-635. (pp.89-90).

Wing, J.K. and Brown, G.W. (1970). Institutionalism and Schizophrenia: A Comparative Study of Three Mental Hospitals, 1960-8. Cambridge University Press. (pp.2, 4, 48-50).

Wiseman, J.P. (1970). Stations of the Lost: The Treatment of Skid Row Alcoholics. Prentice-Hall, Englewood Cliffs, New Jersey, (pp. 47, 84).

Yablonsky, L. (1965). The Tunnel Back: Synanon. Macmillan, New York. (pp.12, 83).

Zelditch, M. (1955). Role Differentiation in the Nuclear Family: A Comparative Study. In: T. Parsons and R.F. Bales (Eds.). Family, Socialisation and Interaction Process. Free Press, Chicago. (p.151).

# SUBJECT INDEX